Night-Whispers 'New Antiochs' Volume 02-Q3

July-August-September

Edition 01-Revision 05

Victor Robert Farrell

NightWhispers
All current
Contact & Sales Information
Can be found at
www.Night-Whispers.com

Night-Whispers

'New Antiochs'

Volume 02–Q3

July-August-September

ISBN Number 978-1-910686-12-6

First published in this format

June 2016 by WhisperingWord

All current contact and sales information can be found at

www.Night-Whispers.com

Printed in The United Kingdom

for

WhisperingWord Ltd.

Night-Whispers

'New Antiochs'

Volume 02-Q3

July-August-September

Dedication

This book is dedicated, very simply,

To the now four most important people

In the whole wide world to me.

My daughter Gemma,

My son Jonathan,

My grandaughter Ellie May,

And of course,

My wife

Bridget.

PREFACE

I am Pastor, Rev. Victor Robert Farrell, and these everyday Bible insights called 'Night-Whispers' have long since been a global endeavor to communicate the God of the WHOLE Bible in very raw terms to very real people. This is my passion and the reason why I founded The 66 Books Ministry, who, through our 66 Cities project, over the course of the next 25 years, by the grace of God and according to His will and favor, shall be preaching consecutively from each of the 66 Books of the Holy Bible, the Gospel of the Lord Jesus Christ in 16,500 of the most influential cities of the world on an annual and ongoing basis! In this regard, these Night-Whispers accompany our endeavors by providing Every Day Insights into the whole Bible.

These Night-Whispers are presented in such a way as to be read each day. They are produced on a regular basis, and the 366 daily readings for each year are presented with a unique volume number. That 'Volume' year is then divided into four Quarters. For example:

Year 01= Volume 01-Q1 | January-February-March
Year 01= Volume 01-Q2 | April-May-June
Year 01= Volume 01-Q3 | | Vol 02 | Q3 | NW00458 | July 01st |-| Vol 02 | Q3 | NW00580 | August 01st |-September
Year 01= Volume 01-Q4 | October-November-December
Year 02= Volume 02-Q1 | January-February-March
Followed by Volume 3, 4, 5, 6 etc., and the associate four Quarters for the consecutive years. I am sure you get the picture!

The point is, that you can start any volume of Night-Whispers IN ANY YEAR you wish, and AT ANY TIME you choose, because whilst these Everyday Bible Insights are fresh and relevant to each day, they are not interconnected in a way, which means you have to read one volume before another. Indeed, Night-Whispers are produced as stand-alone products rather than connected volumes. Therefore, if you wish, you can also consecutively read any Quarter from any Volume you choose! For example: Volume 02-Q3 might easily be followed by Volume 05-Q4, because each book is a standalone product. Got it? Excellent!

So, now that I have most thoroughly confused you, may I say that along with the team at The 66 Books Ministry and Whispering Word, I do hope and pray that these particular ***Night-Whispers,*** will be an enormous blessing to you in ***revealing just a little more to you of the God of the WHOLE BIBLE.***

Rev. Victor Robert Farrell, June 2019, England.

INTRODUCTION TO NIGHTWHISPERS

VOL 02-Q3- 'New Antiochs'

This is our seventh standalone quarterly volume of Night-Whispers and we hope that these Every Day Bible Insights will be mighty food supplements to arm you for the present spiritual conflict and the coming fight of this dark night.

When the church moved out from the hub of Jerusalem it was not only to provide a post AD70 fall of that city, new command base for the propagation of the Gospel it was to provide a new effort of global evangelism that would now include the gentiles, and mainly the gentiles. Antioch became that 2nd hub, that new command base, that original platform of operation where the followers of The Way now became known as Christians. Antioch was the new center and hub for the gathered and going church, where the apostolic and prophetic pool bubbled with the Great Commission.

Our Kingdom within these fallen and falling states we now occupy must be peppered with a million 'New Antiochs,' places of protection, provision, and a base for propelling the people of God out into the world with the Gospel. This volume of Night-Whispers is dedicated to the need for 'New Antiochs' galore!

As usual, all we earnestly desire is that you especially check the Scriptures to see if these things are so, and also to do your own digging both there in particular and elsewhere in general. May God the Holy Spirit truly guide you in this.

Some global and historical acknowledgements

Now then, I have been writing these Bible Insights for many years and I have gleaned in a multitude of fine meadows and otherwise. For me to give credit where credit is due then, would not only increase the size of this quarterly volume many, many times, but I would undoubtedly miss many more people out of that massive list of those which I have not tried to give credit to. It is Solomon who said that *"there is nothing new under the sun"* and I believe it! Therefore, please then take it for granted that when someone like myself, who almost sees 'cut and paste' as an unspoken gift of the Holy Spirit, says that he might have gleaned from another person's work, in someplace, somewhere, and at some point in time and has done so without giving appropriate credit where credit is due, that I probably have! If this is the case, it was not my intention to rob you of any rightly due glory, but if I have, then please inform me of the same and the necessary changes and/or credits will be made. Remember, I have borrowed from everywhere; I have taken from everyone. 'Everywhere' and 'everyone;' there you go, that should have you covered!

US, UK or elsewhere, or, "How do you spell that?"

To be British, is to be somewhat like 'the last of the Mohicans.' The United Kingdom I grew up in is breaking apart. Even so, I am of Irish & Scottish great-grandparents, grandparents and parents, and I was also born in England. Therefore, I am British and a Celt at that. Even so, I love North America. Does this make me a Yankophile, or loving the South and its battle flag, more especially a Dixiophile? Alternatively, maybe I could be an Americophile or a Canameriphile? Who knows? Suffice to say, that as our nations are divided by a common language, America being the residence of the majority of our English readers, I have tried to adopt the spelling and grammar of the Americas. Even so, I have no doubt failed, and in the so doing, both mixed and matched the UK and US spelling and grammatical styles as I have compiled these Night-Whispers. I confess that I am a double-minded man, unstable in all my editorial ways. The purists, either side of the pond, I am sure will never forgive me. The rest do not care. Either way I need your help. So, if you spot any 'howlers,' do let me know. Please Email me your corrections on:

getyouracttogetherman@whisperingword.com

Bible Versions & Text Form

Ah, the Bible. The true meta-narrative of the real world and therefore all things meta-physical. Well, preferring the 'Textus Receptus' or the 'Majority Text,' I have tried to use the New Separatist Bible (NSB), which is a confluence Bible based on the 1560 Geneva Bible and the 1611 Authorized version, (Pure Cambridge Edition) when I have referenced the Bible, though where necessary, for mere contemporary clarity of course, when I have I have deviated from this norm, at that time I have clearly indicated which other Bible Version has been referenced.

In addition to this, though I have removed verse numbers from the Bible text, I have retained the Capitalization of the beginning of new lines within the text, which would indicate its NKJV poetic form as well as the start of a new verse.

NIGHT-WHISPERS ARE WRITTEN FOR........

There is so much 'devotional' material available nowadays for the Christian that a great part of me says that no more should be written. Yet I do believe that we are moving speedily to the time of the end. What devotionals are written to truly address the needs of Christians living in the approach to this period, or in this period? In my opinion, there are none. Night-Whispers then, are written for those people of this darkening time in particular. Therefore, you will find that Night-Whispers are battle rations that demand your time, attention, study and consideration. If you need a little ear tickler folks, a quick little cuddle before you go to bed at night, a sleeping pill even, indeed, if you have sold out the truth, your calling and your very self for ten shekels and a shirt, then these Bible Insights are NOT for you. They demand your thoughtful consideration and further investigation and ardent application. They need your time! Night-Whispers are written for those seekers who are looking for the God of the whole Bible. They are written for those who hate the color grey but love black and white. They are written for those who want to know the truth, even if it is unpalatable to them. They are written for the awakened; that is, for those people who know that the darkness is alive and like a black incoming tide, is infiltrating every area of present life. They are written for those people who know that a Night is coming when no man can work. They are written for those people who refuse to be spoon-fed. They are written for Bible hungry people. They are written for those who are done with distractions. They are written for those people who have not sold out to cultural compromise and refuse to sell themselves to social niceness and religious self-righteousness. They are written for those who want to cease being unpaid social workers for the unthankful and want to love and arm the saints. They are therefore written for fighters, even that growing band of brothers who are no ragged or rag-tag remnant, but rather, are the released people of 'The Revolution,' that back to the Bible, boots on the ground, present movement of God, who are done with everything that has silenced the one true church and with the removal of its voice, have killed our nations. They are written for the sold out the followers of Christ who have at last found their proclamation voice. They are written for the rooted, fruited and flowering stump. Therefore, to all you great and holy people then, who, even in this darkness might just turn the world right ways up once more, I say then this to you this very night: ***"Welcome to Night-Whispers, Volume 02-Q3- 'New Antiochs' "Be strong and keep looking up for your salvation draweth nigh."***

JUST A HUCKSTER

Some young preacher will study until he has to get thick glasses to take care of his failing eyesight because he has an idea he wants to become a famous preacher. HE'S JUST A HUCKSTER buying selling and getting gain. They will ordain him and he will be known as Reverend and if he writes a book, they will make him a doctor. And he will be known as Doctor; but he's still a huckster buying and selling and getting gain.

And when the Lord comes back,
HE will drive him out of the temple
along with the other cattle.

A.W. Tozer

(from 'Tozer on Christian Leadership,' compiled by Ron Eggert)

John 3:30 He must increase
but I must decrease.

STILL LOOKING

Wise men speak of trees
From the Cedar to the Hyssop
Springing from the wall
From the Aspen to the Alder
Beside the water fall

Wise men speak of animals of creeping things and fish
Of birds and bees and smooth black cats
That lap the dainty dish

Wise men sing of love and capture moments in a jar
Wise men suck the juice of days
Wise men shop at Spar!

Wise men count the fallen ticks
Of old clocks running down
Wise men number muscles
That help create the frown

Wise men follow after
Wise men follow far
Wise men seek the Savior still
Beneath the wandering star

1 Kings 4:33 Also he spoke of trees, from the cedar tree of Lebanon even to the hyssop that springs out of the wall; he spoke also of animals, of birds, of creeping things, and of fish. (NKJV)

The Old 100th!

All people that on earth do dwell,
Sing to the Lord with cheerful voice.
Him serve with fear, His praise forth tell;
Come ye before Him and rejoice.

The Lord, ye know, is God indeed;
Without our aid He did us make;
We are His folk, He doth us feed,
And for His sheep He doth us take.

O enter then His gates with praise;
Approach with joy His courts unto;
Praise, laud, and bless His name always,
For it is seemly so to do.

For why? the Lord our God is good;
His mercy is for ever sure;
His truth at all times firmly stood,
And shall from age to age endure.

To Father, Son and Holy Ghost,
The God whom Heaven and earth adore,
From men and from the angel host
Be praise and glory evermore.

From 'Fourscore and Seven Psalms of David'
(Geneva, Switzerland: 1561); attributed to William Kethe

CONTENTS

| Vol 02 | Q3 | NW00549 | July 01st |

Night-Whisper | ACTION

"Let England Beware!"

It was a 17th Century English non-conformist. parliamentarian puritan preacher and, personal chaplain to Oliver Cromwell, John Owen, a man seemingly wedded to loss (all of his 11 children died, he lost his living and his position and no doubt at some time, his marbles) who preached to parliament on the day of the execution of Charles 1st.

Acts 13:38-52

.. 'Behold, you despisers, Marvel and perish! For I work a work in your days, A work which you will by no means believe, Though one were to declare it to you.'" .... On the next Sabbath almost the whole city came together to hear the word of God. But when the Jews saw the multitudes, they were filled with envy; and contradicting and blaspheming, they opposed the things spoken by Paul. Then Paul and Barnabas grew bold and said, "It was necessary that the word of God should be spoken to you first; but since you reject it, and judge yourselves unworthy of everlasting life, behold, we turn to the Gentiles. .....But the Jews stirred up ...the city, raised up persecution against Paul and Barnabas, and expelled them from their region. But they shook off the dust from their feet against them, and came to Iconium. NKJV

Immediately, at the end of the Civil war, John Owen is supposed to have preached a sermon to parliament entitled, "A VISION OF UNCHANGEABLE, FREE MERCY, IN SENDING THE MEANS OF GRACE TO UNDESERVING SINNERS: Wherein God's Uncontrollable Eternal Purpose, In Sending And Continuing The Gospel Unto This Nation, In The Midst Of Oppositions And Contingencies, Is Discovered; His Distinguishing Mercy In This Great Work Exalted, Asserted Against Opposers, Repiners." Interestingly, Owen's title is longer than most modern day seeker sensitive sermons, sorry, talks. Just saying.......

In the reading of this sermon, Owen's focus is three-fold. First that the house of England beware in being prideful and taking glory to itself for its recent victories in the Civil war. Secondly that there was much of the country still very much untouched by the Gospel and thirdly, that England should beware of rejecting the Sovereign grace of God. Listen to how he puts it,

"How comes it that this island glories in a reformation, and Spain sits still in darkness? Is it because we were better than they, or less engaged in antichristian delusions? Doubtless no. No nation in the world drank deeper of that cup of abomination. It was a proverbial speech amongst all, 'England was our good ass' (a beast of burden) for (Antichrist whom they called) the Pope. Nothing but the good pleasure of God and Christ, freely coming to refine us, (Malachi 3:1-4) caused this distinction. Though men can do nothing towards the procuring of the gospel, yet men may do much for the expulsion of the gospel. If the husbandmen prove idle or self-seekers, the vineyard will be let to others; and if the people love darkness more than light, the candlestick will be removed. Let England beware!"

If indeed this sermon was preached in 1646 then nearly 400 hundred years have passed since its first rousing warning went out. Most certainly, the legacy church has seen to it that the Gospel has been removed of its power and consequently the whole system is now full of Word rejecters and the whole land is full of Bible ignorant Gospel rejecters and worse than that, Christ has handed us over to our enemies for judgement. The cancer of Islam now gnaws at what is left of England's bones. Again Owen says,

If the husbandmen prove idle or self-seekers, the vineyard will be let to others; and if the people love darkness more than light, the candlestick will be removed. Let England beware!"

"Let England consider with fear and trembling the dispensation that it is now under ; — I say, with fear and trembling, for this day is the Lord's day, wherein he will purge us or burn us, according as we shall be found silver or dross: — it is our day, wherein we must mend or end."

This is the third time that England is come up from the drowning. As Emily Dickenson has said, "DROWNING is not so pitiful as the attempt to rise. Three times, t'is said, a sinking man comes up to face the skies, and then declines forever to that abhorred abode." Protestant England, that solid purity of the British Isles, is now defunct and even dead.

Consequently, this England is about to disappear forever beneath the waves of history.

It is my belief that the remnant people of God are no longer preserved to rise again and reconstitute a Christian land, but rather, are to remain in conflict, preparing whoever's ear has been softened by God to receive the Word in preparation for the return of Jesus who shall judge the living and the dead. The remnant are no longer the shapers of nations, but are the end-time proclaimers of the soon coming of the King of Kings.

The heartlands are lost. The cities of learning, commerce and community are gone. We need to build us some new Antiochs right now!

For the remnant to thrive, (for if we do not thrive we shall not survive) we must build a Kingdom within a State. The remaining people of God must rally their strength and strategically relocate to new Antiochs across the land from where the Gospel can go out once more. The lock jaw of secular humanism shall soon clamp down its teeth upon us. The clash of civilizations, with a strident homeland Islam shall soon be upon our children and our children's children. Wars and rumors of wars shall be our daily bread and our slave owners (to whom we have been sold) shall soon come to claim what's theirs.

For Christian cities to rise, Christians must dominate the landscape in proclamation, people, politics, provision, protection and policing. These islands are divided, but in this division we might also find our safety and our strength. Let us embrace it then. The present politicians and preachers are mostly liars. Do not listen to them. Rather, let us pray that God will send us some new Pilgrim fathers, some new providential move of God, that will gently shepherd us to being gathered together in one place, even in several places as one body. My fear is that if we do not do this obediently and willingly, we shall be forced to do so under the terrible hand of persecution and disaster. Compulsion is not a gentle shepherd. .

Listen: *At that time a great persecution arose against the church which was at Jerusalem; and they were all scattered throughout the regions of Judea and Samaria, except the apostles. And devout men carried Stephen to his burial, and made great lamentation over him. As for Saul, he made havoc of the church, entering every house, and dragging off men and women, committing them to prison. Therefore*

*those who were scattered went everywhere preaching the word. Then
Philip went down to the city of Samaria and preached Christ to them.
And the multitudes with one accord heeded the things spoken by
Philip, hearing and seeing the miracles which he did. For unclean
spirits, crying with a loud voice, came out of many who were
possessed; and many who were paralyzed and lame were healed. 8
And there was great joy in that city. (Acts 8:1-8 NKJV)*

Pray: Father, send us shepherds who shall speak the truth to us and lead us. Father, reveal to us these new Antiochs of Your choosing, guide direct and provide for us to get to them. Then O Lord, send us out in strength! In Jesus name I pray, amen, and let it be so.

Night-Whisper | ACTION

Of poles on the mountain tops, and banners on the hills

And so the church of the living God has most recently and in far too many cases, been run by pimps and served by prostitutes. Indeed, even hirelings that have fleeced the sheep, have long been shipped in by the devil to pole dance their spiritual wears before a gagging audience longing to be entertained and titillated, for they find no satisfaction in their wife of the Word of God.

Isaiah 30:8-11

Now go, write it before them on a tablet, And note it on a scroll, That it may be for time to come, Forever and ever: That this is a rebellious people, Lying children, Children who will not hear the law of the Lord; Who say to the seers, "Do not see," And to the prophets, "Do not prophesy to us right things; Speak to us smooth things, prophesy deceits. Get out of the way, Turn aside from the path, Cause the Holy One of Israel To cease from before us." NKJV

The congregation's spiritual sexual pleasure has been an exceptionally simple one, "Say nice things to me. Say nice things about me. Speak of goodness and honor to come, speak of greatness and of settledness in the land of the living at the gates of Sodom. Justify my buying into the world and its wares. Justify my pleasure please. " The truth of the matter is clear to see, most of the people of the Book no longer want the God of the Book, but would rather have the God of their own making, even the divinity of their own spiritual sexual desire. The church is always destroyed from the inside.

In early 2016, the BBC reported that "Iraq's Mosul Dam, inaugurated in 1984 during the era of Saddam Hussein, is today falling into disrepair as a result of neglect over the past 18 months after the Kurds wrested it back from Islamic State. Budget shortfalls due to the slump in oil prices and political rivalry between the central government in Baghdad, and the regional government of the semi-autonomous Iraq Kurdistan, have hampered urgently needed repairs.

There is also a desperate shortage of workers. Half the workforce has left the dam for other jobs on account of not being paid for up to five months."

The problems of the Mosul dam are fourfold: 1) The foundations are giving way. 2) Outdated machinery us being used to try and fix the foundations. 3) "The joints at the two main gates have been dislocated vertically and horizontally, which could lead to the collapse of the dam, but we don't know when. It could happen next month, next year or in five years' time. We actually don't know when." 4) There is no safe or serious investment of money, materials and especially of excellent manpower.

Isaiah 30:12-14

"Because you despise this word, And trust in oppression and perversity, And rely on them, Therefore this iniquity shall be to you Like a breach ready to fall, A bulge in a high wall, Whose breaking comes suddenly, in an instant. And He shall break it like the breaking of the potter's vessel, Which is broken in pieces; He shall not spare. So there shall not be found among its fragments A shard to take fire from the hearth, Or to take water from the cistern." NKJV

When the dam collapses, whole cities will be washed away. If I was in those cities, I would move now.

Oh how the fortunes of the people of the Lord are reversed in these lands of ours. Instead of one of us chasing a thousand, one enemy is chasing a thousand of us! In the face of just five enemies, a whole nation is fleeing and nothing shall be left of them, save a pole on a mountain and a banner on a hill. I tell you now, on the one hand, this is a picture of all that shall be left of that composite, mixed and compromised, accepting lukewarm legacy church, for its caretakers are now carrying the keys to all its closing doors, and they are nothing but sodomites, old ladies, children of every sort, men in frocks and authoritative women. All blind leaders of the blind. All falling in the ditch of destruction, for there is no reproduction within them.

I remember an old preacher describing these Israeli banners we read of tonight, these 'Standards, these 'poles,' these gathering points for the armed forces of God on earth. He said that these poles were embedded with a reflective glittering, indeed, with anything that could catch the 'light shine.' Therefore, on the other hand, I wonder if we can say that this picture of poles and banners might also represent that currently elusive and hidden remnant that shall occupy the high ground? They shall initially be but a mast without a sail, but never the less, be a reflective banner of light, a gathering place, a rallying place, a spot to rebuild from, even the 'New Antiochs' of the Lord.

There are people who shall read this Bible Insight after the uncared for and ignored foundations of the dam have been destroyed, thus causing the churches' final collapse. Many of you shall be washed from your cities. Driven before the floods. When this happens, no, before this happens, look to the mountains and the high hills! Look to the heights and seek out the New Antiochs. Look for the reflective glittering of the people of God, the Word of God, and there you shall find the provision of God, the protection of God and the strength of God. From these New Antiochs, the true church of God shall go forth once more.

Find the heights and be it ever so small, set up a standard, raise the pole, lift high the banners and call the people of God to the New Antiochs. Are you a founding Father? Are you a founding follower? Go!

To those reading this Bible Insight before the final collapse of the dam with rotten foundations, I say again that it is time to strategically relocate yourself. Find the heights and be it ever so small, set up a standard, raise the pole, lift high the banners of the Lord Jesus Christ and call the people of God to the New Antiochs.

Are you a founding modern day 'Patriarch?' Are you a founding Father of some new Antiochs? Are you a founding follower? Go! Go! Go!

Listen: *For thus says the Lord God, the Holy One of Israel: "In returning and rest you shall be saved; In quietness and confidence shall be your strength. "But you would not, And you said, "No, for we will flee on horses" — Therefore you shall flee! And, "We will ride on swift horses" — Therefore those who pursue you shall be swift! One thousand shall flee at the threat of one, At the threat of five you shall flee ,Till you are left as a pole on top of a mountain And as a banner on a hill. (Isaiah 30:15-17 NKJV)*

Pray: Father, You have asked us to return to You. This we do with repentance and resolve. We turn from our sin and in the power and with the aid of God the Holy Spirit we resolve to do what is righteous, holy and according to Your word. We remarry ourselves to You O God, the Lord of the Word and the Word of the Lord. Make us then, O God our Father, builders of New Cities of refuge, these New Antiochs of rescue and rejuvenation, even these 'Glittering Antiochs' from where the Word of the Lord shine forth and go out in strength once more. Amen and let it be so.

Vol 04 | Q1 | NW00551 | July 03rd |

Night-Whisper | ACTION

Get ready to run

The spiritually awakened now need to scout out the high places of refuge. When we get there, let's put some poles on the mountain tops and some banners on the hills. Let us prepare for what is to come.

Matthew 24:15-22

"Therefore when you see the 'abomination of desolation,' spoken of by Daniel the prophet, standing in the holy place" (whoever reads, let him understand), "then let those who are in Judea flee to the mountains. Let him who is on the housetop not go down to take anything out of his house. And let him who is in the field not go back to get his clothes. But woe to those who are pregnant and to those who are nursing babies in those days! And pray that your flight may not be in winter or on the Sabbath. For then there will be great tribulation, such as has not been since the beginning of the world until this time, no, nor ever shall be. And unless those days were shortened, no flesh would be saved; but for the elect's sake those days will be shortened." NKJV

In a society with no moral base whatsoever, with no moral order, with no discipline, with no respect for the humanity of others, when the fun, the finances and the food run out, disaster will follow. In a few short weeks without these things, people turn to robbery, rape, murder and even cannibalism. Not only is there ample evidence of these things in our world today, and evidence of the same in general human history, but the Scriptures are full of relevant examples of the them. Look now, for when fun, finances and food run out, madness consumes the land. Are you prepared for what is to come?

In our text for tonight, Jesus when speaking about an 'end time' revelation, instructs people who shall be in Judea to 'flee to the mountains.' This running is an immediate event. It is an event that does not allow for the 'wait and let's get a few important things together before we go' kind of scenario. No, it is an event that demands an immediate departure. Knowing these things then, knowing that at some point people are going to have to run to the hills, should we not then get ready to run? Should we not have a destination to run to, a route to run by, and a 'bug out' bag to grab and go with? Should we not have a personal and strategic plan to escape the coming madness? I put it to you, that whether we live in Judea or not, we the church of the living God, knowing what is to shortly come upon us, need to have 'mountain Antiochs' to run to, a prepared and planned way to get there, and a means to do so. This is strategic planning for the individual and for local churches and the gathered 'New Antiochs.' Though we may already be too late, this preparation needs to be done right now. Why? Well, because God favors the prepared!

If you are in the madness when it happens, then you shall not escape the madness. You need to get ready to run.

THIS is your responsibility!

Prayer is vital in the planting of poles on mountain tops. Prayer is vital in all disaster recovery preparation. Indeed, in our text for tonight, Jesus says that prayer is also vital even in the determination of the day and even the weather conditions of our getting ready to run. Knowing that judgment is coming, knowing that disaster is destined for us by God and highly likely in the very near future, are you prepared for this brother? Are you ready to run?

Ellicot says regarding this very Jewish prayer for not fleeing on the Sabbath day that, "Rules were given for flight where the conditions lay within their own power. Other incidents which lay outside their will might lawfully be the subjects of their prayers. ..... Living as the Christians of Judea did in the strict observance of the Law, they would either be hindered by their own scruples from going beyond a Sabbath day's journey (about one English mile,) which would be insufficient to place them out of the reach of danger, or would find impediments—gates shut, and the like—from the Sabbath observance of others." Therefore, let me ask you again tonight then dear brother, what 'scruples,' what pride, what psychological self-calming, what so called sensible reflection, what convenient cultural embarrassment even, what religious respect is to be gained from settled others, what investment in earthly cities, is keeping you from even talking about and from getting ready to run? Babylon fell. So will your city.

The words of the dead Japanese's soldier's buried face, speaking from the ground in the 1998 film 'The Thin Red Line' are pertinent and poignant for today,

"Are you righteous? Kind? Does your confidence lie in this? Are you loved by all? Know that I was, too. Do you imagine your suffering will be any less because you loved goodness and truth?"

Brother, if you and your family are in the madness when it happens, then you shall not escape the madness. You need to get ready to run.

Those of you who are commanded by God the Holy Spirit to build some New Antiochs upon the mountain tops, to plant some new banners on a few good hills, need to do so now. May God enable you to do so, and provide you with favor and finances to make it possible. Lift up Christ and He shall draw all people to Himself.

Those of you who are commanded by God the Holy Spirit to build some New Antiochs upon the mountain tops, to plant some banners on a few good hills, need to do so now.

Those of you who God the Holy Spirit moves to join these folks, need to do so now. Strategically relocate.

The rest of us, obediently working in the place prepared for us by God, need to have connections with these New Antiochs, knowledge of how to get there, and a listening ear and open eyes to know when to run. Judgement is coming on the West, even on the whole world.

Brother, are you ready to run? Church, are you preparing places for the people of God to run to?

Listen: *Now when they had departed, behold, an angel of the Lord appeared to Joseph in a dream, saying, "Arise, take the young Child and His mother, flee to Egypt, and stay there until I bring you word; for Herod will seek the young Child to destroy Him." When he arose, he took the young Child and His mother by night and departed for Egypt, 15 and was there until the death of Herod, that it might be fulfilled which was spoken by the Lord through the prophet, saying, "Out of Egypt I called My Son." (Matthew 2:13-15 NKJV)*

Pray: Father, the storm clouds are now above our heads, the taste of unrighteousness is in our mouth, and the smell of death is in our nostrils. The day as far spent and we need Your favor to hold back the wind that we might get ready to run, So then please, hold back the wind O God, that we might get ready to run. Amen and let it be so.

| Vol 02 | Q3 | NW00552 | July 04th |

Night-Whisper | **REJOICE**

Preparations for midnight

On this occasion, the disciples returned from their mission with happiness; their conquest complete and victory on their lips. On other occasions, the battle would go hard against them and maybe like John the Baptist they would, in the darkness of the dungeon, have to send an urgent plea to Messiah saying, "Are You really who we thought You were?"

?Luke 10:17-20

Then the seventy returned with joy, saying, "Lord, even the demons are subject to us in Your name." And He said to them, "I saw Satan fall like lightning from heaven. Behold, I give you the authority to trample on serpents and scorpions, and over all the power of the enemy, and nothing shall by any means hurt you. Nonetheless do not rejoice in this, that the spirits are subject to you, but rather rejoice because your names are written in heaven." NKJV

Today, out of the silence and darkness of your lives, maybe many of you are asking that very same question. Fear not little flock, Jesus does not want you to be so desperate, despite the heat of battle or the damp of dungeon cells, though at times, we shall undoubtedly feel desperate in them both.

Jesus never kept the fact of hardship from his followers.

"If anyone desires to come after Me, let him deny himself, and take up his cross, and follow Me." (Matthew 16:24).

The cross of suffering is a dark place and can be as black as midnight in the noonday sun. So, here in tonight's text, Jesus prepares His disciples for such a midnight. The battle will ebb and flow, victories will come and go, but "Know this though," He says: "the enemy is ultimately defeated and you are saved, so, rejoice because your names are written in heaven." "Rejoice because your names are written in heaven." "Rejoice because your names are written in heaven."

"Rejoice because your names are written in heaven." "Rejoice because your names are written in heaven." "Rejoice because your names are written in heaven." Have you got that?

Many times the fact that our names are written in the book of life may not seem good enough to cause us to rejoice but oh my brethren, often times it's really all we have to hang on to. Make sure that these particular words are a nail in a sure place for you today and also that you know where to find that nail when midnight comes, for it's the only place you shall be able to hang your heavy troubles upon and thus be enabled to bring a rejoicing lightness to your oh, so, stumbling steps once more.

Rejoice because your names are written in heaven." Have you got that?

Listen: *"Then the multitude rose up together against them; and the magistrates tore off their clothes and commanded them to be beaten with rods. And when they had laid many stripes on them, they threw them into prison, commanding the jailer to keep them securely. Having received such a charge, he put them into the inner prison and fastened their feet in the stocks. But at midnight Paul and Silas were praying and singing hymns to God, and the prisoners were listening to them. Suddenly there was a great earthquake, so that the foundations of the prison were shaken; and immediately all the doors were opened and everyone's chains were loosed." (Acts 16:22-26 NKJV)*

Pray: Father, may my happiness be rooted in eternity and may its certain smile shake the earth again and release me from my chains and release those also chained with me. In Jesus name I ask this, Amen.

| Vol 02 | Q3 | NW0553 | July 05th |

Night-Whisper | **REJOICE**

Blue frog pie

Now it goes without saying that, ***"Like one who takes away a garment in cold weather, And like vinegar on soda, is one who sings songs to a heavy heart." (Proverbs 25:20)***

> ***Proverbs 17:22a***
>
> *A merry heart does good, like medicine.*

We would all agree that someone who would act like that is extremely thoughtless and exceptionally offensive! Yet, I feel we are very rarely in danger of committing such a "faux pas" as singing songs to a heavy heart, for Christians on the whole, are not marked by the world as being the "the happy bunch." Except that is, the much maligned and looked-down-the-nose-at "happy clappy" type of Christians, you know, the ones that live in 'never-never land' and not the real world like you and me! Ha! Who do those silly, happy clappy, strange and wappy, unreal folk think they are? Surely, the Christian should be marked by a profound seriousness? Yes, a seriousness of demeanour that is marked by pious misery. Especially if he's a minister!

You know, unfortunately, there is the Celtic part of me that isn't really content unless it is miserable! Yes, there is a part of me that isn't happy unless it has got something to worry about. Now is that bizarre or what! Because of this, I find a song entitled, "The Happy Song" by the former British Christian band 'Delirious' to be really challenging. I mean challenging in a quite annoying kind of way, because a part of me is exceptionally offended about the exuberance that this song tries to instigate. Shame on me though! For something very Celtic in me, something very reserved and broody, something cynical, something that is quite happy to be miserable, rebels and sneers from a haughty vantage point within my spirit upon such a preposterous attempt at a stirring of exuberant emotion. I'm not too worried though, not too many Christian folk will challenge me in my error because we all know that a really happy Christian is as rare as "blue frog pie." Think about that. A really happy Christian, not a worked up one, not a plastic smile Christian but a really happy Christian is as rare as blue frog pie. It's the truth and it's very sad isn't it?

This brooding melancholy, this satanic cynicism, this damp and critical mess of restrictive emotional visceral fat, lining the belly of our spiritual life must be gotten rid of, must be lipo-suctioned out and flushed away down some surgical drain somewhere! Yes, we must begin to thrust into our beings a living and righteous hypocrisy to poke and stir jubilance from its deep slumber, its forced hibernation within us and provoke the dampness in our souls to be actively danced away and friends, even Baptists must do this! Indeed, we must all let our mornings begin with such shouts of joy that they roll back all the glooming clouds that gather so early on our doctrinally correct, rightfully reformed, conservative and evangelized, oh so unhappy horizons! Go on, shock the neighbors today! Open the windows, take a couple of lung-fulls of air and force yourself to sing some lyrics from the happy song:

"I just can't stand it anymore, all that laughing, all that singing, all that earth shaking, wall vibrating, frivolous dancing. Who do those Christians think they are being so happy?"

"I want to shout it out from every rooftop scene
For I know that God is for me not against me
Oh I could sing unending songs of how you saved my soul
Oh how could dance a thousand miles because of your great love
Oh everybody dance!"

It's time to get the neighbors complaining friends and listen to them telling the police that they "just can't stand it anymore, all that laughing, all that singing, all that earth shaking, wall vibrating, frivolous dancing. Who do those Christians think they are being so happy?"

Unless we spike everyone's morning coffee with a tab of ecstasy it's almost impossible to believe that this can happen among Christians isn't it? However, why not ask God for faith and vision to believe and act in this way and then, imagine every seminary president and principle, hands raised, boogying down in their study, praising God! Stomping around like "good'uns". Imagine then what their lessons and their discourse would be like after that! Imagine every Christian graveside becoming a graduation event of raucous rejoicing, and every Pastor refusing to wear black ever again, ripping off white collars of captivity and burning all their "Des

O'Conner" cardigans, donning their forgotten Jesus sandals and painting their toenails red, whilst leaping like leviathans and bouncing like behemoths, and rolling around with such outrageous laughter, that with their giggle machines, now overflowing with such heavenly hilarity, that they can hardly speak through their happiness because Jesus, Jesus, Jesus, truly is their realized Savior, their inseparable friend, their Almighty mate, and they now know in truth that they are working with Him and He with them, both of them now singing together and bringing in His eternal harvest. After all, He did say, ***"I have called you friends."*** Imagine that! He did say, ***"I have called YOU friends."***

Imagine a happiness that is rooted deeply in the overwhelming experiential knowledge of God as our true friend! Would that make you sing today? Would that make you happy today, make you merry today, make you shout today, make you sing and make you dance today? I think it should.

Imagine a happiness that is rooted deeply in the overwhelming experiential knowledge of God as our true friend! Would that make you sing today? Would that make you happy today, make you merry today, make you shout today, make you sing and make you dance today? I think it should.

Religious people hate making merry but I tell you friend, spiritual people cannot live without merry making. So, let me ask you: Are you sick of church, sick of a denominationally and doctrinally correct Jesus and longing for a slice of blue frog pie? Then start making a merry heart; yes MAKE a merry heart! Go on, take your medicine right now you old misery guts and get the neighbors banging on the wall! Be happy right now beloved of Jesus, FORCE YOURSELF TO BE HAPPY!

Today, I challenge you to choose singing, to choose shouting, to choose dancing, to choose happiness and to choose life!

Listen: *"Happy are the people whose God is the LORD!" (Psalm 144:15 NKJV)*

Pray: Lord let Your blessedness arise in me in the morning and o'er flow my lips in praise and smiles; miles and miles of smiles! O Sovereign Savior, dancing King, teach me to make war with Your joy and so conquer all my darkness with rooted and well-practiced happiness. Amen and Hallelujah!

| Vol 02 | Q3 | NW00554 | July 06th |

Night-Whisper | **BALANCE**

Gluttonus Maximus, Big Boys and The Giant Greedy

Gluttonus Maximus was a Roman butcher who kept a small shop on the Appian Way. Famous for his sausages, livers and lambs legs, he nevertheless died aged just 28 years and weighing 412lbs. A nice man, but being lavish and unrestrained, he died of a heart attack brought on from gargantuan greed and elephantine excess. Many of our generation shall follow his direction and demise on our way to 'Krispee Kreme,' 'Home Town Buffet,' 'TGI Friday's,' 'Frisch's' or wherever else we can fill our plates up to the ceiling with weighted wantonness.

Deuteronomy 21:20-21

And they shall say to the elders of his city, "This son of ours is stubborn and rebellious; he will not obey our voice; he is a glutton and a drunkard." NKJV

Frisch's restaurant chain was founded in America nearly one hundred years ago in the city of Cincinnati and of course in 1946, introduced their full '1/2lb Beef Double Decker Big Boy' onto the market. The big-eyed plastic waiter, sporting his red checked dungarees over his porky little pot-belly, has become their national icon for the 'Big Boy' and today the plastic icon and the 'Big Boy Burger' are still both on sale behind every Frisch's counter!

Now let me tell you friends, that I am partial to an "all you can eat" menu, and my Scottish blood likes to get more than its money's worth. So, just the other day, in we went to trawl the breakfast bar. It was a holiday and the place was packed. Those leaving, even though they waddled out of the door, were still getting 'to go. bags, or 'to go' cups so they could continue munching in the car, (America is a country that walks very little.) Meanwhile, the food that was left behind on the plates, if gathered up, could feed a small African nation and most of economic migrants flushed across our open borders. The Big Boys were not just on the shelves waiting to be purchased, oh no, they were right here on two fat legs, perambulating and bouncing alongside numerous big mommas all on their way to their third or fourth helping. And where were we? Well I was also stuck in, right up to my elbows in the rough with the rest of them, chewing up and chow downing! It's got to be said, we're a fat nation! We're killing ourselves, and I'm sorry but it's gluttony and it'sa sin!

Now let's clear some issues out of the way. As a former fitness instructor, I advised many people on their diets and remember meeting a man who had lost 60lbs in six months. "Yup, once the doctor gave me the correct medication for my thyroid," he remarked, "all my right eating and exercising kicked in and the weight fell off." Hmmm? It's obvious that maybe some of us have a medical problem that needs checking out. I do believe that every overweight person should first visit the doctor before starting any exercise program. However, if you check out OK with the doctor friends and you're still fat, then brother, sister, you are simply eating too much. End of story! Again, the Bible calls this gluttony.

It's got to be said, we're a fat nation! We're killing ourselves, and I'm sorry but it's a gluttony and it's sin!

If under pressure, we continually and habitually turn to drugs, we are classed as an addict. If under pressure, we consistently turn to drink, we are classed as an alcoholic. If under pressure, we continually turn to chocolate or ice-cream or cake, or food in general, then at the most, we are classed as "a bit of a joke," a silent laugh line in a comedy sketch maybe. However, don't be deceived friends, for gluttony is in the end rebellion, idolatry, excessiveness and a lavishness that leads to both slavery and to death. Gluttony is all of this, for it is a seeking of satisfaction and comfort in something other than God. I am not innocent here, for I am a chocoholic and it is no joke! Ask my dentist. Ask my bank manager.

Look, enjoy your food and even pig out a little sometimes, but if food is overtaking you, overcoming you, eating you up and has become the comforter you turn to in times of trouble, then your excess is a sin that needs repenting of and by now, probably a physical problem that needs attending to. God helps all repentant sinners; and so in this, He can help us gluttons as well. Turn to Him when He calls you. If you don't, then it's bad manners and you might just end up busting a blood vessel and falling into the pig trough.

Listen: *"Your words were found, and I ate them, and Your word was to me the joy and rejoicing of my heart; for I am called by Your name, O LORD God of hosts." (Jeremiah 15:16 NKJV)*

Pray: Jesus I am sorry when I turn to candy and brandy instead of You. O Lord my God, let my soul delight itself in true fatness, because I know You and am always a familiar and open mouthed at Your most healthy table.Amen.

| Vol 02 | Q3 | NW00555 | July 07th |

Night-Whisper | **DISCOVER**

A standing ovation

One time when our son left home and went on his travels, he left his guitar for us. It was a nice one, an Ovation hard back. It stood in the corner against the wall and frankly, wasn't played at all. I wanted to play but just couldn't. You see the problem for me was that the strings were around a quarter of an inch from the fret board. Blessed with little fingers, I found pressing them down securely to get the correct note to be a virtual impossibility! When I tried it, it was painful, it sounded awful, I didn't really enjoy it, and I looked really clumsy. So, the guitar was pretty much left alone and had become the wrong kind of "standing ovation." It was a great guitar, but it was left lying in a corner, mocking me. Let me ask you tonight, what good stuff do you have that you cannot use correctly or effectively and is lying in a corner, mocking you?

1 Samuel 17:38

So Saul clothed David with his armor, and he put a bronze helmet on his head; he also clothed him with a coat of mail. David fastened his sword to his armor and tried to walk, for he had not tested them. And David said to Saul, "I cannot walk with these, for I have not tested them." So David took them off. NKJV

It happens a lot doesn't it? People in the wrong jobs, with beautiful armor on their backs, all approaching giants and making a right pig's ear of it! It takes a lot of courage to say to failing folks like that, "Friend, it's not working is it?" It takes even more courage to address that observation to ourselves.

The armor in our text tonight might look great on Saul, but only five stones and a sling will do the job in your case David. So, I ask you again, what have you got in your hand that is not working, that is uncomfortable or makes you stumble? Let go of it, put it down, and take up what is truly yours. You can guarantee that you will feel better, move smoother, walk lighter and be more effective than you ever thought possible.

Stephen (see Acts 6 and 7), the first recorded martyr of the Christian church, took to himself the Word of God and the shield of faith and so was enabled to march through the ranks of the religious with mighty signs and wonders, being enabled to dispute so irresistibly with certain of the Jews, that it was like heaving the broad sword of God across their ranks and laying bear their stinking hearts! Stephen died in battle friends but never the less, died effectively and gloriously, his face bright and happy, gleaming with the reflected glory of God. He died this smiling way because he used that which was his and so received from his mostly seated and admiring Master, a standing ovation in heaven.

The first recorded martyr of the Christian church, took to himself the Word of God and the shield of faith and so was enabled to march through the ranks of the religious with mighty signs and wonders, being enabled to dispute so irresistibly with certain of the Jews, that it was like heaving the broad sword of God across their ranks and laying bear their stinking hearts!

Maybe, getting to heaven just isn't enough? Maybe, how we arrive and are addressed and greeted when we get there should mean so much more to us? Let me ask you one more time tonight then, "Just what do you seek in glory?" Think about that O warriors of God, and worriers of hell, "What do you seek from the King of Glory? Look! What has He put in your hand today? Use it. It's mightier than you think."

Listen: *"Look! I see the heavens opened and the Son of Man standing at the right hand of God!" (Acts 7:56 NKJV)*

Pray: Lord. Grace alone has got me to Christ, has got me to heaven and will keep me secure in both, yet Lord! Rewards await. Lord, help me to use the talents You have given me in the most effective and pleasing way possible. Let me discover my gifts and usefulness today Oh God, in Your great name I ask it, amen.

Night-Whisper | **MERCY**

The look of life

Imagine a newborn child abandoned in an open field, left alone and naked, its umbilical cord still attached to the discarded placenta. The mother has gone and the carrion circle around in the morning sun waiting for the pitiful cries of the thrashing and increasingly cold and stinky specimen of a child to stop, and be still, before feasting on the newly opened eyes. This child has been left to die, to die despicably, and alone.

Ezekiel 16:6

"And when I passed by you and saw you struggling in your own blood, I said to you in your blood, 'Live!' Yes, I said to you in your blood, 'Live!'" NKJV

So God paints the picture of Israel's true state before His Sovereign intervention and friends, in so doing, He paints a true picture of our true state without His Sovereign intervention; all of us dead in trespasses and sins; all of us thrashing around like abandoned and screaming, bloody little children.

I do not want to take away from the clear Scriptural teaching of personal responsibility but tonight I want to point to this wonderful scriptural and comforting truth, that when God says, ***"Live!"*** then friends, people live! It is as Spurgeon puts it, "an irresistible mandate." Once God speaks, it is accomplished!

Jesus, I recall, was recorded in the Scriptures on being open mouthed in marveling on but two occasions: One was at the unbelief in His own area, His own relatives and in His own house and the other time, was at the belief of a Roman Centurion whose discovered faith literally "wow'd" Jesus into an amazing proclamation:

"Assuredly, I say to you, I have not found such great faith, not even in Israel!" (Matt 8:10).

The faith Jesus referred to was encapsulated in the Centurion's reply to the walking feet of Jesus then headed to his house,

"Lord, I am not worthy that You should come under my roof. But only speak a word, and my servant will be healed." Matthew 8:8

Do you see it friends? Here is the embracing of a truth that in practice, both firmly and fantastically laid hold of the soul of the Sovereign Savior and made Him squeak in delight! Lay hold of His soul again tonight dear friends, and in so doing, lay hold of His heart and change your world of worry to one of watching wonder.

Change your world of worry to one of watching wonder.

"Lord, regarding my child…please say the word and..."
"Lord, regarding my spouse…please say the word and…"
"Lord, regarding my doctor's words …please say the word and…"
"Lord, my bank manager, the letter, …please say the word and…"
"Lord, the enemy, he is saying that.….please say the word and…"
"Lord, this great and blocking mountain…please say the word and…"

Listen: *"Live!"*

Pray:

Hungry, I come to You for I know You satisfy.
I am empty, but I know Your love does not run dry
and so I wait for You. So I wait for You.
I'm falling on my knees. Offering all of me.
Jesus, You're all this heart is living for.
Broken, I run to You, for Your arms are open wide
I am weary, but I know your touch restores my life,
and so I wait for You. So I wait for You.
I'm falling on my knees. Offering all of me. Jesus,
You're all this heart is living for.

(Kathryn Scott - "Hungry")

| Vol 02 | Q3 | NW00557 | July 09th |

Night-Whisper | **PEACE**

Secret ways and hidden paths

I don't know if you noticed but in the trilogy production of Tolkien's Books, *The Lord of the Rings* there is an awful lot of imagery around doorways. It begins with the door to a hobbit house and ends with a shot of that very same door. In addition to this, the story is full of secret passageways traversing up and over mountains and even through the mountains. I particularly remember the hidden door of 'Durin' which led to 'Khazad-dum,' the domain of the Dwarves, the doorway of which could only been seen in moonlight.

Psalm 77:19

Your way was in the sea, Your path in the great waters, and Your footsteps were not known. NKJV

The second film portrayed most fearfully both the mystique and danger of approaching these same doors, of Durin and Khazad-dum, for they had both monsters outside and death inside!

I recall Browning's children's poem, 'The Pied Piper of Hamelin' and find the abduction of the children of Brunswick to be far more malevolent than many things in Tolkien's trilogy. Look…

And to Koppelberg Hill his steps addressed,
And after him the children pressed;
Great was the joy in every breast.
"He never can cross that mighty top!
He's forced to let the piping drop,
And we shall see our children stop!"'
When, lo, as they reached the mountain-side,
A wondrous portal opened wide,
As if a cavern was suddenly hollowed;
And the Piper advanced and the children followed,
And when all were in to the very last,
The door in the mountain-side shut fast.

Now that's scary!

Friends it's not only the nasty that have their secret pathways. You will be pleased to know that God also has His hidden ways, His secret paths, His ways of escape, His places of refuge. Ask Noah about the door being shut on the Ark. Ask Obadiah how he hid and protected the hundred prophets, ask David, ask Moses, ask Paul, ask a thousand others, even the millions of Israel, who in a desert place came to the sea's edge and worried and wept to find themselves boxed in by water and mountains and pursued an angry and on-coming Pharaoh! Worried that was, until God opened up a prepared way, a secret and hidden path, a way not previously known, beneath the foaming waters, where they all crossed over on dry land!

Tonight friends, as you face your violent seas and your enormous mountains, know this, and know this for sure, that though you might not see it, before you yet lays a prepared path, a hidden way of escape, a secret place of refuge.

Tonight friends, as you face your violent seas and your enormous mountains, know this, and know this for sure, that though you might not see it, before you yet lays a prepared path, a hidden way of escape, a secret place of refuge. At the right time, it shall be revealed to you. Look for it. Ask God for clarity of sight to see it. This your night, look for God's secret paths; look for God's hidden ways.

Listen: *"No temptation has overtaken you except such as is common to man; but God is faithful, who will not allow you to be tempted beyond what you are able, but with the temptation will also make the way of escape, that you may be able to bear it." (1 Corinthians 10:13 NKJV)*

Pray: Lord, All Mighty Master, reveal to me Your secret ways, Your dry path through my raging seas and the firmness on which to place my following and fearful feet. Amen O Lord, Amen.

| Vol 02 | Q3 | NW00558 | July 10th |

Night-Whisper | **HOPE**

Framing butterflies

Our opening text today is spoken to Job by his 'friend' Eliphaz the Temanite. The spoken words appear to be true and should have encouraged the beleaguered and plagued Job deep in his spirit. Unfortunately, they were but a mere pre-amble to some harsh and judgmental words that followed. Job's friend would become an Elephant of a Termite and walk all over Job's already sad and sickened soul, eat at his heart and bring down his house upon his now enfeebled little head.

Job 4:4

Your words have upheld him who was stumbling, And you have strengthened the feeble knees. NKJV

Words are powerful things friends, they are either solid and foundational, slow and steady in building, or they are fast and swinging like a wreckers ball, filling lives with devastation and dust; Yes sir, words are as sweet as honey or as bitter and repugnant as rancid butter.

Despite nursery rhymes that tell of words that "never hurt us," we all know by experience the sometimes hurtful power of words, of even a single word! In a greater respect, we also need to recognize the awesome and awful fact that words also breed. You see, when they depart our mouths, they spread their wings, enter the body through the ears, and lay their eggs in the heart. The way those words are spoken, or maybe even received, means that years later, when the larvae eventually burrow up and leave, they either emerge as ravaging locusts that eat us away from the inside, or as beautiful butterflies, that visit each memory of our mind and mend the weeping hurts of many a present distress. Did you know friends as well that, words, especially final words, last words spoken, are words that haunt people?

Many of you have spoken some words to loved ones that you wish you could take back. I say to you, "You cannot!" However, in the coming years you can so overwhelm the loved ones you have hurt, with words of such winged beauty that in time, the butterfly shall overwhelm the locust!

If it is too late, to deliver words of beauty, if death has made the distance too far for your words to travel, then dear friend, repent and make your peace with God. Such repentance will turn your own horrid haunting to repentant regret and in time, Jesus Himself may reveal to you some of the loving and living power of other words you had spoken to those now departed, some good words forgotten, powerful words, that you had spoken to them but had ceased to remember. Yes, God can take the smallest smile in any word and turn it into a firefly in a loved one's darkness. God is gracious, more than we can ever realize. Do not be destroyed by the haunting of your past horrible words to folk now gone. Repent and move on.

However, in the coming years you can so overwhelm the loved ones you have hurt, with words of such winged beauty that in time, the butterfly shall overwhelm the locust!

So, may I encourage you today to begin collecting your words as framed pictures? Words that encapsulate pictures of what could be. Invest time, love, compassion and genuine care in these words which you speak to others now. Make them like apples of gold in frames of silver and deliver them packaged with a prepared possibility, even to those who yet do want to receive them.

Life has taught me, that in time all words turn to parceled up pictures and either in rooms of regret, or halls of happiness, they are eventually unwrapped examined and held to the heart, before being hung on our inner walls as a perpetual reminder of the good or evil wished upon us or observed within us. Today my friend, fondly frame the fluttering butterfly. Have done with locust words.

Listen: *"Your words were found, and I ate them, and Your word was to me the joy and rejoicing of my heart." (Jeremiah 15:16 NKJV)*

Pray: Oh God in my mouth lays an unruly evil and a world of fire, even a flask of dripping poison! Oh Lord, tame my tongue, remove its whipping ways and make it like a lovers hand. In Jesus name I beg it, amen and let it be so.

| Vol 02 | Q3 | NW00559 | July 11th |

Night-Whisper | **HOPE**

Happily haunted

You know that words, especially final words, last words, are words that haunt people. Every mother remembers the last words she said to her son as he went out to school, into the world, off to war and then never came back.

Revelation 22:17

And the Spirit and the bride say, "Come!" And let him who hears say, "Come!" And let him who thirsts come. Whoever desires, let him take the water of life freely. NKJV

Many men still hold tight to words which they wished they had released into the lives of their loved ones, their departed mothers, their struggling sons, their sweet and beloved daughters.

"Before they had gone, I wish I had told them just how I... just how much I... that I forgive... that it's ok... that..."

You know that words, especially final words, last words, are words that haunt people.

And so today, we find ourselves happily haunted by the final words of our Savior. They are prepared words, packaged like apples of gold in frames of silver, and as each day passes more towards our end and even the end of all things as we know it, we hopefully find that we take them out more frequently, and gaze into the depths of the certain and hurried hope they carry. These final words of Jesus are for me, indeed, they are for us.

When the battle is getting hot, these last words spoken are a trumpet sound of rapid re-enforcements. When loneliness overwhelms us, they become His loving arms, embracing us. When hunger opens our mouth and thirst parches our tongue, they are poured out waters from the well of Bethlehem delivered by the mightiest of living men. When the mundane meddles with our joy, they tickle our soul and force a smile; when demands of the day destroy our peace, they come and speak calm to the raging seas; when that which is but rust and rot appears to glitter like gold, they uncover the desert and show us the sand trickling away inside the trinkets of this fast and fading world. Yes, these words are for me, they are for us.

"Surely I am coming quickly."

You know that words, especially final words, last words, are words that haunt people. Be then happily haunted today friends by the final words of your Lord.....

Listen: *"...Surely I am coming quickly."*

Pray: Amen. Even so, come, Lord Jesus! (Revelation 22:20)

Night-Whisper | **BLESSING**

Last words spoken

The small hamlet of Bognor Rocks on the south coast of England, in the 20th century became the select seaside resort for the convalescence and recovery of the very 'well to do.' It 'aint like that now!

Genesis 49:32-50:1

And when Jacob had finished commanding his sons, he drew his feet up into the bed and breathed his last, and was gathered to his people. Then Joseph fell on his father's face and wept over him, and kissed him. NKJV

King George V, when in good health, liked the place so much that he granted the town the suffix of 'Regis.' Bognor Regis had now come of age. You would have thought that this Kingly accolade would have made the place famous but you would be wrong. However, what has marked the town forever, are the final words of the same King, who, when on his death bed was asked if he would like to spend his final days in his favorite resort of Bognor Regis, retorted "Bugger Bognor!" and died at the mere thought of going there!

Another Englishman, born in Kent to wealthy parents, after serving out his time as an accountant in the city of London, was pensioned off to fulfil his desires of writing. "Goodbye" is one of the poems of Walter De La Mare and tonight, ends our present theme of powerful words.

The last of last words spoken is good-bye -
The last dismantled flower in the weed grown hedge,
The last feeble rumour of a bell far ringing,
The last blind rat to spurn the mildewed rye.

A hardening darkness glasses the haunting eye
Shines into nothing the watchers burned out candle
Wreathes into scentless nothing the wasting incense

Faints in the outer silence the hunting cry

Love of its muted music breathes no sigh,
Thought in her ivory tower gropes in her spinning
Toss on in vain the whispering trees of Eden
The last of all last words spoken is, Good-bye.

Words have power and our lives are full of them. Few of us shall have the rare opportunity, with great clarity of mind, to be able to speak with power, our final words. A car accident, a debilitating disease, imprisonment, separation, and a multitude of other silences may rob us of the power of our final words.

Prepare Your final words. Live your final words.

Think on then friends, think on, for I have determined that "goodbye" shall not be my final words but "au revoir" and "We shall meet again in far better days than these," for this certain hope of a promised tomorrow shall now dress my lips each day and clothe my pen at night, with an invitation to always follow me, "even as I will always follow Christ."

How about you? Will your life be the pen that always writes in power, your final words to those you love?

Listen: *"This I recall to my mind, Therefore I have hope. Through the LORD's mercies we are not consumed, because His compassions fail not. They are new every morning; Great is Your faithfulness." (Lamentations 3:21-23 NKJV)*

Pray: Let Your honor and Your praise Oh God, wing my words each day and clothe them with inviting hope each night, amen.

Night-Whisper | **HOPE**

Between silk and cyanide

Leo Marks wrote the fascinating book called, '*Between Silk and Cyanide: A Code Makers War, 1941-1945.*' Aged just 22, Marks began working for the SOE (Special Operations Executive) creating secret codes for heroes dropped into occupied Europe. Marks wrote over five hundred poems for such agents to use. Those dropped behind enemy lines would memorize the poem given to them and then simply transmit it back to headquarters, which, with the simple repositioning of a word or words within the text, would then relay the desired message. Violette Szabo was one such poetic agent.

> ***Matthew 11:4-6***
>
> *"Go and tell John the things which you hear and see: the blind see and the lame walk; the lepers are cleansed and the deaf hear; the dead are raised up and the poor have the Gospel preached to them. And blessed is he who is not offended because of Me."*
> *NKJV*

The film '*Carve Her Name With Pride*' tells the story of Violette Szabo, this remarkable woman, who would later be arrested and executed in Ravensbruck concentration camp. The film features "*The code poem for the French Resistance,*" which was personally given to her. Interestingly, Violette had a problem, which was that for the life of her, she could not correctly memorize the first poem she was given to use as her code! So, Marks apparently gave her this very particular poem, a poem dear to his own heart, which was dedicated to his own fiancée who had tragically been killed in a plane crash. Here it is:

The life that I have is all that I have
And the life that I have is yours.
The love that I have of the life that I have
Is yours and yours and yours.

A sleep I shall have
A rest I shall have,

Yet death will be but a pause,
For the peace of my years in the long green grass
Will be yours and yours and yours.

This poem touched Violette's heart and she did not forget it.

I have no love for Hollywood or its overly rich liberal fawning faulty human beings, never the less, I am convinced that God speaks today through communication 'codes' hidden in Hollywood films, or even set in secular books, or in seemingly unwise words dripping from the drawl of donkeys… of which there are many. Even so, I believe God still speaks, tapping out His love poems on the souls of all men everywhere by whatever means He can!

I believe God still speaks, tapping out His love poems on the souls of all men everywhere by whatever means He can!

A dark dungeon and a brutal death gripped the greatest of preachers, John the Baptizer. Hope fading, he urgently tapped out a desperate message to the Savior,

"Are you the coming one or do we look for another?"

Jesus in turn tapped out a loving response to John, a code if you will, that encapsulates not only John's desired answer but also every promise and prophecy of the past concerning Jesus, and every certain hope of the future concerning John! When John the Baptizer received the words of Jesus, I wonder if it also contained for him a very personal code from the heart of the Savior clearly speaking to John's own broken, wounded and fearful soul? I wonder if that code John was given would also translate and read,

"And John remember, the peace of My years and the long green grass will be yours and yours and yours."

Listen: *"In My Father's house are many mansions; if it were not so, I would have told you. I go to prepare a place for you. And if I go and prepare a place for you, I will come again and receive you to Myself; that where I am, there you may be also." (John 14:2-3 NKJV)*

Pray: For Your tender message of hope, I weep. My Lord, my eyes, my eyes overflow with water, that the Comforter would restore my life, draw near to my soul, restore and prosper all of my children and crush the enemy as I walk between these pressing hills of silk and cyanide. Let me know Oh God, the certain hope of Your victory today. In Jesus name I pray, Amen and let it be so.

| Vol 02 | Q3 | NW00562 | July 14th |

Night-Whisper | **FIGHT**

Before the bout begins: receive and believe!

You've probably heard the sayings "He is as much use as an ash tray on a motorbike!" Or maybe "He's as much use as a chocolate tea pot!" Both of which most picturesquely portray failure, ineptitude and uselessness.

Joshua 5:1

So it was, when all the kings of the Amorites who were on the west side of the Jordan, and all the kings of the Canaanites who were by the sea, heard that the LORD had dried up the waters of the Jordan from before the children of Israel until we had crossed over, that their heart melted; and there was no spirit in them any longer because of the children of Israel. NKJV

The Lord is a warrior and part of a warrior's tactics is to intimidate his foe. If the battle can be won before you take to the field, then all the better. After all, overcoming is often a matter of the heart, that is, what you thoroughly believe, concerning the definiteness of the outcome will help you overcome. If you can translate this belief into both spiritual and psychological intimidation to so minimize, crush and wither the heart of an opponent before the battle, then the dispatching of the enemy from the field will be a far simpler than if their hearts were stout and ready for your onslaught. This is a valuable and Biblically well-used tactic, for mark this well today, determined, defiant and fleshly confident hearts, are still the most formidable fortresses for any warrior of God to go up against.

As a former boxing coach, I can tell you that I have seen the defeated before they ever stepped through the ropes. A glimpse of their muscular and intimidating opponent, his prowess and tales of his ferocity had taken the fight out of them before the bout ever began, even when the tales that they were told, were blatant lies! You see victory is first and foremost, a matter of the heart.

For example, our Warrior God on one occasion when preparing a person for a fight, begins by implanting a troubling dream in the heart of a then unknown enemy soldier, who, then began to become so quietly concerned, that he voiced his trouble abroad in the quiet, dark, Midianite encampment. The recounting of this dream by a disturbed enemy soldier to one of his nervous mates, is then overheard by the watching Gideon, as he squirms in his troubled and trembling wait. Listen and observe, look and feel what happened in the chest of Gideon, when these things came to his listening ears:

"And when Gideon had come, there was a man telling a dream to his companion. He said, 'I have had a dream: to my surprise, a loaf of barley bread tumbled into the camp of Midian; it came to a tent and struck it so that it fell and overturned, and the tent collapsed.' Then his companion answered and said, 'This is nothing else but the sword of Gideon the son of Josh, a man of Israel!' Into his hand God has delivered Midian and the whole camp."

Can you see what's happening in Gideon's heart? You see, when the faint hearted and hidden Gideon heard the telling of the dream and its interpretation, his own most pitiful and quivering heart then became powerfully pumped and so, in strong expectation he then began to worship God in wonder, awe, and hopeful expectancy.

Cripple the heart, cripple the man. Turn the heart, turn the battle.

Two things happened here:

First, the enemy's heart was made fearful and expectant of defeat and second, the heart of Gideon was made strong and expectant of victory!

May I say, it was at this intersection of Gideon's receiving and believing that the battle was won. Friends, at this point even before a pot was shattered, the battle was all over bar the shouting! Gideon returned to the camp of Israel and proclaimed to his companions,

"Arise, for the LORD has delivered the camp of Midian into your hand."

See it friends? Whilst making great the heart of Gideon, our warrior God also deflates the heart of the Midianites. Cripple the heart, cripple the man. Turn the heart, turn the battle. This method is replicated throughout Scripture and may I add, is seen on both sides of conflict! (see 1 Samuel 4:5-11).

Warriors of God, may I ask you tonight concerning the state of your heart and the level of your hope in God and the depth and the firmness of your confidence in our Almighty commander? If your heart is not right friend, don't even step through the ropes. However, if you will first get your heart full of expectant victory tonight, then I tell you, "Some giants are going down! Some strongholds are going to be shattered and pulled to pieces" that is, providing your hearts are full of faith, full of confidence and can see the victory from afar. Receive and believe! Get to that intersection tonight, receive and believe today!

"Some giants are going down! Some strongholds are going to be shattered and pulled to pieces"

Listen: *"Keep your heart with all diligence, for out of it spring the issues of life." (Proverbs 4:23 NKJV)*

Pray: Lord, who can stand before You? Who can resist You? You are great O Lord, You are the promised "head crusher". So Lord place your feet and mine, on the necks of all our enemies, deflate and defeat them today O my mighty Jesus and so fill my heart with faith, amen.

| Vol 02 | Q3 | NW00563 | July 15th |

Night-Whisper | **FIGHT**

Faith in the forger

Mere bravado and self-confidence does not constitute pre-battle intimidation. If you have not trained, if you do not know your enemy, if you have not walked wisely and obediently in your preparation, such ignorant bravado is but mere stupidity.

Joshua 7:1-5

Now Joshua sent men from Jericho to Ai, which is beside Beth Aven, on the east side of Bethel, and spoke to them, saying, "Go up and spy out the country." So the men went up and spied out Ai. And they returned to Joshua and said to him, "Do not let all the people go up, but let about two or three thousand men go up and attack Ai. Do not weary all the people there, for the people of Ai are few." So about 3,000 men went up there from the people, but they fled before the men of Ai. And the men of Ai struck down about thirty-six men, for they chased them from before the gate as far as Shebarim, and struck them down on the descent; therefore the hearts of the people melted and became like water. NKJV

David, that ruddy young man of renown, was no doubt fearful in approaching Goliath of Gath. Yet his heart was in the trim because his method and weapons were tried and tested.

"Your servant used to keep his father's sheep, and when a lion or a bear came and took a lamb out of the flock, I went out after it and struck it, and delivered the lamb from its mouth; and when it arose against me, I caught it by its beard, and struck and killed it. Your servant has killed both lion and bear; and this uncircumcised Philistine will be like one of them, seeing he has defied the armies of the living God." (1 Samuel 17:34-36)

David was ready! You see, the intimidation and mocking of our enemies before the battle, the shaping and shattering of hearts before a stone is thrown or a sword is swung is not mere bravado. It must come from the fact that we have already thoroughly tried, trained and tested what we are about to use. We know the strength and value in what God has given us to fight with.

The weapons of our warfare are not carnal, but mighty! Do you know that? Have you felt the shuddering impact of a weapon of God used by you against His enemy? More than this though friends, our confidence must be in more than the weapon and the known wielding. Our faith must be in the Forger of such weapons.

"Moreover David said, 'The LORD, who delivered me from the paw of the lion and from the paw of the bear, He will deliver me from the hand of this Philistine'." 1 Samuel 17:37

Now many of you not only do not have a clue about what I am speaking but may also find my use of fighting words deeply troubling and against what you believe to be the mind of Christ? May I encourage you to examine the Scriptures and find the Christ of the Scriptures? He is the Commander of God the Father's magnificent Hosts of angel armies. He is the ultimate warrior and He's engaged in a tremendous conflict with the great enemy. He was dead but now is alive and He's coming soon to bring a sword of flaming judgment to the earth!

Jesus is the Commander of God the Father's magnificent Hosts of angel armies. He is the ultimate warrior and He's engaged in a tremendous conflict with the great enemy. He was dead but now is alive and He's coming soon to bring a sword of flaming judgment to the earth!

Intimidate, mock and make the enemy shake, make the darkness tremble friends, don't just sing about it but do it! However, do make sure that such talk and dancing is not mere bravado rooted in a big mouth and a bombastic untried head and heart! Let thorough preparation, knowledge of self and intimacy with the Almighty God, clothe your words with steely strength, both tomorrow and in all the days thereafter.

Listen: *"Now I saw heaven opened, and behold, a white horse. And He who sat on him was called faithful and true, and in righteousness He judges and makes war. His eyes were like a flame of fire, and on His head were many crowns. He had a name written that no one knew except Himself. He was clothed with a robe dipped in blood, and His name is called The Word of God. And the armies in heaven, clothed in fine linen,* *white and clean, followed Him on white horses. Now out of His mouth goes a sharp sword, that with it He should strike the nations. And He Himself will rule them with a rod of iron. He Himself treads the winepress of the fierceness and wrath of Almighty God. And He has on His robe and on His thigh a name written: KING of KING and LORD of LORDS." (Revelation 19:11-16 NKJV)*

Pray: Lord, help me to live in the reality of who You are. Teach me how to kick some enemy ass, in Your great name I pray, amen and let it be so.

| Vol 02 | Q3 | NW00564 | July 16th |

Night-Whisper | **FIGHT**

Seek out the "smithies"

To finish off this wee trilogy on warfare, let me point out a great plan of the enemy. He wants to remove the weapons from our hands so we can neither attack nor defend ourselves and the best way to do this, is to remove the blacksmiths from the land.

1 Samuel 13:19-22

Now there was no blacksmith to be found throughout all the land of Israel, for the Philistines said, "Lest the Hebrews make swords or spears." So it came about, on the day of battle, that there was neither sword nor spear found in the hand of any of the people who were with Saul and Jonathan. But they were found with Saul and Jonathan his son. NKJV

A minister of the Most High, a Pastor, is in fact a vital member in the support and supply corps of the Lord's army. It is part of the Pastor's job not just to fight and defend the flock of God but to so supply them with sharp double-edged swords, so that it's not only two people who enter the battle sufficiently armed and prepared, but the whole band, even the whole local nation as it were.

"Every man armed with a sharp two edged sword."

Now there's an interesting church motto I have yet to see in any Pastor's study!

Our enemy has done a thorough job in eliminating blacksmiths from the land. When did you last think of your Pastor as someone you can go to learn how to fight, or as an armorer 'par excellence' that will give you the most effective and appropriate weapons to fight with, or is able take what you have already got in your hands and have it sharpened, re-forged, re-tempered and made stronger still? Too many Pastors are adept at the art of political maneuvering, social studies, demographic science, tea drinking, nice talking, wet fish handshaking, deacon dodging and trustee training than they are at laboring over God's hot coals of supplying service and producing weapons of warfare, weapons of both defense and destruction for their local battalion. Many a Pastor's persistent motto has been,

"Be Nice. Smile. Offendeth Not and most of all, Covereth thine own back!"

No, I am afraid that the old blacksmiths are long gone from the land.

To those who are sick of losing, I counsel you to seek a man who has a furnace and is known for having the wind of the Holy Spirit pass over his coals to make them white hot. Seek out a Pastor whose house is filled with the sound of a rushing mighty wind, the clash of arms and the felt heat of forged steel. Seek out a true spiritual blacksmith then, whose hallway is full of harness and halter, breastplates and helmets, not of old ladies coats, nice curtains and pink puffy pelmets. Seek out some real men then, men that are hot with God!

Seek out a Pastor whose house is filled with the sound of a rushing mighty wind, the clash of arms and the felt heat of forged steel.

Seek out The Smithies!

Listen: *"Behold, I have created the blacksmith who blows the coals in the fire, who brings forth an instrument for his work." (Isaiah 54:16 NKJV)*

Pray: Lord, lead me to the blacksmiths and equip me for the war. In Jesus name I ask it, amen.

| Vol 02 | Q3 | NW00565 | July 17th |

Night-Whisper | **LOVE**

Night-Whisper | CONSIDER

Are you an idiot?

Someone once said to me that "Even if heaven was a lie and there was no afterlife, Christianity would be worth it because it is still such a great way to live." I get the point, however, the apostle Paul says exactly the opposite! "If Christianity is all bunkum," he says, "then of all men we are the most pitiable!" That is, we are altogether wretched and miserable and without any compassion being shown to us. In other words, if Christianity is all bunkum, we are like well-needled heroin addicts, covered in our own vomit and left out to die on the cold wet streets of the city, whilst vicious passersby, pee and spit on us.

1 Corinthians 15:12-19

Now if Christ is preached that He has been raised from the dead, how do some among you say that there is no resurrection of the dead? But if there is no resurrection of the dead, then Christ is not risen. And if Christ is not risen, then our preaching is empty and your faith is also empty. Yes, and we are found false witnesses of God, because we have testified of God that He raised up Christ, whom He did not raise up — if in fact the dead do not rise. For if the dead do not rise, then Christ is not risen. And if Christ is not risen, your faith is futile; you are still in your sins! Then also those who have fallen asleep in Christ have perished. If in this life only we have hope in Christ, we are of all men the most pitiable. NKJV

The apostle Paul and the early Christians fallen asleep and especially 'put to sleep' in Jesus, and in the most violent of ways, left gaps in the front line ranks of the church militant that were readily filled with more spiritual cannon fodder. Tell me, if the claims of Christianity were not true, then was this a good way to live, or simply just a stupid but certain way to die?

Look now, to be a Christian in the early church was more often than not a death sentence. For a multitude of Christians now in the Islamic world, to be a Christian is to be a target for similar dissolution. In the time to come in the West, to be a Christian shall once again be a death sentence. Therefore, if the resurrection and rewards to come are not true, then being a Christian in the face of terrible death would make us the most pitiable of deceived people. Brother, there is no middle ground for the true disciples of Christ. If Christianity is not true, you are a pitiable idiot with an imaginary friend! However, if Christ and His claims are both real and true, then He is worth dying for and you probably will. Might I suggest, that if you think Christianity is just a great way to live, then you probably aren't living it, for, to be a Christian is a costly, sacrificial, and deadly way to live. Are you just a chameleon in a culture club?

If Christianity is not true, you are a pitiable idiot! If it is true, then it's worth dying for and you probably will!

It looks as though the devil has moved his earthly throne back the middle east. He's been spiraling anticlockwise and to the left from Pergamum in Turkey for a couple of thousand years now and recently gone all across Europe in two world wars. Now, he's coming back to where he started some 2,000 years ago. Look now, when this happens, all hell will break loose around the satanic seat. Fear and fury are always greater the closer you get to Caesar. Do you know what I mean? My point is this, that the darkness has, and is, warring against the light. The vanguard of the church militant is always pressing against the gates of hell. Therefore being a Christian will cost you dearly and you will wonder if the price is worth the paying. I tell you that the Scriptures say it is! Resurrection and rewards follow the faithful people of God.

Brethren, count the cost and press on, and before you press on, take time to count the cost. The days of cultural Christianity and choosing Christianity as a profitable lifestyle are drawing to a close in the West. Its time to really trade in and Biblically ' trade up!'

Listen: *I look death in the face practically every day I live. Do you think I'd do this if I wasn't convinced of your resurrection and mine as guaranteed by the resurrected Messiah Jesus? Do you think I was just trying to act heroic when I fought the wild beasts at Ephesus, hoping it wouldn't be the end of me? Not on your life! It's resurrection, resurrection, always resurrection, that undergirds what I do and say, the way I live. If there's no resurrection, "We eat, we drink, the next day we die," and that's all there is to it. But don't fool yourselves.*

Don't let yourselves be poisoned by this anti-resurrection loose talk. "Bad company ruins good manners." (1 Corinthians 15:31-33 from THE MESSAGE: The Bible in Contemporary Language © 2002 by Eugene H. Peterson. All rights reserved.)

Pray: Father, who would live for facts, except they would be profitable, but my Lord, what a dry way to live. Father, who would die for mere facts? Ah but Father, to live with the living God, to walk with You in daily experience, what a way to live! Amen and let it be so. Then Lord, who would deny Your reality and loveliness, Your greatness, goodness and promises in the face of death? So, let us know You, that death would be to us, nothing but the doorway You have spoken of. Amen and let it be so.

| Vol 02 | Q3 | NW00566 | July 18th |

Night-Whisper | **WITNESS**

Night-Whisper | FREEDOM

Of created and movable chocolate feasts

The Evangelical Dictionary of Biblical Theology says that "the major festivals of Old Testament Israel were, in calendar order, Passover, Unleavened Bread, First-fruits, the Feast of Weeks (Pentecost), the Feast of Trumpets, the Day of Atonement, and the Feast of Booths (Tabernacles or Ingathering). After the exile, the Jews added memorial days for the fall of Jerusalem (eventually fixed as the Ninth of Ab), Purim, and the Feast of Dedication (Hanukkah). In addition, the Israelites observed the Sabbath every week and the feast of the New Moon every lunar month." The old testament theocratic nation of Israel celebrated a great deal as a community. In the New Testament there are of course, ooh, how many feasts and feast days was it again? Oh that's right. None.

Deuteronomy 23:1-3

He that is wounded in the stones, or hath his privy member cut off, shall not enter into the congregation of the Lord. A bastard shall not enter into the congregation of the Lord; even to his tenth generation shall he not enter into the congregation of the Lord. An Ammonite or Moabite shall not enter into the congregation of the Lord; even to their tenth generation shall they not enter into the congregation of the Lord for ever: KJV

Even so, as the New Testament church has trudged through two thousand years of time, it has in its various institutional forms acquired more feasts than you could throw a ferret at, more seasons than the four that God gave us, and more rotating holy-days than there are days in a year! With this conglomeration of congregational events, there lies a great selection of garbs and colors, of ceremonies and cultural events and traditions. In addition to this, two thousand years of additional consumer magic has also led most of the manmade major Christian festivals to be remembered and fitted to the shape of an open wallet. I have two questions to ask tonight, the answers, if put into practice, might reshape the church of the near future.

My first question is, "Did God the Holy Spirit, over time, give additional unrecorded commands and direction to the church to initiate, commemorate, celebrate, and participate, in various feasts and holy-days not recorded in the Scriptures?" If the answer to that is 'yes,' then it's all a bit of a mess, or, it looks at bit of mess because God has obviously adapted Himself to various historical splits, expressions and cultural mores. If this is the case, then the intent of such Holy Spirit direction in the initiation of the feasts etc., is for them to be a didactic remembrance episode for the ever-forgetful people of God. If, however, the answer to this my first question is a resounding 'No,' then we are being cluttered, gutted and misled in the nicest of ways.

In this, we the church, have become static, institutionalized, and inbred. We have produced nominal citizens of the Kingdom of God rather than true converts of grace.

My second question is, "As there are no recorded New Testament church feasts etc., should this new body of Jew and Gentile still celebrate the Old Testament feasts?" I believe the answer to this is NO! Now then, before my messianic brethren string me up, let me tell you why.

The Old Testament theocracy of Israel was a 'come and see' spectacle of how and who God was. For the Gentile, he could see 'from afar,' and maybe, providing he could adhere to and pass the laws and regulations of conversion to Judaism, he might observe God a little more up close and semi-personal. I think that our Christian liturgical calendars and two thousand years of envy of other religious spectacles, coupled with competition to retain congregations and even control monarchs, has led to a similar 'come and see' mentality even in the modern day celebration worship extravaganzas of the local church. In all this false feasting, we the church, has become static, institutionalized, and inbred. We have produced nominal citizens of the Kingdom of God rather than true converts of grace.

The early church travelled light and boy they travelled! The 'Go and Tell' mentality of the two-ordinance light brigade made them fleet of foot, as active as yeast, and as powerful as a right hook from Manny Pacquiao. Look now, two thousand years and the world is still not evangelized? There are many reasons for this, but one of them is that we have settled down to a church calendar 'come and see mentality.' Going back to celebrating Jewish feast days is just as bad, if not worse.

Biblically, the church has but the two ordinances of baptism and the breaking of bread. That's it. Sure, we have instructions on how we should gather, (not when) and how we should be governed. However, these instructions are for the 'go and tell' Great Commissioning people of God. If you turn into the 'come and see' people of God, then I suppose two thousand years will allow you enough time to make some stuff up. (Ouch!)

As for me, providing I am 'going and telling,' then I delight inso called 'Christian Feasts.' Who doesn't like Chocolate eggs at the time to remember the resurrection of our Lord. I have no problem with it. When it comes to Christmas time, somewhat reluctantly, you will also find me celebrating the landing of our Lord on our shores. Why? Well, because it's a good family time and yes, I love gifts of chocolate.

I judge no one on their participation in feast days, new moons or Sabbaths. Keep what you will and keep it to the Lord. However, if the end of these things is simple indulgence and a 'come and see' mentality, then you're on your own fat boy, because you are out of step with the Holy Spirit and the Word of God.

If the end of these things is simple indulgence and a come and see mentality, then you're on your own fat boy, because you are out of step with the Holy Spirit and the Word of God.

Let me simple ask you tonight you 'Go and Tell' disciple....who are you going to share this Gospel with tomorrow?

Listen: *In Him you were also circumcised with the circumcision made without hands, by putting off the body of the sins of the flesh, by the circumcision of Christ, buried with Him in baptism, in which you also were raised with Him through faith in the working of God, who raised Him from the dead. And you, being dead in your trespasses and the uncircumcision of your flesh, He has made alive together with Him, having forgiven you all trespasses, having wiped out the handwriting of requirements that was against us, which was contrary to us. And He has taken it out of the way, having nailed it to the cross. Having disarmed principalities and powers, He made a public spectacle of* *them, triumphing over them in it. So let no one judge you in food or Let no one cheat you of your reward, taking delight in false humility and worship of angels, intruding into those things which he has not seen, vainly puffed up by his fleshly mind, and not holding fast to the Head, from whom all the body, nourished and knit together by joints and ligaments, grows with the increase that is from God. Therefore, if you died with Christ from the basic principles of the world, why, as though living in the world, do you subject yourselves to regulations — "Do not touch, do not taste, do not handle," which all concern things which perish with the using — according to the commandments and doctrines of men? These things indeed have an appearance of wisdom in self-imposed religion, false humility, and neglect of the body, but are of no value against the indulgence of the flesh. (Colossians 2:11-23 NKJV)*

Pray: Father, let each new day for me, be a feast day with You. Amen and let it be so.

Night-Whisper | CONISDER

For those who are straining at the gates of Gerizim

The redeemed Old Covenant people would now pass through a valley on their way to possess the promised land. A natural amphitheater to host the spiritual theater which they were now all to partake in. On one side would be the six square miles of mount Ebal, a naked and barren mountain, cold and rocky in structure and look. On the other side, Mount Gerizim, apparently abounding with springs, gardens, and orchards, and covered in verdant loveliness.

Deuteronomy 27:1-3

Now Moses, with the elders of Israel, commanded the people, saying: "Keep all the commandments which I command you today. And it shall be, on the day when you cross over the Jordan to the land which the Lord your God is giving you, that you shall set up for yourselves large stones, and whitewash them with lime. You shall write on them all the words of this law, when you have crossed over, that you may enter the land which the Lord your God is giving you, 'a land flowing with milk and honey,' just as the Lord God of your fathers promised you. NKJV

Joshua, on Mount Ebal would build an alter and make sacrifice in the place of cursing. With the Ark of the Covenant occupying the center of the valley and the tribes divided by six on each side of it, all ascending either up Mount Ebal or up Mount Gerazim, the cursing's and the blessings of disobeying and obeying the law would be pronounced, and from these great whitewashed standing stones, upon which 'in relief' the words were written, would also bear testimony to this first convocation of a national gathering in a land which was now theirs.

Look now, a nation stands in the valley, the presence of God in their center, the law above them, and a continual choice of witnessed cursing and blessings before them.

I write in 2016 when Ireland is commemorating its birth as a an independent nation. Fergal Keane, commenting on Ireland's violent Easter Rising of a century ago, remarks that, "Almost every state exists because of violence. Over the centuries world wars, civil wars, revolutions and genocide have helped create nation-states across the world. Great empires were built on the violence of superior firepower."

For sure, Israel now would enter into the promise of God through judgement genocide, violence, war and brutality, yet even so, this nation was to be built upon a Divine promise, and the new nation would not have its own representatives nor statesmen poets to read out its covenantal intentions, no, God through His prophet Moses commanded this first national initiation to be celebrated in this way, with all seriousness and national agreement. This land legacy was from God, it was His land and they were His new national tenants.

"Behold, the Lord comes with ten thousands of His saints, to execute judgment on all, ... "

At the coming of the Lord for His church, a similar national convocation shall take place, but this time it shall be 'in the air.' The living shall be translated and caught up with the dead in Christ in a Holy convocation in the clouds which shall be filled with people from every nation, tribe and tongue redeemed from the earth. Then, God in our midst, shall establish us as He sees fit in all reward of ranks and privileges. Following this, after being well fed in all rejoicing at the Marriage supper of The Lamb, the gates of this earth's Gerizim shall be opened once more to us and we shall return to take it.

Saints of God, the rebel occupiers of this earth are using our stuff! However, be assured that the promised land shall be ours and we shall return to take it.

"Now Enoch, the seventh from Adam, prophesied about these men also, saying, "Behold, the Lord comes with ten thousands of His saints, to execute judgment on all, to convict all who are ungodly among them of all their ungodly deeds which they have committed in an ungodly way, and of all the harsh things which ungodly sinners have spoken against Him." (Jude 14-15)NKJV

Meanwhile, we must break our 'sleep cycle.' Look now, the average Christian comes into the world, gets an education, gets a career, consumes in the name of Jesus, biologically reproduces, prepares financially for retirement, dies in hope and sleeps in Jesus. All of this is being done without any reckoning to judgement and reward and the life to come. Our sleep cycles have left us in the grave. The 2nd coming of Christ in the air, shall lead to the judgement seat of Christ, the great convocation of Kingdom nationhood, and the forceful retaking of the earth. The thousand years and the eternities of thousands of years thereafter together with our place and position in it, all have their roots in our here and now.

Christian you must awake from your sleep cycle. There is more to come and very much at stake. Christian you must live with Mount Ebal at your back and the gates of Gerizim before your face. Are you straining like a greyhounds in slip collars? Are you neighing like a horse for battle? Are you ready to possess the land? Wake yourself from Laodicean lethargy! Mightily stir yourself, else at the time of the coming burning, your pension will go up in smoke, and you along with it.

Wake yourself from Laodicean lethargy, mightily stir yourself, else at the time of the coming burning, your pension will go up in smoke, and you along with it.

Meanwhile, for those straining at the gates of Gerizim, I say, “Look, the land lies ready before you. Go and take it.”

The game's afoot my friends, follow the Holy Spirit, and upon this charge cry out, “"That the Lamb may receive the reward of His suffering. Amen!”

Listen: *"Moses My servant is dead. Now therefore, arise, go over this Jordan, you and all this people, to the land which I am giving to them — the children of Israel. Every place that the sole of your foot will tread upon I have given you, as I said to Moses…….No man shall be able to stand before you all the days of your life; as I was with Moses, so I will be with you. I will not leave you nor forsake you. Be strong and of good courage, for to this people you shall divide as an inheritance the land which I swore to their fathers to give them. Only be strong and very courageous, that you may observe to do according to all the law which Moses My servant commanded you; do not turn from it to the right hand or to the left, that you may prosper wherever you go. This Book of the Law shall not depart from your mouth, but you shall meditate in it day and night, that you may observe to do according to all that is written in it. For then you will make your way prosperous, and then you will have good success. Have I not commanded you? Be strong and of good courage; do not be afraid,* *nor be dismayed, for the Lord your God is with you wherever you go." (Joshua 1:1-9 NKJV)*

Pray: O God that we might prove our Divine nobility, and our breeding as the blood bought of Jesus. Help us not dishonor Jerusalem our mother, even the Holy City of God, but please Lord, let the luster of the life to come be seen in our eyes and in the going forth of our limbs and the true possession of our hearts. In Jesus name we ask it, amen and let it be so.

| Vol 02 | Q3 | NW00568 | July 20th |

Night-Whisper | **LOVE**

"This is the end. For me, the beginning of life."

The Allied breakout from the Normandy landings inspired an assassination attempt today in 1944 when Count Von Stauffenberg placed a briefcase with a bomb inside Hitler's command post for the Eastern Front in the city of Rastenburg, otherwise known as his 'Wolf's Lair.' The bomb used by these Germans was one of many British bombs confiscated by German intelligence. Stauffenberg placed the primed bomb under the conference table and left.

John 15:12

This is My commandment, that you love one another as I have loved you. NKJV

After the explosion, both Stauffenberg and the other plotters believed Hitler was dead and so prepared to seize Berlin with home army troops. However, Hitler, though seriously injured, survived the bombing. Stauffenburg and thousands of others died in the purging that took place after this failed assassination.

Remarkably, this attempt on Hitler's life had been in the planning for more than six years and a German Lutheran Pastor, Dietrich Bonhoeffer, had been involved in this plot from the beginning. Nazi officials would shortly discover the diary of another co-conspirator, Admiral Canaris and Hitler in his rage, would order the annihilation of the Admiral and his entire resistance group, which by the way, included Pastor Bonhoeffer, who was by now already in prison for aiding the escape of Jews to Switzerland and keeping his own underground Pastors out of the military.

There are three things of note here:

First, that it is difficult for people of peacetime to understand the desperate necessities forced on others in times of war, especially when they are facing such overwhelming horror. Bonhoeffer's Christian conscience was clearly rooted in his theology, which demanded he respond to such evil whatever the cost. I pray that God is raising up some new Bonhoeffers to stand against the coming wave of persecution from the little teeth secular humanism and the big teeth of Islam.

Secondly, Bonhoeffer knew and that he had bravely counted the cost to himself, his family (three other close family members were executed shortly after him) and to many other people associated with him. Not only would he have to take responsibility for his life before His Lord but he would be accountable for the lives of many others before His Lord as well.

I pray that God is raising up some new Bonhoeffers to stand against the coming wave of persecution from the little teeth secular humanism and the big teeth of Islam.

Thirdly, Bonhoeffer knew he was ultimately safe in the hands of Jesus and that death, though it may be very tortuous and very horrible, would nevertheless be the portal to his eternal home and eternal life. Nevertheless, this side of heaven, he was bound in his inmost being to fight evil. Be sure friends that this brave Pastor knew and lived out all three of my pitiful observations from me, presently a peacetime Pastor.

On April 9 1945, Bonhoeffer stripped naked before his gallows and faced the consequences of his love for Jesus and his fellow man. It is reported that before he walked out of Flossenburg concentration camp barracks for the last time, he had whispered to a fellow prisoner, "This is the end. For me, the beginning of life."

Listen: *"Greater love has no one than this, than to lay down one's life for his friends." (John 15:13 NKJV)*

Pray: Lord, You call us to a life of love and sacrifice for others. Give us courage here, and wisdom. Let us not be ardent for some desperate glory but no matter what the cost to us, let us be faithful and true to our deep love for You, amen.

| Vol 02 | Q3 | NW00569 | July 21st |

Night-Whisper | **VISION**

Millions of Magoos

So she looks at me and says, "I'm sorry the ticket is for a flight next week at this time, not today!" Now this was the second time in two months this had happened to me. I booked the flight over the internet, checked the documents thoroughly only to find later that something vital to the journey was incorrect. The date! I didn't trust the electronic booking system and these mistakes were becoming expensive. So, another $100 later, I was found a seat on my flight and boarded the same, this time even more tired and grumpy.

Proverbs 29:18a

Where there is no vision, the people perish. KJV

My seat was 16A and as I approached it, I could see it was occupied by some giant of a man. I sat in the vacant seat next to him leaned over and showed him my ticket. "I think you're in my seat." He looked at my ticket, and then looked at me with that "Are you out of your mind?" kind of look. I looked at my ticket again; 16A, then looked up at his seat number. It read, 15A! Thoroughly embarrassed, I apologized, withdrew graciously and took my real and empty seat behind him!

My flight back home gave me opportunity to reflect on what was happening in my life, with the wrong flight bookings, wrong seat identification, etc. Other incidents of reading words at a distance, only to find they read something completely different close up indicated that I might have had some problems with my eyesight. A visit to the optician confirmed this and getting older meant that I now had to wear my prescription glasses more often.

It took so long to identify the problem because my brain took many of the blurred images and translated them for me as best as it could, as near as it could. In other words, I was not seeing what I thought I was seeing! My brain was tricking me as I was just unconsciously interpreting, and many times incorrectly, the blurred images I was now observing.

In our society, our eyesight is so far gone that we cannot but fail to misinterpret that which we see. Even as Christians we so often fail to clearly see what is going on. Friends, we need to put on the prescription glasses of God's Holy Word and have our vision corrected by the Holy Spirit, for the older we get as Christians, the clearer we should really see. It would seem that this is not the case though and the failing eyesight in the natural, is all too often reflected in our increasing darkness in the spiritual. Surely this should not be the case friend should it? Of course not! However, the cares of this world and the deceitfulness of riches have cast their pollinated darkness into the very depths of our vision and millions of Christian Magoos with big 'bi-focal' eyes and outstretched arms, follow each other into one deep pit, one after another. So, let me ask you today dear friend, "What do you see? I mean, are you wearing your prescribed spectacles of the Word of God?"

Millions of Christian Magoos with big 'bi-focal' eyes and outstretched arms, follow each other into one deep pit, one after another.

Listen: *"I counsel you to buy from Me gold refined in the fire, that you may be rich; and white garments, that you may be clothed, that the shame of your nakedness may not be revealed; and anoint your eyes with eye salve, that you may see." (Revelation 3:17-18 NKJV)*

Pray: Lord, open my ears and open my eyes, for I walk along the precipice of my life and am in need of the clearest of vision. Oh Holy Spirit help me, in Jesus name in that you make me a true seer, amen.

| Vol 02 | Q3 | NW00570 | July 22nd |

Night-Whisper | **VENGEANCE**

The lady in red

Anna Sage, a Romanian born brothel keeper living in Chicago was actually wearing an orange dress to identify her leaving the Biograph Theatre. Under the cinemas entrance lights her dress appeared to be red. Sage's beau for the evening was America's then public enemy number one, the bank robber and murderer Mr. John Dillinger. Leniency in an upcoming deportation hearing and the prospect of cashing in on the $10,000 bounty meant Anna turning him in to the FBI a very attractive proposition. Dillinger however, refused to surrender and was gunned down by twenty waiting FBI agents. A multitude of murders, bank robbing and daring jailbreaks had finally come to an end. It was 'the lady in red' who had led this rascal to his public Police execution.

Judges 4:18

And Jael went out to meet Sisera, and said to him, "Turn aside, my Lord, turn aside to me; do not fear." And when he had turned aside with her into the tent, she covered him with a blanket. NKJV

I love the way the Scriptures present life in its beautiful but often times monstrous reality. For example, Rahab the harlot wisely betrayed her own city and country to find forgiveness and mercy and a place in the family tree of the Christ. Bathsheba the beautiful, would for centuries become almost unmentionable for the betrayal of her husband, yet Solomon would emerge from her adulterous womb. Delilah would seduce Samson (and it didn't take much friends!) and topple a judge and blind a powerful leader. Ye, Samson would also topple a kingdom in his redeemed blindness. I could go on but it might be good to get to my point. Am I saying, "Men beware of women dressed in red?" You're dead right I am!

However, that is not my main point. I truly believe that the message we need to embrace is that God will get the bad guys in the end! He is a God of judgment, and all things are naked and laid bare before Him with who we have to do. God will get the bad guys in the end.

Researchers claim that autopsy findings on the corpse dragged from outside the Biograph Theatre contradict known medical records of Dillinger and the truth is, in another daring twist, Dillinger once again might have given justice the slip. Even so, I tell you, whether the corpse was Dillinger's or not, he did not escape God's justice. No one ever does.

God's timing and purposes are inscrutable, yet it has to be acknowledged that there is a mountainous multitude of great injustices that go un-dealt with in this life. People think they can hide in a new name, a new country or with a new face and even behind the power and pride of self-justification, or whatever convenient and clever fig leaf that comes to their hand. Though many are quiet and peaceful and seemingly smug and successful in so thoroughly hiding their sin, having so slippery side stepped what is most certainly their just rewards; I still tell you, that they are not successful in their seclusion at all, for God will nail them in the end, for we know Him who said**,**

Our God, is a God of pursuing vengeance.

"Vengeance is Mine I will repay," says the Lord. And again, "The LORD will judge His people." It is a fearful thing to fall into the hands of the living God. Hebrews 10:30-31.

You might not like it but there it is. Our God, is a God of pursuing vengeance.

Tell you what, you had better make sure all your fatal felonies and mocking misdemeanors are nailed to the cross of Calvary along with and in, His sacrificial Son. Because He's coming and when He arrives, it'll be no more Mr. Nice guy. Christian, neither will your persecutors and murderers get away with anything. There is a reckoning coming and God will not forget.

Listen: *"And Jael went out to meet Sisera, and said to him, 'Turn aside, my Lord, turn aside to me; do not fear.' And when he had turned aside with her into the tent, she covered him with a blanket. Then he said to her, 'Please give me a little water to drink, for I am thirsty.' So she opened a jug of milk, gave him a drink, and covered him. And he said to her, 'Stand at the door of the tent, and if any man comes and inquires of you, and says, "Is there any man here?" you shall say, "No".' Then Jael, Heber's wife, took a tent peg and took a hammer in her hand, and went softly to him and drove the peg into his temple, and it went down into the ground; for he was fast asleep and weary. So he died. And then, as Barak pursued*

Sisera, Jael came out to meet him, and said to him, 'Come, I will show you the man whom you seek.' And when he went into her tent, there lay Sisera, dead with the peg in his temple." (Judges 4:18-22 NKJV)

Pray: So Lord, help us to give You all our injustices. So Lord help us to be mightily empowered to love our enemies knowing that You, The Great Judge will do right. For we know that those who do not find refuge under the nails of Jesus, will indeed be nailed by Him in the end. Amen.

Night-Whisper | ACTION

God's coming iconoclasm and gifts to UNESCO

N owadays, despite Greece and other countries wanting the return of artifacts which they see as their heritage, including parts of buildings which they consider to have been their national property long stolen from them, the United Nations Educational, Scientific and Cultural Organization, UNESCO, currently defines such heritage as "our legacy from the past, what we live with today, and what we pass on to future generations," and further that, "our cultural and natural heritage are both irreplaceable sources of life and inspiration," and finally that, "World Heritage sites belong to all the peoples of the world, irrespective of the territory on which they are located." I think UNESCO would be at odds with the destructive action plans of the Lord God Almighty found in our text for tonight.

Deuteronomy 12:2,3

You shall utterly destroy all the places where the nations which you shall dispossess served their gods, on the high mountains and on the hills and under every green tree. And you shall destroy their altars, break their sacred pillars, and burn their wooden images with fire; you shall cut down the carved images of their gods and destroy their names from that place. NKJV

Inspired by the mad mullahs of Islamic State, these black hearted and black clothed monsters have recently destroyed yet another World Heritage site that used to reside in Palmyra, Syria. The destruction being that of the long standing and much utilized temple of Baal. As a United Nations reaction to such destruction, the Roman Archway of the temple shall be reproduced by 3D printer and placed in the capital city of many of the world's nations. Yes indeed, a portion of the temple of Baal was reconstructed in a capital city near you, any day now.

Over the centuries this particular Palmyra Baal building, once used for religious orgies including the summoning of the demonic and the sacrifice of children being burnt alive, has then been subsequently used in a most utilitarian fashion down the centuries to house many other things, including a church and a mosque. Therefore, why shouldn't it be regarded as a piece of world heritage to be preserved and glorified? Why? Well, because we can see that when Israel failed to follow God's command in utterly destroying the World Heritage sites of Canaan, their failing to do so led to within a couple of generations, to them utterly corrupting themselves and thus bringing themselves under an even greater judgement than that which had been applied to the promised lands previous residents. All idols are gateways to the demonic.

Idols are a generational snare. However, in this world, only when Christians are in the ascendance and moved to take action, should they have the idols legally and orderly removed and transported to whoever wants them. UNESCO can have them all!

In Britain, we seem to now have a fat stone Buddha sitting on every third front doorstep! Golden Hindu temples abound, as do mosques and minarets, together with the long time, long bearded druid dancing around the great henge on Salisbury plane. In the light of UNESCO's fascistic 'acquisition by naming' of what it deems to be 'World Heritage,' what then should be the Christian reaction to the growing idolatry we find all around us and to the unrescinded 2nd commandment of the Lord which reads,

"You shall not make for yourself a carved image — any likeness of anything that is in heaven above, or that is in the earth beneath, or that is in the water under the earth; you shall not bow down to them nor serve them. For I, the Lord your God, am a jealous God, visiting the iniquity of the fathers upon the children to the third and fourth generations of those who hate Me, but showing mercy to thousands, to those who love Me and keep My commandments." (Exodus 20:4-6 NKJV)

Well, I think there are four tings we should do:

First then, if the idol is personally ours, let us personally destroy it.

Secondly, if the idol is resides in the community of the people of God, then by orderly and legal means let us seek to have it destroyed, but be prepared to take the consequences. The fallen people of God love religion, especially of its syncretized. If UNESCO demand to have it, gift aid it to them.

Thirdly, if the idol is not yours, and is in the sphere of the wider and mixed community of religions, then you must leave it alone. Avoid it, do not pay homage to it, neither its priests, nor anything flowing from it. Meanwhile, should God be pleased to prosper Christianity then allow the idols to fall into disuse and disrepair. Then, move it, brick by brick if needs be, into storage, and if again UNESCO want it, then let them have it to store with all the other idols removed from Christian lands. When Christ returns to destroy these idols, and He will, it would be easier for them to be found on one place.

Remember that idols are a generational snare. However, in this world, only when Christians are in the ascendance and moved by God to take action, should they have the idols legally and orderly removed and transported to whoever wants them. UNESCO can have them all.

Look now, do you think upon the return of Christ that any of these 'Idolatrous Heritage sites' and their Idols shall be left to stand? They shall not. Never-the-less it is not now our present responsibility to destroy that which is not ours. Let Christ do it when He returns. In the meantime, avoid them, do not hallow, honor, nor pay for them. Do not visit them nor knowingly accept anything from them.

Listen: *Therefore, my beloved, flee from idolatry. I speak as to wise men; judge for yourselves what I say. The cup of blessing which we bless, is it not the communion of the blood of Christ? The bread which we break, is it not the communion of the body of Christ? For we, though many, are one bread and one body; for we all partake of that one bread. Observe Israel after the flesh: Are not those who eat of the sacrifices partakers of the altar? What am I saying then? That an idol is anything, or what is offered to idols is anything? Rather, that the things which the Gentiles sacrifice they sacrifice to demons and not to God, and I do not want you to have fellowship with demons. You cannot drink the cup of the Lord and the cup of demons; you cannot partake of the Lord's table and of the table of demons. Or do we provoke the Lord to jealousy? Are we stronger than He? (1 Corinthians 10:14-22 NKJV)*

Pray: Father, help us to cast down our own idols first of all. Lord the spiritual ones we have erected in our hearts and minds are both an offence and stench to You and a great stumbling block to we ourselves and others. Help us therefore to cast down our own idols. As to the external ones in our community and nations, Lord, let anarchy subside and the rule of law and order triumph until You come and so prosper Your people O Lord, that we might gift UNESCO with as many of these snares as we can. Amen and let it be so.

The master of my own ship?

Robert Graves was born today in 1895. His classic memoirs of his time with the Royal Welch Fusiliers during the First World War, have worried my mind since I read them when I was in school, and that was many years ago!

Exodus 19:18

Now Mount Sinai was completely in smoke, because the LORD descended upon it in fire. NKJV

Graves is not of my favorite poets, yet from his book, '*Fairies and Fusiliers* (1918),' the poem entitled "Smoke-Rings" presents a penetrating and perturbing picture of God.

BOY:

Most venerable and learned sir,
Tall and true Philosopher,
These rings of smoke you blow all day
With such deep thought, what sense have they?

PHILOSOPHER:

Small friend, with prayer and meditation
I make an image of Creation.
And if your mind is working nimble
Straightway you'll recognise a symbol
Of the endless and eternal ring
Of God, who girdles everything
God, who in His own form and plan
Moulds the fugitive life of man.
These vaporous toys you watch me make,
That shoot ahead, pause, turn and break—
Some glide far out like sailing ships,
Some weak ones fail me at my lips.
He who ringed His awe in smoke,

When He led forth His captive folk,
In like manner, East, West, North, and South,
Blows us ring-wise from His mouth.

I imagine some comfortable and placid person may find comfort in such pictures of God blowing us like smoke rings for His own pleasure! However, it is only a comparative few that seem to possess such an *interesting* attribute, such a desirable situation maybe. The vast majority of us appear to be intent on scrambling ever higher up the heap with all the vigor and dash that we can muster, to see what we can do, to see what we can make of ourselves on this perturbing and beautiful rock, bathed in blue, hanging like a forgotten Christmas bauble in the vastness of cold and empty space. Most of us are not content to muse and rest as smoke rings from the mouth of God.

He who ringed His awe in smoke,

When He led forth His captive folk,

In like manner, East, West, North, and South,

Blows us ring-wise from His mouth.

As for me, well probably like you, I am not a "sit down and wait for it to happen" kind of guy. The double witness of my bowels and grey hair will testify to that! Oh no, I like to make things happen! So friends a large part of my character doesn't particularly appreciate this poetic picture. Are we not after all, the master of our own ship? Are we not all after all, the masters of our own fate?

Listen: *"So then it is not of him who wills, nor of him who runs, but of God who shows mercy. For the Scripture says to the Pharaoh, 'For this very purpose I have raised you up, that I may show My power in you, and that My name may be declared in all the earth.' Therefore He has mercy on whom He wills, and whom He wills He hardens." (Romans 9:16-18 NKJV)*

Pray: Great King, You who ringed Your awe in smoke, forgive me when I forget myself. You are the potter and I am the clay. You are both master and commander of this my little and creaking ship. You are the Creator and I am the creature. Yet Lord, I am a creature borne of and bearing Your image. Father, help me to rule wisely and humbly my own heart and Your great creation; the day and the darkness, the light and the shadow of my life before you dear Jesus, majestic Lord over all. You are the Lord; yes, You are the

Lord and for Your pleasure was I created. Help me to live to feel Your pleasure upon my upturned and waiting face, as You blow me from your lips into the center of Your will for me. Amen and let it be so.

| Vol 02 | Q3 | NW00573 | July 25th |

Night-Whisper | **KNOW**

Those awful agnostics

The vicar stood at the exit of the church shaking the hand of each parishioner as they left the service. Spotting an elderly new comer, he reaches out his hand and taking hers thanks her for coming and asks if she enjoyed the sermon? She looks him in the eye and forgetting the word "acoustics," whilst adjusting her hearing aid she replies, "Well my dear. I'm sure it was very good but what with all the bad agnostics you have in these old buildings, it made it very difficult to understand precisely what you were saying."

Romans 1:18-23

For the wrath of God is revealed from heaven against all unGodliness and unrighteousness of men, who suppress the truth in unrighteousness, because what may be known of God is manifest in them, for God has shown it to them. Although they knew God, they did not glorify Him as God, nor were thankful, but became futile in their thoughts, and their foolish hearts were darkened. Professing to be wise, they became fools. NKJV

Bertrand Russell says that, "An agnostic thinks it impossible to know the truth in matters such as God and the future life with which Christianity and other religions are concerned. Or, if not impossible, at least impossible at the present time." On the surface this description might present agnosticism as a peaceful "live and let live" kind of philosophical position, you know, liberal but without the teeth. Just like the little old lady. No sir, beware! Agnosticism is like a hungry alligator. It's got teeth and it'll eat you up if given half the chance.

Many so-called free thinkers may now join a multitude of libertine organizations ready to utilize all the bags of disdainful rocks such free thinkers have gathered throughout the years. (And believe me friends, in our stupidity and naivety we have left a lot of ammunition lying around for them!) For example, the Universal Church Triumphant of the Apathetic Agnostic. (Tag line: 'We don't know and we don't care') may have started out as a joke and an exercise in irony but their published papers against Christianity and the knowable existence of a supreme being, show such barbed intensity against people who acknowledge "revelation" and the "knowing that they have in their knower" about God, that it's obviously way past time for us to wake up, suit up and stand up!

Beware though friend, for if we stand up we then need to follow up! We have to practice what we preach, we have to exhibit that which we proclaim and we need to come up with unshakeable proof that God is indeed among us. The world has both nothing but disdain for the practitioners of religion and disgust for those that do not practice what they preach. Maybe we should have the same approach? I think the time has come for us to come up with "the Christian goods" for I wonder if the world is truly groaning in its longing to see the authentic and supernatural evidence of Christ in the redeemed people of God. Please God let it be so, for our true Gnosticism is not the whispering of secrets in high walled cloisters but shouts from the rooftop concerning the revelation of God in the face of Christ Jesus! The true Gnostics of God need to have a raging resurgence in our day.

The world has both nothing but disdain for the practitioners of religion and disgust for those that do not practice what they preach. Maybe we should have the same approach?

So let me ask you today, "Do you know God? Can your enemies maybe say that you at least appear to know God? Do you have an answer to give for the hope that is within you? Is your relationship so vital with Jesus, so vibrant in connectivity, so visionary in insight, so voluminous in possession that you are called a 'city on a hill', 'salt', 'light', 'mercy' and even, 'love come down'?"

You will agree with me I am sure that "The true Gnostics of God need to have a raging resurgence and those of us who claim to have possession of God need to come up with the evidence of such a possession." What are you going to do about that friend?

Listen: *"And we know that the Son of God has come and has given us an understanding, that we may know Him who is true; and we are in Him who is true, in His Son Jesus Christ. This is the true God and eternal life." (1 John 5:20 NKJV)*

Pray: Lord. In good fruit and wonderful works, show me the signs of my possession by You. Amen.

REST

Sensible selfishness

Even the pre-flight presentations are now mostly presented on video. The fun of the small pantomime at the front of the aircraft is almost gone so let us share some memories of those happy times!

Song of Solomon 1:5,6

I am dark, but lovely, O daughters of Jerusalem, like the tents of Kedar, like the curtains of Solomon. Do not look upon me, because I am dark, because the sun has tanned me. My mother's sons were angry with me; they made me the keeper of the vineyards, but my own vineyard I have not kept. NKJV

For me it was always the shock of making sure that, should the oxygen masks fall, even if you are sat next to a small child, even the darling of your life, you must put your mask on first. Even if you are sat next to your wife - your very heart and soul you must put your mask on first. In fire, flood, crumpling metal and tightest of lungs, you must take care of yourself first, so you can then take better care of others.

Evangelical Christianity does a lot of travelling on guilt trips. The pressure from the pulpit to be involved in this or that ministry can be immense. The Pastor's local heroes are of course those dedicated souls who run themselves ragged and still smile for Jesus. Until one day, they wake up, look in the mirror and see panda eyes and cheeks draped like heavy curtains weighing down their now meagre smiles. The Pastor often does not fare much better; you know? Bitter, fatter, balder. You know it's the truth! In this respect, in the end we are responsible for our own vineyards, yet the church in all its busyness must beware not to destroy the vineyards of its members. Think about it. In addition to this, the church must take care of itself. Saints must come first in all social giving and in all pastoral care, church comes first. Let the world come long second to church finances and social care.

Spanish poet Antonio Machado says in his poem 'The Wind One Brilliant Day,'

The wind, one brilliant day, called
To my soul with an odor of jasmine.

'In return for the odor of my jasmine,
I'd like all the odor of your roses.'

'I have no roses; all the flowers
in my garden are dead

'Well then, I'll take the withered petals
and the yellow leaves and the waters of the fountain.'

The wind left. And I wept. And I said to myself;
'What have you done with the garden that was entrusted to you?'

Friends the church is dying through lack of self-care. Let's put the church first and make sure we do not wear ourselves out in taking care of a world that does not give a toss. Church first!

Listen: *"Jesus said to him, 'You shall love the LORD your God with all your heart, with all your soul, and with all your mind.' This is the first and great commandment. And the second is like it: 'You shall love your neighbour as yourself.' On these two commandments hang all the Law and the Prophets." (Matthew 22:37-40 NKJV)*

Pray: Lord, walk with me in my garden in the cool of my day, hold me in my desolation and let us together, begin again to make something beautiful. Lord, truly revive Your church that it might take care of itself first of all. Amen and let it be so.

| Vol 02 | Q3 | NW00575 | July 27th |

Night-Whisper | **REST**

His way of walking

So this is interesting. God is heard before He is seen when He walks in the gardens of His making. So, we need to ask the question, what sound does God make when He walks in our garden? What are the audible indicators of His approach? Adam and Eve new the sound of every creature that walked the woods of their abode and God's arrival was distinct among His creation. How can we learn to mark the sound of His appearing in the garden of our hearts, hear Him walking in the grounds of our spirit, and smell Him in Freesia fragrance of the wet rains of our troubled souls? Indeed, what does His knock at the door of our soul sound like? We should know. Shouldn't we?

Genesis 3:8a

And they heard the sound of the LORD God walking in the garden in the cool of the day. NKJV

This is more important than we realize. You see I am a man of words. I love them. I expect to hear God speak in words. I even believe in the primacy and power of the proclaimed Word! Yet God speaks in other ways. In quiet looks, in careful colors, in old friends, muses in movies, in knowing sounds, and in oh so many other ways as well. Oh, methinks we miss so much, so very much indeed concerning the voice of the Lord.

Be sure friends this particular arrival in our text for tonight was not a voice, but a sound. The voice came later in searching pleas for the shamed and hidden Adam and Eve. Before the voice though there came simply the sound of His arrival and it was that time of day, amidst all the other sounds that this one sound was known and expected. I say again, do you know the sound of your Savior walking in your garden?

I suspect it was the best of walking, you know, barefoot walking, His spirit, soul and flesh touching the naked earth. It was a knowing touch a communicating contact of Holy footprints, it was evidence of His being there; it was choice walking, it was weighty walking that only true uprightness brings and yet light walking, you know, enough to tread the storm tossed waves of water and not sink, for this walking is Divine my friend, this walking is distinct! This walk I wonder was not to the accompanying rumble of thunder and lightning crack, no trumpet proclamation here of approaching judgment and doom but maybe a walking accompanied with such a gentle singing, that it trembled open the revealing leaves before it. Maybe it was the sound of tinkling water, a flute or singing harp that paints in our hearts a waters brook, caressing smooth pebbles backed by the sound of a distant deepness and the faint murmur of a giant powerful gushing waterfall. Ah yes, He leads me beside still waters. Ah yes, deep calls to deep at the noise of Your waterfalls.

Maybe this kind of walking is a walking that carries something with it. For God is no unpleasant guest, He always arrives with something good.

Maybe this kind of walking is a walking that carries something with it. For God is no unpleasant guest, He always arrives with something good. The best of bread, the sweetest of wine and the choicest of dainties on which we might dine. Maybe the swish of His picnic basket is also heard amongst the trees. Yes, He prepares a table for us even in the middle of our enemies.

Surely then, the approaching sound of God in the good garden of the regenerate soul is the sound of such a walking, that it brings with it the singing favor of fresh food and rest, comfort, comfort and of joy, the best, the best, the best, the very best indeed. Tell me, have you heard Him walking in the gardens of your spirit just lately?

Listen: *"The LORD your God in your midst, the Mighty One, will save; He will rejoice over you with gladness, He will quiet you with His love, He will rejoice over you with singing." Zephaniah 3:17*

Pray: I did not expect you to arrive this way, but Lord I look and wait today, for the sound of goodness today arriving in my poor garden. Amen.

Sweetness Always

Well it finally happened. At a communion service, a church from the now conservative Southern Baptist Convention offered two cups to the congregation. One alcoholic, the other one just juice.

Psalm 104:14,15a

He causes the grass to grow for the cattle, And vegetation for the service of man, That he may bring forth food from the earth, And wine that makes glad the heart of man. NKJV

This emerging church plant of the 21st century believes itself to be more Biblical in offering an alcoholic alternative at communion time. In England, my part of the world, this is not even an issue but in Kentucky, which has been called the "Buckle on the Bible Belt," this no doubt, was quite a step.

Believe me when I tell you my family has been more than burned regarding the deep problems that arise from drunkenness. However, culturally and more importantly Biblically, I find no basis for alcoholic prohibition on any front. Rather, I do find many warnings and commands against drunkenness, for drunkenness friends is a trigger cocked and loaded, on a cold metal weapon pressed deep inside the open mouth of our very self.

Now, the more I consider the reason for drunkenness, and consistent drunkenness, the more I am drawn to the pain of desperate people that need to anaesthetize themselves against the hurt they carry and for a while no matter what, must forget, must relieve the pain. Brad Paisley and Alison Crouch sum it up so well in their song "Whiskey Lullaby":

The rumours flew but nobody know how much she blamed herself
For years and years she tried to hide the whiskey on her breath
She finally drank her pain away a little at a time
But she never could get drunk enough to get him off her mind
Until the night
She put that bottle to her head and pulled the trigger

And finally drank away his memory
Life is short but this time it was bigger
Than the strength she had to get up off her knees
We found her with her face down in the pillow
Clinging to his picture for dear life
We laid her next to him beneath the willow
While the angels sang a whiskey lullaby

Anesthetic drunkenness is a big problem, especially amongst women and especially amongst women at home by themselves. The problem is big enough for me to say to some who even read these words today, "dear friend if you are caught in this numbing cycle, Jesus your healer can heal your pain, can remove the darkest stain, can restore from little to more, much, much more." You see, much like the majority of things, sex, money and alcohol aren't the problem. What you do with them is!

Anesthetic drunkenness is a big problem, especially amongst women and especially amongst women at home by themselves.

So, if you are today caught in a drunken trap, then you need to begin to find a deeper desire to replace the destructive one that you have in your heart and hands right now and that deeper desire my friend, would be Jesus. Alcoholism is a very serious issue not dealt with by magic mantras but by you and the power of God Almighty. As a beginning and an end to the finding of this greater desire may I suggest that you get on your knees today, my brother my sister, and uncork His grace and hold Him to your lips and drink deeply of His help. Every time the bottle calls, turn to your Father and say the following words:

Listen: *"Let him kiss me with the kisses of his mouth - for your love is better than wine." (Song of Solomon 1:2 NKJV)*

Pray: Lord, forgive me when I have taken a bottle rather than the blessing of Your sweetness to my lips. Forgive me when I have sought another numbing solution to the product of my bad choices and the hurts of this fallen world and then pushed those hurts even further, even so deep into my soul only to leave them rotting, like compacted faeces at the center of my being. I stink Lord and I hurt. Jesus, today I ask you to kiss me with the kisses of Your mouth and breath healing to my spirit. Give me better desires today O Lord and an enema of love for the relief of my hurting and bloated self-protection. Jesus I take Your name to my lips today, please let me find You to be, always sweetness to my soul. Amen and let it be so.

| Vol 02 | Q3 | NW00577 | July 29th |

Night-Whisper | **PURE**

Listening for the lisp

I walked into the printing shop to pick up my photocopying and the guy who I usually deal with comes over and says, "Thigh!" I'm sure he meant to say "Hi" but it really sounded like "Thigh!" His speech seemed to be a little slurred. I soon found out that as a founder member of the Church of Body Modification he had by himself, the previous night with some ice, a little gauze and a scalpel, performed a central bifurcation of his own tongue. He had split that bad boy right down the middle! He assured me that in a few days after the swelling had gone down that I would hardly notice the slight lisp he now had. He opened his mouth and showed me his new lizard tongue. It matched the four spikes he had protruding from the flesh of his right arm, really well. He assured me that this would also help him on his journey into spirituality, which turned out to be a veritable smorgasbord of everything that was not Christian. He seemed happy, excited and quite at peace about things. This coming weekend he and a few of his friends were going to have some pizza and then hang themselves for a few hours on flesh hooks. I couldn't really compete with that. Pizza, friends and a movie would be enough for me. So I thanked him for the photocopying and went on my astonished little way. His values were of a different weight to mine, his apparatus of judgment was indeed marked by a very different scale and that was dangerous, for the weighing of flesh always needs to be upon the Masters measured scales. Remember that.

Proverbs 20:10

Diverse weights and diverse measures, they are both alike, an abomination to the LORD. NKJV

Concerning different weights and measures, I believe God speaks on two levels about this but on both levels, he calls it "abomination." This is a strong word. It means, "disgusting" or even "a thing of horror." If I could utilize the British way of understatement to so mark the seriousness of what is being said by this verse I might say, "The LORD finds all kinds of double-dealing, most distasteful!"

What is double-dealing? Essentially, it is saying one thing but actually doing another. It's intentionally having a forked tongue so as to deceive the other person. Double-dealing is just that, it's deception and God finds such forked tongue deception, most distasteful.

On the first level all teaching that spouts a true spirituality but is contrary to God's revealed will, is an abomination! It is from the serpent himself, it is death and not life. It is Grandma Goldilocks with sharp teeth and bad breath and no matter how weirdly cute it might look it will eat you up in the end. There is no subtlety here, it is what it is and brazenly so. Such teachings contrary to the Scriptures are but Sulphur-coated sayings that purport sound spiritually, real growth, true freedom, and even life, but in the end, they deceive and deliver perversion, diminishment, bondage and death. Watch for such contrary teachings for in our day, they abound!

What is double-dealing? Essentially, it is saying one thing but actually doing another. It's intentionally having a forked tongue so as to deceive the other person. Double-dealing is just that, it's deception and God finds such forked tongue deception, most distasteful.

On the second level, such double-dealing is often hidden. You have to listen for the lisp. Snake like and serpentine double-dealing is everywhere and God help us, if we listen closely we shall find that it is sometimes present even in us, and especially in our churches. Here we often say one thing, whilst we actively do another. We praise God but then we curse men. We smile with our face but hate wriggles within our hearts. We shake hands in the open but shake fists in the darkness. May God forgive us! For the Father finds our church wide double-dealings most, yes, most distasteful. Careful now.

Listen: *"Woe to those who call evil good, and good evil; who put darkness for light, and light for darkness; who put bitter for sweet, and sweet for bitter!" (Isaiah 5:20 NKJV)*

Pray: Oh God. Who of us has not spoken with a forked tongue, through snakeskin and lizard lips? From this day Lord, we seek the pure water from our regenerate hearts to break out and freely flow from our mouth and so to disinfect, our often most distasteful mealy mouths. Amen.

| Vol 02 | Q3 | NW00578 | July 30th |

Night-Whisper | **EMBRACE**

Refluxology

It's a nasty condition and the effect on the esophagus can be profound. Acid bubbling up out of the stomach into the esophagus can burn lesions into the tissues. For a preacher, one of the more disconcerting aspects of acid reflux disease is its tendency to reach up to the vocal cords and eat them away. At night time, many people take their teeth out and put them in water; for those people with acid reflux however, just eat the wrong food at the wrong time and it's like putting your vocal chords in acid overnight. After a while it becomes painful to speak and your power of projection is virtually gone and many times, even your ability to maintain a healthy sounding discourse is also ruined. Acid reflux is nasty.

Luke 15:28

But he was angry and would not go in. Therefore his father came out and pleaded with him. NKJV

It is obvious to me that there is a parallel, I may even suggest a connection, between physical acid reflux and spiritual acid reflux. Just the other day I took note of how regularly I became aware of my thoughts regurgitating painful scenarios of past conflicts. The emotions associated with each revisit were acidic. Not just one type of bad thought either but a whole panoply of nasty stuff. You know, anger, disgust, astonishment! Spiritual acid reflux is like trying to pick up a single hook from a bowl full of the same but you can never get just one without pulling up a whole bunch of others! This regurgitated mass of kicking and screaming emotions has a dreadfully debilitating effect on us. We become aware of a lump in our throats, a difficulty in swallowing what others might have to say to us, a lack of enjoyment of certain foods of fellowship, an avoidance of issues and worst of all a loss of power in that voice which is ours. The projection of our personhood and the totality of our wholeness are indeed diminished when you suffer from spiritual acid reflux disease.

There are several ways of dealing with physical acid reflux. Eat the right things at the right time, raise your bed head up four to six inches and of course take medication, which neutralizes the acid, until finally you find a medication to turn the acid off, and slowly gain some healing! You deal with Spiritual acid reflux in exactly the same way friends. What I am about to say next is good theology and excellent refluxology. So listen up!

While the process of the healing of past hurts takes place, you may have to avoid scenarios which aggravate the issue. For sure, you may well have to deal objectively and righteously with issues of great concern (2 Tim 4:14) but it must be at the right time. So, be sure then to objectively tackle things at the right time and with that of course, learn to never stick your hand in a bowl full of hooks! Address issues objectively and do so while taking large measures of vocal forgiveness and including positive substitutionary thoughts in your mind and heart. With this you can then neutralize the acid of bitterness whenever the bile rises.

Now, all of this works well friends but it's very tiring when you continually have to do it! So, we need to find a way of stopping the bitter and angry, deadly and depressive regurgitation today! So, just how do we turn the acid off? How do we stop the bile rising? Well, may I suggest that the best of medicine is the embracing our own sin and then the thorough embracing of our Savior, followed by the embracing and loving of others, very much indeed. In other words, once you own your own sin, confess it and repent of it you must then thoroughly embrace the Savior. Yes, like a legless drowning man would squeeze any buoyant object to himself, so we must thoroughly and desperately embrace the Savior! I wonder if that when you begin embracing Jesus as your Savior in this thankful, desperate and life giving manner, then, and only then, are you one who realizes that He has forgiven you much. Very much indeed! This gripping embracing is so necessary, for you see, it's only once you are aware of just how much you have been forgiven, that you can then begin to forgive and to love other's as you should. Once you get that sense of being so very deeply forgiven yourself, only then can you truly forgive those who have trespassed against you. Does this mean you avoid the issue with the sins of other people against you? By no means! They must

Once you own your own sin, confess it and repent of it you must then thoroughly embrace the Savior. Yes, like a legless drowning man would squeeze any buoyant object to himself, so we must thoroughly and desperately embrace the Savior!

be objectively tackled both for yourself and the whole body. However, it is only in the forgiving of others, then and only then, that the bitter bile can be neutralized.

The truth is that some of you have got terrible spiritual acid reflux disease because you have yet to realize just how much you have been forgiven. Do you dare to begin to enter and own the darkness which is yours today? Maybe you need to, for I am convinced that it's only by doing this, that you are enabled personally, from your heart to truly love the Savior and then objectively begin to confront the persons and issues of the trespasses against you and that you might begin to love them rightly? It's not easy, but then again, good cures never are!

It is only in the forgiving of others, then and only then, that the bitter bile can be neutralized.

Listen: "*Do you see this woman? I entered your house; you gave Me no water for My feet, but she has washed My feet with her tears and wiped them with the hair of her head. You gave Me no kiss, but this woman has not ceased to kiss My feet since the time I came in. You did not anoint My head with oil, but this woman has anointed My feet with fragrant oil. Therefore I say to you, her sins, which are many, are forgiven, for she loved much. But to whom little is forgiven, the same loves little." (Luke 7:44-47 NKJV)*

Pray: Lord, lift up my head. I have been forgiven much and no doubt, much more than I know or care to truly acknowledge. Father, help me to embrace my sin and my Savior in such a way that I would love others well. In Jesus name I ask this, amen!

PAUSE FOR PRAYER | 66CITIES

Well, I do pray that the first month of this quarters Night-Whispers written with you in mind, have prospered you spiritually and pushed you on a little farther down the road in knowing, obeying and immediately following the commands of the God of the whole Bible. This is my desire.

I am Victor Robert Farrell and I am the author of Night-Whispers. I also have the privilege of being the President of The 66 Books Ministry and I want to tell you a little bit about our major project which is: 66Cities. I believe one of the problems with the rapid moral decline of the West coupled with the influx of other religions, has been the compromise of the local church. It is as though we leaders have watered down the wine of the Gospel with the methods and culture of the world and have done so to such an extent that all we are left with is an anemic and slightly rose colored, fluoride-filled cup of poor tepid mouth wash. It is good for nothing except to be poured down the drain. This compromise I speak of, was to stop speaking about the God of the whole Bible and to such an extent that Christians were left in a strange kind of idolatry, worshiping the God of a cultural constructed Christianity, and so much so, that when these same Christians came into contact with the real God of the Bible, He troubled them and offended them. Indeed, they were embarrassed by Him and wanted Him excluded from their parties. The world of course, found more substance in the other gods, especially that kind of unbiblical Trinitarian spirituality which allowed science and hedonism to mate with the X factor of their own particular choosing.

We at The 66 Books Ministry intend to preach the Gospel of Jesus Christ and the God of the whole Bible, from each of the 66 Books of the Bible in the 66 most influential cities of the nations of the world. That's 16,500 cities in an annual and ongoing basis. To make this happen we are prayerfully raising up teams of proclaimers and 'prayer rangers' to go into these cities. We see this is a true prophetic witness to the glory of God. Indeed. This is the main reason why we are doing this: that God the Father and God the Son may be seen and Glorified in the power of God The Holy Spirit. We hope and pray, that many will see the Father, trust in the Son and be saved by the power of the Holy Spirit as well. Brethren, **we covet your prayers as we do this.** Check out WWW.66Books.TV

| Vol 02 | Q3 | NW00579 | July 31st |

Night-Whisper | **FREEDOM**

The real slam papi

In 1987, Mark Kelly Smith, born on the east side of Chicago began a new strand of performance poetry at the Green Mill Tavern. His unflinching realism and innate sense of rhythm made him a compelling performer of "Slam Poetry." Narrating "The Spoken Word Revolution" he tells of the arrival of slam poetry on Chicago's near West side, as "breaking with convention" and "daring to be entertaining and inclusive, allowing audiences the option of booing, stomping, snapping or hissing the poets off stage". He says, "It was anarchy, it was outrage and it was Holy Holy Holy!"

John 7:46

The officers answered, "No man ever spoke like this Man!" NKJV

In Galilee, after a hidden 30 years The Promise reveals Himself. The Head Crusher steps quietly, confidently and mightily, through this planet's possessed and drooping ropes into the center of the ring and with His Words, He lays His mighty grip on the shoulders of the adversary and every other cobelligerent who for years had blinded hurting eyes and corked bleeding, pleading ears, slams the enemy on his back. They are all treated with the same disrespect.

"White washed walls." SLAM!
"Brood of Vipers." SLAM!
"The Sabbath day! So what! The Sabbath was made for man." SLAM!
"Stretch forth your hand friend." SLAM!
"Even the rocks would cry out." SLAM!
I said "Even the rocks would cry out." SLAM, SLAM, SssLAM!!

Look again now at the angry Jesus! For there He goes, striding into the temple, table tossing, yes, turning and throwing the money changers out on their ear and on their ass,

"My Words, my Words they shall remain," He cries, ***"though everything else shall pass, shall pass!"*** Slam! Whipping their backs and booting them up the Heine throwing them out of the temple shouting, ***"My Father's house shall be a house of prayer for all nations and not a den of thieves!"*** Slam! A crowded house leads to the roof being peeled off and a quadriplegic being lowered down and He says in front of them all, **"I forgive you your sins!"** Slam! And just so they know He can, He says**, "Take up your bed and walk!"** Slam! Then the caught, shamed and bear breasted woman is brought before Him, the mouthy mob all weighed down with killing stones baying for her blood is dispersed, slapped across the chest with words that exploded like a percussion bomb in their hearts, **"You who are without sin, throw the first stone!"** SLAM! And then turning to the woman, He says **"Woman where are your accusers? Yeah! Where are your accusers? Go and sin no more."** *Do you see that?* Slam! Slam! Sssssssslam!

Grace and forgiveness you see, when truly embraced when truly applied, stirs up the foul messes of our lives and move us into His restorative order and I tell you, I tell you when this truly happens "It's anarchy! It's outrageous and it's Holy Holy Holy!"

My God! Jesus, think on what He did! Think on what He does today! Grace and forgiveness you see, when truly embraced when truly applied, stirs up the foul messes of our lives and move us into His restorative order and I tell you, I tell you when this truly happens "It's anarchy! It's outrageous and it's Holy Holy Holy!"

Listen: *"The Spirit of the Lord GOD is upon Me, Because the LORD has anointed Me to preach good tidings to the poor; He has sent Me to heal the broken hearted, to proclaim liberty to the captives, and the opening of the prison to those who are bound; to proclaim the acceptable year of the LORD, and the day of vengeance of our God; to comfort all who mourn, to console those who mourn in Zion, to give them beauty for ashes, the oil of joy for mourning, the garment of praise for the spirit of heaviness; that they may be called trees of righteousness, the planting of the LORD, that He may be glorified." (Isaiah 61:1-3 NKJV)*

Pray: Slam down lies today O Lord. Slam me down today. Wrestle me dear Jesus, fight with me, grapple with me and at the break of this my coming day and dead leg me forever! Make me limp and lean on You Lord Jesus, yes, come and tell it like it really is. So, raise Yourself up in my life O God and rock of ages, come so rock my world today, that I may never be the same again! Mighty Savior make today my slam time. Amen and let it be so.

Coiled cobras

Bohun Upas, the 'tree of poisons' is a mythical plant of the middle ages. The first travelers returning from South East Asia returned with tales of a tree that gave out such toxic fumes that it would kill plants and animals for miles around. Like old fishing stories, the power of the Upas tree seemed to grow more with the telling. One such story was that "prisoners sentenced to death would be forced to sit the night under the tree of poisons and so were gruesomely dispatched" or "out of twenty warriors sent to harvest the sap of the tree of poisons, well, only two or maybe three would return alive!"

2 Samuel 13:30-32

And it came to pass, while they were on the way, that news came to David, saying, "Absalom has killed all the king's sons, and not one of them is left!" So the king arose and tore his garments and lay on the ground, and all his servants stood by with their clothes torn. Then Jonadab the son of Shimeah, David's brother, answered and said, "Let not my Lord suppose they have killed all the young men, the king's sons, for only Amnon is dead. For by the command of Absalom this has been determined from the day that he forced his sister Tamar. NKJV

The Upas tree does in fact exist and yes, its latex sap is extremely deadly and has been used to make the tips of arrows and spears and blowpipe darts, definite and certain instruments of death over the years. William Blake's poem, 'A Poison Tree' is based on the existence of the Upas. His opening stanza is most instructive:

I was angry with my friend:
I told my wrath, my wrath did end.
I was angry with my foe:
I told it not, my wrath did grow.

And I water'd it in fears,
Night & morning with my tears;
And I sunned it with smiles,
And with soft deceitful wiles.

And it grew both day and night,
Till it bore an apple bright;
And my foe beheld it shine,
And he knew that it was mine,

And into my garden stole
When the night had veil'd the pole:
In the morning glad I see
My foe outstretch'd beneath the tree.

King David's son Amnon had raped and disgraced his half-sister, Absalom's full sister, Tamar. Amnon had "loved" her in unrequited lust and then hated her with a passion, once he had his way. Tamar was brutally and culturally shamed. Absalom said nothing that terrible day but he planted a tree of hateful revenge in his own heart and meticulously watered it. The growth and grotesque beauty of his poison tree was enough to have Amnon take a bite of its fruit and in the morning be found underneath it. Dead.

Poison trees are host to all the chickens that will eventually come home to roost.

Look! Poison trees grow stronger once their fruit is picked. Amnon did not kill the tree, or rather the tree did not die when Absalom's revenge was poured upon him but rather, its blood-leeched roots now reached deeper still within the heart of Absalom, the bitter avenger. In just over 40 years' time, Absalom's now deeper rooted poison tree will fully blossom and cause so great a stench on the plains of Israel that it will split the kingdom and break his father's heart. Yes, Israel will never be the same again after Absalom's pure latex poison shall pierce the flesh of David. Mark this well friends and be afraid. Poison trees are host to all the chickens that will eventually come home to roost.

Do you feel its serpentine root formation around those festering areas of your own offended heart? Today, all those dreams, all those projects, all those people you are touching, are they living or dying beneath your leafy but poisonous boughs? Tell me: what particular slimy snake is trying to coil itself around your hurting heart today dear friend? Do you not know, that it is simply trying to squeeze out your poison and drip it on all and everything that walks beneath your tree? If you see the snake today, then kill it, before death permanently encamps beneath the beastly boughs of those hate-dripping holes of your own pierced and scarred little heart.

Deal with the damage else it shall most surely deal with you.

Listen: *"Though evil is sweet in his mouth, and he hides it under his tongue, though he spares it and does not forsake it, but still keeps it in his mouth, yet his food in his stomach turns sour; It becomes cobra venom within him." (Job 20:12-14 NKJV)*

Pray: Lord. Help me to acknowledge my hurt, and command and vent my poisonous wrath into Your cleansing and waiting wind. Bring up all the coiled cobras of my twisted soul, O Lord that I might kill them dead! Amen and let it be so.

| Vol 02 | Q3 | NW00581 | August 02nd |

Night-Whisper | **BELIEVE**

The estate agent and the real estate

> ***Genesis 13:17***
>
> *"Arise, walk in the land through its length and its width, for I give it to you."*

So I said to him "I'm looking for a new house." He smiles shakes my hand sits me down and begins "the financial probing." This guy has been around a bit. I can tell this by measuring the time it takes to get from the handshake to the seamless discovery of what I can afford to spend. He doesn't want to offend me but "time is money" for him and he doesn't want to waste his time showing me a property I cannot afford. "Ah, I've got just the home for you," he says with an "I can't believe the coincidence of this" look on his face. "And you won't believe it," (he's right) "but it only recently came on the market. I tell you if no one snaps this up soon I'm going to buy it for my daughter. Tell you what, take the keys, it's not far from here and take your time. Walk through the house, take it all in and make sure the wife is with you, she will just love it. Then, when you see why this house is so perfect for you, bring back the keys and let's talk." Getting real excited now he exclaims, "Man! I just want you to see this place before we go any further. It's gonna blow you away!"

God is no sleek realtor, no professional estate agent, yet it seems to me in our text for today that He does say to Abraham. "You gotta see this place Abe baby, you're gonna love it!" Abraham had to take time to take in the magnitude of the promise. The stars in the sky, the sand on the ground, the length and breadth of the land. He had to look and he had to see and believe and then bring back the keys to the Lord God Almighty. "I tell you" says God "It's enormous, it's magnificent, it's beautiful for situation, it's ample room for you, the kids, the grand kids, the whole massive family, man it's yours and you know what? I am giving it to you baby. It's not gonna cost you a cent, no sir, it's yours, it's a free gift from Me, I promise, and I tell you what Abraham, take the keys, go and see, walk up and down, in and out, cross the rivers, climb the mountains, feel the grass, smell the roses, cause it's all yours. What do I want?" The Lord says incredulously, "What do I want? I want some anticipation Abe baby, I want some expectancy, I want some joy before the promise, I want to see you happy, I want to see you drooling, I want you hungry in belief, I want to see some deep inward longing, wanting, believing. Then, when you see why this house is perfect for you, bring back the keys and let's talk. Man! I just want you to see this place before we go any further. It's gonna blow you away!"

We need to take time to meditate on the Scriptures, to think on Jesus and allow the dimension of our divine inheritance to make its eternal impression upon us.

Friends we need to take time to walk through the land of our inheritance. We need to take time to meditate on the Scriptures, to think on Jesus and allow the dimension of our divine inheritance to make its eternal impression upon us. We need to walk through the land. I tell you, if your expectant belief and drooling hunger is not giving you heartburn this side of heaven in the long dark night of your soul, then you need to get out and start walking friends. Start walking and start looking, start drinking, start exploring and start talking about the real things, the unseen things, the eternal things. You've got the keys; so now for the first time in your life maybe, go take a good long look. Here is what Jesus says to you today: "Good grief friends! I just want you to see this place before we go any further. It's gonna blow you away."

Listen: *"These all died in faith, not having received the promises, but having seen them afar off were assured of them, embraced them and confessed that they were strangers and pilgrims on the earth. For those who say such things declare plainly that they seek a homeland. And truly if they had called to mind that country from which they had come out, they would have had opportunity to return. But now they desire a better, that is, a heavenly country. Therefore God is not ashamed to be called their God, for He has prepared a city for them." (Hebrews 11:13-16 NKJV))*

Pray: Lord. I do declare that I am a stranger and a pilgrim in a foreign land. Please begin the guided tour today of all I posses in you Lord Jesus. Amen andf let it be so.

Night-Whisper | **PLACE**

Thrones, footstools and cities

Sometimes those of us who hate the urban sprawl and have made the daily and debilitating journey into commuter packed cities where the prices are high and the streets are hot and bustling with glazed eye, briefcase carrying drones, well sometimes, those of us experiencing that, get discouraged with the book of Revelation. You see, we want to get back to the garden. However, the problem is that the Bible may start with a garden but it ends with a city. The city of God. Yes, the city of the Great King! The book of Revelation you see, is about the city of God.

Matthew 5:34-36

But I say to you, do not swear at all: neither by heaven, for it is God's throne; nor by the earth, for it is His footstool; nor by Jerusalem, for it is the city of the great King. NKJV

It's my understanding that the Scriptures refer to the city of God in four contexts:

First of all, old Jerusalem in the land of Israel is of course 'the city of The Great King.' Why else would there be so much warfare around such a seemingly insignificant sandy and stone-infested real estate?

Secondly, the New Jerusalem which shall descend at the end of the age and this, our new and eternal base of operations, home, community and center, well this as well of course is also referred to as 'the city of The Great King.'

Thirdly, the church, in its collective gatherings, both local and universal is also 'the city of The Great King,' a city like Jerusalem of old, a city set on a hill that cannot be hidden.

Fourthly and finally and most importantly, our hearts, our center, have also become the dwelling place of the Most High God. As individuals, we too are cities set on a hill.

In any of these four contexts, make no mistake about it, the city of God is called just that and is desirable for that one fact alone that God, is in residence there!

In England, whenever the monarch is present and in residence, the Royal colors are flown high. It is the responsibility of the keeper of the colors, not the monarch, to watch for the monarchs approach and raise their colors high when they enter through the gates. Have you got that? It's not the monarch's responsibility to raise their colors but the servants!

It's not the monarch's responsibility to raise their colors but the servants

An older Christian chorus, usually sung by children, talks of a "flag flying high in the castle of my heart, for the King is in residence there". We older children have sadly forgotten this. The castle, the fortress, the inner keep of ourselves, has often no outward acknowledgement by us that the King is actually and personally in residence there. At best we take this great truth simply as a positional argument or a theological fact to be mentally acknowledged, except occasionally, when we are in gardens, quiet and away from the bustle of life, we feel we catch a glimpse of His royal robes swishing along our cold inner corridors searching for us, angry at our absence. Then we wish we had raised His royal standard!

You see, in the warmth and the stillness, in the beauty and gently chirruping of the sparrows, in the reflecting pool of stillness at the center of our own inner garden, when we get there, when we look there, as we do, it will reveal Him standing just behind us, even at our elbow, hand on our shoulder, always there, never leaving nor forsaking us, waiting, questioning, sighing and shaking His head a little, maybe? When we feel His presence, when we sense His presence, when we see His love, when we feel His touch, it is then that we now appreciate that the King is in residence here and actually, always has been! For those of us who have failed to raise His standard and keep His standards, this realization of His holy presence can fill us with such defeated shame and such frustrating regret, that it is with embarrassment rather than joy that we slowly begin to turn our face toward Him.

Friends, there may not be many gardens in a city, but in His garden are billions and trillions of cities, a vast and innumerable number and Jesus is in the cities friends. Jesus is in the center. His Royal arms from now on must fly high, in the hustle and bustle of all the life that goes on around the gates of our heart. His Royal standard must now fly high, over all incoming and outgoing trade, traders and traitors; over every siege, over every arrow that is fired from every engine of war pitted against us; over every word from false prophets of personal doom and even over the big battering rams of our own despairing emotion. The flag of Jesus must still fly high, fluttering and waving in the wind of His brooding Spirit hovering high over our ramparts. Oh Hallelujah! The King is in residence here, right here in the middle of our city, in the middle of your city, in the middle of my city.

The flag of Jesus must still fly high, fluttering and waving in the wind of His brooding Spirit hovering high over our ramparts

Yes, Christ's throne is presently in heaven at the right hand of the Majesty on High and the earth is becoming His footstool, as the Father, through bloody war and dreadful conflict, is reclaiming that which His own Son, our Savior Jesus has purchased with His own blood; but never forget this and tonight especially remember it, that you also are His redeemed city, in which He has come to reside. Look to Him in now and the morning and then raise High His Royal Colors.

Listen: *"Walk about Zion, and go all around her. Count her towers; Mark well her bulwarks; consider her palaces; that you may tell it to the generation following. For this is God, Our God forever and ever; He will be our guide Even to death." (Psalm 48:12-14 NKJV)*

Pray: There is a flag flying high in the castle of my heart, in the castle of my heart, in the castle of my heart. There is a flag flying high in the castle of my heart, for the King is in residence here! Let it fly in my sky and let the whole world know, that the King is in residence here. Amen and let it be so.

| Vol 02 | Q3 | NW00583 | August 04th |

Night-Whisper | **CALLING**

Dribbling and your dentine destiny

Well it's happened much earlier than expected but I have started dribbling. Not all the time but of course inevitably, at the most public and therefore most embarrassing of times. All of a sudden, I'm just aware of a dribble on my chin. It's "mucho grosso" really!

1 Corinthians 12:21

And the eye cannot say to the hand, "I have no need of you," nor again the head to the feet, "I have no need of you." No, much rather, those members of the body which seem to be weaker are necessary. NKJV

Thankfully, I've figured out the problem and with some awareness training, I think I can limit the embarrassment. You see I am the proud owner of fixed bridge across the front of my mouth. It's magnificent! I can bite through ice cream with no pain, chomp into apples and chow down on baby back ribs like a glutton on speed! The sensation of pressure is still there but it's obvious that the sensitivity and awareness feelings that my natural teeth once gave me are now gone. Hence, sometimes it's dribble city for me because I just don't feel it leaking out as it were! Who'd have thought that a couple of home grown enamel covered nerve endings were such an important anti-dribbling device?

You know where I am going with this don't you? But it's the truth and because it's something we so easily forget, it is worthy of a remembrance. Let me put it like my teeth, bluntly, by saying that if you are a vocal and open mouth in the church, you must not despise the quieter members that never the less bring sensitivity and awareness to your proclamations, for their kind prayers and gentle hints, will stop you looking like a dribbling fool! Consequently, may I say that if you know you are but a "small tooth" in a big mouth, then be sure that God has put you just right where you are to fulfil your dentine destiny! You might be next to a large molar called Albert who grinds away daily, but believe me, he needs you.

So finally today, I want to say a word to those who feel so inconsequential in the shadow of all the mouth might be proclaiming and indeed, so much so, that maybe they just want to up and leave. Please don't go for you are such a necessary part of the body. Keep backing up by speaking up, for after all, we all know that a dribbling fool is not really taken seriously! Keep being sensitive! Keep stopping the dribble and Oh, by the way, thank you.

Keep backing up by speaking up!

Listen: *And the eye cannot say to the hand, "I have no need of you" nor again the head to the feet, "I have no need of you." No, much rather, those members of the body which seem to be weaker are necessary. (1 Corinthians 12:21 NKJV)*

Pray: Today Lord, where I am, show me my value and my necessity to the body of Your church, amen.

| Vol 02 | Q3 | NW00584 | August 05th |

Night-Whisper | **FAITH**

Dealing with "Blue Moons"

> ***2 Kings 4:23***
>
> *So he said, "Why are you going to him today? It is neither the New Moon nor the Sabbath." NKJV*

Nanci Griffith may have sung it but, it was written by Patrick Alver and Gene Levine. A delightful country music ballad called 'Once in a Very Blue Moon.' Of course, there is no such thing as a 'blue moon.' Originally, it meant "something that would hardly ever happen," as in "We will have a blue moon, before such and such..." Moving on from the old saying though, a blue moon eventually became the name for the third full moon in a season (three months) of four full moons. Then, in the early to mid-1900s it became the name of the second full moon in a month. Complicated isn't it? My point is this friends, in the great scheme of the intergalactic timing of things, blue moons may be reasonably common but they are not everyday occurrences! Have you got that?

In the same way, concerning or lives, there is nothing that happens to us that is not common to mankind. However, occasionally we all experience to some degree something that is not an everyday occurrence. It's unusual, it's a blue moon kind of occurrence and there is something in its unexpectedness, in its unusualness that just might cause us to halt, shudder, fail or fall. Nancy Griffiths sings:

There's a blue moon shinin'
When I am reminded of all we've been through
Such a blue moon ... shinin'
Does it ever shine down on you?
You act as if it never hurt you at all
Like I'm the only one who's gettin' up from a fall
Don't you remember?
Can't you recall?
Just once ... in a very blue moon

In our verse today, a Shunammite woman has for years been providing lodging for the itinerant ministry of Elisha the prophet. A childless mother for years, for her concern, by the grace of God and through the prayerful intervention of the prophet, she had received a "prophet's reward" and it was in the form of a lovely little son, even a son of her husband's old age. This son of their old age, she both loved and hungrily embraced.

All blue moons should send you to Jesus. Go and get Jesus. Go and get Him now.

Once in a very blue moon day this marvelous and unexpected gift of God, early one bright mid-morning, complained of a terrible headache. He was taken indoors and with his head in the lap of his mother and with his eyes squeezed up in pointed pain, he groaned and groaned and then quickly died. With pent up fury and the silent determination of a nuclear submarine leaving harbor for some deep waters of conflict, this mad mother, rises from her sobbing seat, quietly closes the door behind her and sets her face towards both the cause and the answer to all her problem. Her countenance betrays her speedy but organized exit, yet when asked about the possibility of trouble in her life, she determinedly replies "all is well" to those who voice their concern. Saddling her donkey, silently she slips out of her devastated harbor. The Shunamite sets sail in but one direction. Elisha the prophet.

Ignoring everything and everyone, she arrives at her destination and literally launches herself at his feet, tackling the unsuspecting prophet almost to the ground. Boom! "Did I ask a son of my Lord?" she says, boom! "Did I not say, 'Do not deceive me'?" Boom!

These explosive questions are the summary of all the painful pleadings, all the fearful longings and shattered expectations of her broken heart. What has been hidden from Elisha as he viewed the determined and directed steps of the approaching storm of sadness raging with anger and crashing against the staring eyes of the Shunamite, submerged and dangerous in the periscope depth of her attacking distress, is now fully revealed to him and in that revelation, he responds and so departs to attend to the problem.

Friend, when a blue moon rises in your sky, close the door on the problem, saddle up your horses, go to Jesus, launch yourself at His feet, let it all out, hang on to Him and do not let Him go. Insist He comes personally to attend to the matter. Insist on it I tell you!

Call this approach to your unusual problems, your unexpected and blasted blue moons what you will, but I call it a solution! Go and get Jesus. Go and get Him now.

Listen: "*He returned and walked back and forth in the house, and again went up and stretched himself out on him; then the child sneezed seven times, and the child opened his eyes. And he called Gehazi and said, 'Call this Shunamite woman.' So he called her. And when she came in to him, he said, 'Pick up your son.' So she went in, fell at his feet, and bowed to the ground; then she picked up her son and went out." 2 Kings 4:35-37*

"Now when He concluded all His sayings in the hearing of the people, He entered Capernaum. And a certain centurion's servant, who was dear to him, was sick and ready to die. So when he heard about Jesus, he sent elders of the Jews to Him, pleading with Him to come and heal his servant. And when they came to Jesus, they begged Him earnestly, saying that the one for whom He should do this was deserving, 'for he loves our nation, and has built us a synagogue.' Then Jesus went with them." (Luke 7:1-6 NKJV)

Pray: Lord, help me to run to You and hang on to You when any blue moons lay low and large in the midnight of my sky. Help me to pray and pray and pray and listen for the solutions in all the sneezing's of my life! I plead and implore, beg and insist that You come back to my house dear Jesus and fix all my blue moons today. Lord I will not let You rest until You do this for me. Amen and let it be so.

| Vol 02 | Q3 | NW00585 | August 06th |

Night-Whisper | **REJOICE**

Pensions, pasta and personal accessories

The Lord did not say do not plan for tomorrow, He said, "Don't worry about it." That is, don't let it break into today and rob you of fully enjoying the present. Friends, we are linear livers and linear thinkers, in that we have a past a present and anticipate a future. Now concerning the future, remember that anticipation of it is all we really have! Let's face it, this time next week any one of us could dead, buried, and dispatched. It's the truth! All we have concerning the future is either anticipation or fear of it.

Matthew 6:34

Therefore do not worry about tomorrow, for tomorrow will worry about its own things. Sufficient for the day is its own trouble. NKJV

We are often comforted, confused expectant or fearful about life after death because on top of this earthly anticipation for a linear future, God has also put eternity in our hearts. We not only anticipate a linear future but also we anticipate and expect, even yearn for and know of the terrible certainty of an eternal destiny. I suppose one of the benefits of such an eternal anticipation, of such a maybe fearful expectation, is that knowing there is a never ending future and that there are never ending consequences in that certain and eternal future, which relates to how we act now, well, it often makes us much more restrained in our excess down here, it reins us in as it were, it sometimes tempers the explosive and consuming nature of our sinful self. You might spend now but you will always pay later. This we know.

Planning for the future is wise. Planning for college, for the care of children etc, all of these things are right and good. However, may I suggest that if these "plans" have reached into our present and dictate and depress us, dominate and drive us; then maybe they are wrong! Many, many people live much of their lives planning for the future, when they retire, when the kids have left home, when, when, when, even though it may never come! Ah but if and when it does, then they are ready for it, then all the worry abd waste of time seems worth it. Maybe. Meanwhile in the now, in this gift of a moment, in this precious point in our lives when time touches eternity, peace it is eaten and opportunity for enjoyment is wasted away in worry, having been so thoroughly consumed by the "when" and the worries of an unknown future. Safety, security, food and possessions, or should I say, pensions, pasta and personal accessories are all very nice to look forward to but friends, quite frankly, they not very good to live for right now. They are in the future, which we can only anticipate and never with full certainty possess. Do you see that?

> *Over meticulous planning, such overly protective planning for the "when" of the future, opens such pensive portals in the time space continuum that it allows fears of every kind to be projected along our linear line of living and be bounced right back at us in the now, only this time, it is now magnified a thousand fold!*

We all plan and rightly so and certainly we should not have the attitude of "eat drink and be merry for tomorrow we die." However, such meticulous planning, such overly protective planning for the "when" of the future, opens such pensive portals in the time space continuum that it allows fears of every kind to be projected along our linear line of living and be bounced right back at us in the now, only this time, it is now magnified a thousand fold! For don't you know that fear cannot live in the future or the past and so it fights to manifest itself always in the now! Future fears like fat little kittens will always try to claw themselves into our souls the moment an opening is presented to them. When we allow this to happen, when devouring fear is in our house, "the maybe then," that monster of our own creation, like a hungry teenager will come and empty our peaceful cupboards, throw its dirty washing around on the ground of our contentment, go to its room and slam the door in the disrespect of our present and turn up its thumping music, very loud indeed, worrying and tormenting us to distracting anger and disbelief! Be very careful what you let in your house dear friends. Be very careful.

Jesus is very clear. In one day under this fallen and failing sun, there is only so much we can handle, or are expected to handle. Yes, be wise and plan when you can, however do not live for the plans you make for frankly, they are out of your control. Grab those scabby and grubby, clawing little kittens by the neck and get teenage fear by the ear friends and throw them out on it. Jesus says: ***"Do not worry about tomorrow!"***

You can't get any clearer than that can you? He says: ***"Seek my kingdom and my righteousness today and all shall be well with you tomorrow."*** You might be saying "yeah, right" – and I tell you the truth in answer to your tired and astonished "yeah right" lack of faith, God is replying, "Yeah right and you'd better believe it for your own good!" God is saying, ***"Yes I mean it, do not worry about tomorrow!"***

The answer to worry concerning the future is chosen rejoicing in the possession of this very moment. "Now" is all you really have, so do make the very best of it!

Listen: *This is the day the LORD has made; we will rejoice and be glad in it. (Psalm 118:24 NKJV)*

Pray: All of your promises Oh God are Yes and Amen in Jesus. Amidst all this technology and temptation to plan and forecast my future, to kid myself into thinking I am in control, teach me Your Way Oh God, teach me Your Way. Amen and let it be so.

Boiling breast milk

The book of Exodus contains some confusing verses for those of us disconnected from such a "bloody" culture. Our verse today and its context left me confused for some time, until one day, I was watching a news broadcast where the mother of a missing child (later found to be murdered) was pleading for the safe return of her daughter. I shall never forget the mother's panicked and tear stained face; overnight she had already aged substantially and her poor terror consumed features were already draped in mourning silk. One poet writes:

Exodus 34:26b

"You shall not boil a young goat in its mother's milk." NKJV

"You shall not boil a young goat
In its mother's milk
You shall not clothe a suckling pig
With chiffon or with silk
You shall not disapprove
Of Section 28
You shall not catch a cod
And demand that he should skate
You shall not cause a robin
To pull ten thousand tons
You shall not stick your tongue out
At penguins, bats or nuns
You shall not twist a knife
Or cause a mother pain
You shall not cut a sapling
Nor murder Sarah Jane
You shall not drape a smiling face
With greys of mourning silk
You shall not boil a young goat
In its mother's milk"

Simeon, a just and devout man waiting in the temple for the consolation of Israel, takes the baby Jesus from the arms of His loving mother Mary and as the Holy Spirit comes upon him prophecies, ***"Lord, now You are letting Your servant depart in peace according to Your word; for my eyes have seen Your salvation which You have prepared before the face of all peoples, a light to bring revelation to the Gentiles, and the glory of Your people Israel." (Luke 2:29-32.)*** Then turning to the marveling Joseph and Mary he speaks directly to them, midway through his proclamation his sad eyes laying for a moment on mother Mary when he says: ***"Behold, this Child is destined for the fall and rising of many in Israel, and for a sign which will be spoken against (yes, a sword will pierce through your own soul also), that the thoughts of many hearts may be revealed."***

Often God warns us of desperate times to come, so that we might prepare ourselves. He is no sadist in such revelation but in love, asks us to strengthen ourselves for that which is both unavoidable and dreadful.

The old seer speaks that which he sees and Mary's coming pain is not forgotten, not laid aside, but deeply felt. Indeed, she is now by the voice of Simeon given over 30 years to prepare herself. She will need this, for her child shall be murdered before her very eyes. He who suckled at her breasts shall be pierced for our sins, while her own soul is pierced in the boiling loss of her own most precious son.

We can learn two things here:

First, that often God warns us of desperate times to come, so that we might prepare ourselves. He is no sadist in such revelation but in love, asks us to strengthen ourselves for that which is both unavoidable and dreadful.

Secondly, that though this may be the case, nevertheless, the Sovereign Father takes no pleasure in our suffering. Indeed, He makes a specific command, that mothers should not be a witness to the cruel death and consuming of those they love so dearly. No child should be tortured and consumed before its mother's eyes.

Maybe some governments should take this verse to heart when dispatching young people to desperate wars? Maybe some legislators should bear this in mind when authorizing the mass destruction of the unborn and turning the word "choice" into a death camp word for women? For it seems the Father has a special love for those He has created to bear and nurture life. It seems to me God loves mothers, for He had one Himself. Young goats should never be boiled in their mother's milk, before their desperate eyes.

Listen: *"Let your father and your mother be glad, And let her who bore you rejoice." (Proverbs 23:25 NKJV)*

Pray: Lord, help us to honor all mothers by not murdering their children before their very eyes. God forgive us for these crimes. God forgive us and help us. In Jesus name precious name we pray, amen and let it be so.

The snuffers of the sanctuary

It is Matthew Henry commenting on Matthew 7:5 which says, ***"Hypocrite! First remove the plank from your own eye, and then you will see clearly to remove the speck from your brother's eye,"*** that makes this wonderful and intriguing observation that "the snuffers of the sanctuary are made from pure gold."

Matthew 7:2-5

For with what judgment you judge, you will be judged; and with the measure you use, it will be measured back to you. And why do you look at the speck in your brother's eye, but do not consider the plank in your own eye? Or how can you say to your brother, "Let me remove the speck from your eye"; and look, a plank is in your own eye? Hypocrite! First remove the plank from your own eye, and then you will see clearly to remove the speck from your brother's eye. NKJV

Lest we be confused here, old Henry is referring to the wick trimmers and their dishes. In other words, the snuffing tools used for the golden lamp stand of the temple that bore seven heads of light. In all likelihood, these probably had to be trimmed every half hour to ensure that they were perpetually lit. This was an office for the priest, who would enter the outer chamber of the first part of the tabernacle to do so (Hebrews 9:6). We should note here that this was an action of service and having a low servant's heart instead of a high and mighty judging heart is of key importance in these things we are looking at, because Matthew Henry here is actually making the point, that as priests, we all need to "be of pure gold" when we are reproving one another, so as to make the light shine ever brighter still.

Yes indeed, there is need for reproof, correction and especially assistance, even the throwing of a rope to a drowning brother, or the laying hold of a sister just about to walk into the flames and isn't this helpful and redemptive reproof friends this just the greatest service we can perform for one another! However, before we do this, to maintain our servant heart, we need to make sure that we have confessed our own sin, reproved our own self and removed the offending article from our own eye. In this way we snuffers, we removers of burnt wick in others that could cause the lamp to go out in our brethren's eyes, well in this way, we need to be like pure gold. Let's trim our own wicks then eh, all seven of them, every half hour before we even think of going to another person's eyes. I don't know about you but I find that keeping myself in order is often a full time job anyway!

For our own safety and for the health of the church, let service and mercy be our watchwords and let's leave the heart judging to God.

The snuffers of the sanctuary never went into the inner court, the Holy of Holies. Maybe we could say that in the same way we must never go into the inner court of our brethren. In other words, we should never judge the motives of heart. We are servants not judges. Remember that. God takes this thing very seriously for not taking care of our own wicks meets with reproof from God, for you see, judging another man's heart meets with the law of reciprocation. This is a terrible, for none of us judge well as none of us fully knows the inner machinations, drives and desires, fears and fretfulness that might lie at the center of another person's soul. Their Holy of Holies is not ours for the entering. It is for the High Priest and for Him alone to enter there. Don't judge the motives of another person's heart, for you will surely get it wrong.

For our own safety and for the health of the church, let service and mercy be our watchwords and let's leave the heart judging to God.

Listen: *"Therefore the LORD has recompensed me according to my righteousness, According to my cleanness in His eyes. 'With the merciful You will show Yourself merciful; With a blameless man You will show Yourself blameless; With the pure You will show Yourself pure; And with the devious You will show Yourself shrewd. You will save the humble people; But Your eyes are on the haughty, that You may bring them down.'" 2 Samuel 22:25-28*

Pray: Lord. Who am I to judge another person's heart? For, you are the knower and revealer of hearts. Help me to be a brave servant of mercy and loving kindness, full of grace and having my own heart trimmed brightly burning before Your well pleased face. Then and only then Lord, give me the courage to trim the burnt wicks of other people's lives. Amen and let it be so.

| Vol 02 | Q3 | NW00588 | August 09th |

Night-Whisper | **PEACE**

Elephantine excreta

Imagine you were born into a family of elephant keepers in India, yet in your heart, you wanted to be a doctor. So each day, after shoveling out the elephant's compound, when the stars came out each night you would sit down under a bright moon, open your books and study, study, study, until one day, you take an exam, get a scholarship and get into medical college and persevere until eventually you graduate and become an MD. In Western terms, you would have aspired and achieved, overcome and conquered even, against incredible odds. In Western terms, you would be a hero! However, believe it or not, in Indian culture you would not have bettered yourself, oh no! On the contrary, you would be creating terrible karma! "After all," they might explain, "you were created to be an elephant keeper. Be a great elephant keeper in this life and maybe in the next life you could be a doctor but to change the course of your destiny in this life is just plain wrong and will have terrible karmic consequences for you in your next re-incarnation! Be very careful because next time around my Indian friend you may re-birthed into something the elephant steps on!" Now, to our Western thinking, this is absurd bondage but to millions of Indians however, this is a way of living, looking and being. Do not aspire beyond your present situation!

Isaiah 43:5-7

Fear not, for I am with you; I will bring your descendants from the east, And gather you from the west; I will say to the north, "give them up!" And to the south, "do not keep them back!" Bring My sons from afar, and My daughters from the ends of the earth - everyone who is called by My name, whom I have created for My glory; I have formed him, yes, I have made him." NKJV

In the West most of us have occupations. Something we do which occupies our time. If we are very fortunate, we may enjoy what we do. However, we mostly do the thing because it brings home the bacon, pays the bills and keeps us out of mischief! In the West, rarely do people now claim to have a vocation, you know, literally something they are called to do. Oh, you do hear about people "called" to the ministry, and I believe that, indeed, God help the poor congregation and the poor person who engages in ministry without such a calling! The rest of us regard this kind of calling however, this kind of vocation as obviously something set apart, spiritual and holy. Of course it is! However, let me tell you this: "If God has called you to be a car mechanic, if that is your vocation, your calling, your pursued destiny, then that too is equally as spiritual and holy. Equally! There is no difference for in either case, you must glorify God, experience His fellowship, and enjoy Him in it! Be happy! Enjoy your calling!"

Now, if you are unhappy at work, then rather than settling for that hateful little existence and your increasing fantasies of escape and vacation, start thinking about your vocation! Maybe there is more peace and glory in fulfilling a vocation rather than doing an occupation? Think about it! Maybe it's better to seek out and occupy your earthly destiny rather than simply occupy your allotted timeslot until it's time to begin "pushing up the daisies?"

Maybe there is more peace and glory in fulfilling a vocation rather than doing an occupation?

Maybe it's better to seek out and occupy your earthly destiny rather than simply occupy your allotted timeslot until it's time to begin "pushing up the daisies?"

Now having said that, though I do acknowledge that there is a peace to be found in doing what we are called to do, gifted to do, delighted to do, I also believe there is even more peace to posses in just, well in just being! Archibald MacLeish in his poem about what a poem should be ("Ars Poetica"), sums it up nicely by saying "A poem should not mean, but be." The most peace we could have, the most glory we could possibly give to God is by simply being who we are! I am not saying we should stop *becoming*, oh no, we need to keep aspiring, possessing and becoming however, we need to become primarily more of who we are, not who they want us to be, or what our parents wanted us to be, oh no! We should at all costs, for our peace and God's glory, be who we are and do what we are called to do. I have observed that these two conduits of peace do go hand in hand.

So today, if you are tired of shoveling out elephantine excreta, then maybe you should begin to seek out your vocation rather than be frustrated in your occupation and maybe, you should also start being who you truly are? So let me ask you right now. “Who are you? What is your name? What are you doing here? Why?” There is an aroma of change in the air. Can you smell it?

Listen: *“Then Peter, turning around, saw the disciple whom Jesus loved following, who also had leaned on His breast at the supper, and said, ‘Lord, who is the one who betrays You?’ Peter, seeing him, said to Jesus, ‘But Lord, what about this man?’ Jesus said to him, ‘If I will that he remain till I come, what is that to you? You follow Me.’” John 21:20-22*

Pray: Lord. Speak to me my own true name. Reveal it to me Lord and show me who I am in You and who You created me to be, help me to be and then help me to do. In Jesus name, Amen and let it be so.

More milk monitors needed

In Britain after WWII and following the 1945 General Election, the then new Prime Minister, Clement Attlee, appointed Ellen Wilkinson as Minister of Education, the first woman in British history to hold the post.

1 Corinthians 3:2,3

I fed you with milk and not with solid food; for until now you were not able to receive it, and even now you are still not able; for you are still carnal. NKJV

A previous investigation in 1937 proved there was a link between low income, malnutrition and under achievement in schools. So, in 1946, Wilkinson, who had long been a campaigner against poverty, managed to persuade Parliament to pass a bill, thus ordering the issue of one-third of a pint of milk, free to all pupils under the age of eighteen. My age means that I was a beneficiary of this magnificent deed and I can still remember the sickly smell of morning milk time.

Milk most definitely had a seasonal taste and texture, for in summer the red plastic crates of milk would stand in the yard until morning break and by that time, the upper half of the bottle was warm and creamy, whilst the lower half was somewhat cool. In winter of course, the summer inversion was reversed and sometimes, the iced up top layer of milk would lift the tin silver red foil right off the top of the small glass bottle and the cold watery ice crystals left floating in the fluid, inflicted brain burn as it slurped and slipped its way down reluctant throats. Winter or summer, all those tin foil tops would eventually be washed off "en masse" and saved in a bag for future "art work". The smell of that strange mixture of old white school glue and bits of sour milk remaining on the red and silver tin foil tops, still hangs in the back of my throat making me gag even today when I think on it. This morning ritual of white top-lipped moustaches and milk burping boys did however for millions of British children carry with it the possibility of a vast place of power and dignity. Well it did, if you became the "milk monitor!"

The job of milk monitor was a most prestigious honor. Like some foreign war correspondent standing on an aircraft carrier counting the war birds departing and arriving, with the same grave countenance the milk monitor would count all the bottles out and count them all back again, empty. In those days, no one had heard of lactose intolerance. You literally had to just suck it up, stop whining and get on and drink your milk, every last drop! I remember for some, getting down that creamy or ice-cold milk was an indescribable and daily ordeal but the milk monitor showed no mercy.

'CARNAL' is an old fashioned word I know but it still carries with it the intended mockery and shame of its first intended use.

Government cutbacks got rid of the free milk and despite the obvious health concerns, pizza, burgers and fries are now the most popular meals at school. The old-fashioned thinking brought free milk to growing children but the new enlightenment brings choice, tolerance, café style menus and condoms. Sexually transmitted disease, teenage obesity and madness in the classroom, sometimes even at the end of pipe bombs and bullets are on the menu in many schools today. It seems education and childcare have come a long way since WWII. Not.

In our text today, Paul berates the childish Corinthians. The need for growing kids to receive milk was an obvious necessity. In this case, the milk was the basic tenets of Christianity. However, that was a for a time and by now, the Corinthians should be way, way beyond that; Christ having been more fully formed in them even, but no, they were not full of either the Word or the Spirit. The Corinthians were carnal.

Carnal is an old fashioned word I know but it still carries with it the intended mockery and shame of its first intended use. The Corinthian Christians, were people who should have been strong in the Lord and in the power of His might. They were Christians who should have had the eyes of their heart opened wider. They were Christians who should have had their heads lifted up to heaven, but were in fact weak Christians of narrow gaze, still focused on their petty little life of sinful and silly self. They were carnal! They missed out on their milk at an early age and were now manifesting all the associated spiritual nutritional deficiencies! Christians with Rickets rarely walk well.

Maybe the church needs some new milk monitors for a while eh? Just to make sure we suck it up, get it down and keep it there. In the end, milk is of more value to you than pizza and fries will ever be. The one will strengthen your heart and bones whilst the other stuff will clog up your arteries and make your knees weak. Let me ask you today then, how are your heart and knees my dearly beloved friends? Maybe it's time to find an udder way of growing? Maybe it's time to avoid all postmodern, post-Christian desperate pizza specialties? Maybe it's time for some of you rickety Christians to get back to a basic milk diet?

Maybe it's time to avoid all postmodern, post-Christian desperate pizza specialties? Maybe it's time for some of you rickety Christians to get back to a basic milk diet?

Listen: *"Therefore, leaving the discussion of the elementary principles of Christ, let us go on to perfection, not laying again the foundation of repentance from dead works and of faith toward God, of the doctrine of baptisms, of laying on of hands, of resurrection of the dead, and of eternal judgment. And this we will do if God permits." Hebrews 6:1-3*

Pray: Lord, if needs be, please take me back to the basics and build up my bent out of shape bones, amen and let it be so.

| Vol 02 | Q3 | NW00590 | August 011th |

Night-Whisper | **PLACE**

The secret place

My father's death was prefixed by strokes. The last one left him comatose and unreachable. He knew the Gospel but I am not sure if he understood it or knew Jesus as his Savior. Though he still inhabited this physical world, he was lost somewhere in that twilight zone of the unconscious or the subconscious realms and as far as I was concerned, he was left undecided, unrepentant and unforgiven in this unreachable secret realm.

Matthew 6:17,18

But you, when you fast, anoint your head and wash your face, so that you do not appear to men to be fasting, but to your Father who is in the secret place; and your Father who sees in secret will reward you openly. NKJV

There are many physical and metaphysical secret realms or places, if you will. Some of them we long for when the dangers and demands of the conscious world beat on us like the unrelenting waves of the sea. Some of them we flee to and hide behind when we are hurt or embarrassed. The reflection of their portals may appear to others to be but a present smile on our face. However, the smile is not us, it's a clone, even an aberration we project, whilst our true self has withdrawn to its own secret place. Our true self may be withdrawn in torment, or withdrawn and shaking stubborn in anger and hurt, swearing at you with secret rebellious fist shaking high on its battlement of disdain, flinging spiritual rocks and curses at the person who feels everything, somewhere deep inside, but beholds nothing but our fair smile. Some of our secret places have become prisons and dangerous places for us to go and friends, for some of you, these secret places of fantasy have become nothing more than deep dark dens of iniquity, a sickening playground for Satan. Selah.

This adjective, "secret" is only found in this verse in the New Testament. Its meaning in this context is simple; "a secret place is a place hidden from others". In this case, Jesus is saying, "When you fast, keep the fact, the inconvenience and even the pain of it hidden from others. Be secret about it." This secret place Jesus talks of here is much more than a closed room, it is a metaphysical place. It is a place we can fully inhabit whilst also inhabiting the physical world. It usually differs substantially from all our other secret places in that we are in it by righteous design and invitation of the Father. Or rather, we inhabit the secret place where we are both being beheld by and beholding the Father. We know we are not alone in the secret place because the Father is communing with us. Indeed, our secret place has become His secret place to meet with us. It has become a secret place of hearing, of helping and of healing.

This secret place Jesus talks of here is much more than a closed room, it is a metaphysical place. It is a place we can fully inhabit whilst also inhabiting the physical world. It usually differs substantially from all our other secret places in that we are in it by righteous design and invitation of the Father.

You will go to one of your secret places today. If it is to sin, know that nothing is hidden before the all-seeing gaze of God. If it is to hurl abuse at others or to simmer sins committed against you in some selfish and surly pot, know that God smells the stench. However, if it is to commune with the Father, to be with Him in righteousness and honor, then know that He is waiting there for you. Rejoice in this!

I spoke despairingly concerning the condition of my comatose dad to the old Salvation Army Brigadier lady that had prayed me into the Kingdom. Lovingly she replied, "Robert, don't worry. There is no place where God is not; even where your father is now, God is there and God can speak to Him and he to God."

Dear friend, fear not. Your Father awaits you in the secret place.

Listen: *"'Can anyone hide himself in secret places, so I shall not see him?' says the LORD; 'Do I not fill heaven and earth?' says the LORD." Jeremiah 23:24*

Pray: Lord. Where can I go from Your Spirit? Or where can I flee from Your presence? If I ascend into heaven, You are there; If I make my bed in hell, behold, You are there. If I take the wings of the morning, and dwell in the uttermost parts of the sea, even there Your hand shall lead me, and Your right hand shall hold me. (Psalm 139:7-10)

| Vol 02 | Q3 | NW00591 | August 12th |

Night-Whisper | **DANGER**

Pig dogs and cataclysmic chiasms!

Matthew 7:6

Do not give what is holy to the dogs; nor cast your pearls before swine, lest they trample them under their feet, and turn and tear you in pieces. NKJV

When I was 11 years of age, I had the opportunity to go to a very posh, fee-paying school. Here you did not progress through your years from the 1st form to the 6th form, or from a lower grade to an higher grade but as a sign of its exclusivity, you progressed through "elements" to "rudiments" and then finally to "syntax". The inference is that you had to be pretty wise and have all the basics of understanding under your belt before you could get to grips with the true grammatical structure of sentences and therefore the syntax of life! (I'm still working on all of these by the way). Anyway, the reason I am telling you this is because some commentators suggest that our text for today, Matthew 7:6 is in fact a "syntactical chiasmus". In other words it's related to a poetic form of writing where a chiasm is suggested by its grammatical pattern conforming to the **">"** shape of the left half of the Greek letter chi, which is drawn like the English letter "X". So, the suggested poetical physical form of the verse would look like this:

A------------→Do Not give what is holy to the dogs

B------------------------------→Nor cast your pearl before swine

C--→Lest

B-------------------------------→they trample them under their feet

A ------------→And turn and tear you in pieces

Nice! Even interesting maybe but so what? Well may I suggest the giving of such instruction in poetic form is there to aid us in our remembering it! In other words, Jesus is saying, "This is important. Don't forget it!"

There is a terrible connection here then, for friends the startling fact is that God regards certain people as both pigs and dogs!

God refers to certain people who have returned to their vomit and eaten it or who have been washed and then returned to wallow in the mire as opposers of the Gospel, abusers, sour, growling, grumbling quarrelling, hungry, ignorant and dangerous curs. "Don't forget this," says Jesus.

Note also that God sees that we possess things which are holy and preciously beautiful. Thoughts, teachings, ideas, bodies, possessions, indeed anything that has been dedicated to Him and His kingdom, are Holy! Good works, kind words, loving reproofs, gentleness and all the other fruits and gifts of the Spirit, are beautiful and precious to Him. Jesus is clearly saying here, "Don't give these things to dogs or cast it before swine."

Pigs and dogs come in varying shapes and sizes. They live in certain patterns, smell in certain ways and are both dangerous to the casters of pearl and to the giver of holy things.

Pigs and dogs come in varying shapes and sizes. They live in certain patterns, smell in certain ways and are both dangerous to the casters of pearl and to the giver of holy things. I think Jesus here in context is showing us that these "pig dogs" are the blind religious and self-righteous hypocrites who have beams in their eyes and think they are a cut above the rest of humanity.

These pig-dogs, outwardly smell nice, look gorgeous and refined in their flowing robes, yet their hearts are full of the sour mud of the pigpen and the soiled dirt of the dog pound. I wonder if Jesus is saying: "Don't bother them, don't even mess with them because they will rip you to pieces as they have done with John and will do so with Me and Stephen, so, leave them alone."

I have seen Christian churches who have their pig dogs honored, talcum powdered down, dressed up in suitable suits, up front, in charge and influential. I have sat in pews with my feet inches deep in the smiling swill; been in members meetings and witnessed the soiled and selfish grunting and felt the sharp ministry of the land of canine. I have seen the blood spattered white washed walls and still can hear the cry of the trampled little ones fallen beneath the trotting and all the fat belly turning, of pink and pompous pigs and wolves in sheep's clothing. To hell with them!

This cataclysmic chiasm, this poetic form frames for us the immense importance of this message. Remember this today.

I have seen the blood spattered white washed walls and still can hear the cry of the trampled little ones fallen beneath the trotting and all the fat belly turning, of pink and pompous pigs and wolves in sheep's clothing. To hell with them!

Listen: *"For dogs have surrounded Me; The congregation of the wicked has enclosed Me. They pierced My hands and My feet; I can count all My bones. They look and stare at Me. They divide My garments among them, and for My clothing they cast lots." Psalm 22:16-18*

Pray: Lord. Who is wise enough in themselves to know when to speak and when to be silent, to know when to embrace and when to cease from embracing, when to give and when to hold back. Lord, guide me in these things that I might not hurt myself or sin against You. Amen and let it be so.

Strongholds footholds and sinkholes

Sinkholes are common in land where the rock beneath the soil surface is carboniferous limestone or salt beds. Essentially, they are found in places where the rock is literally dissolved over time. As rain and circulating ground water eats the rock away, eventually a chasm will develop beneath the surface, until one day, the space grows so large that it can no longer support what is above it and then whooompeta! The ground gives way and all above is swallowed into a giant hole of devastation.

Zechariah 9:11,12

"As for you also, because of the blood of your covenant, I will set your prisoners free from the waterless pit. Return to the stronghold, You prisoners of hope. Even today I declare that I will restore double to you. NKJV

The debate over a Christian's ability to be "possessed" or "oppressed" by forces of darkness is not neatly sidestepped by the term demonization but is rather, far better addressed and understood. The demonization of Christians then, is not a popular subject amongst the body of the church because after all, it brings with it a certain downgrading of our spirituality don't you think? Yet I tell you I have stepped out of bed some mornings and before I've rubbed the sleep out of my eyes, I know the devil is on my case, on my back, indeed there are times when I can feel his hot breath on my neck! I feel demonized in the sense of being attacked, oppressed, unusually depressed, sick without cause, fearful, distrustful, panicky etc. Shall I continue?

Now before you think I attribute all of these things to simply demonic influence, let me tell you that I do not. However, I am coming to know the difference between the ravage of the baggage of my own sin and that, which is stirred up externally and put upon me from without! Friends, we are involved in a spiritual war and it rages over and around our hearts and minds and bodies every single day. This is why we are called to put on armor, resist the devil and to take up especially, the weapons of the Word and all kinds of prayer, brandishing them as destructive implements of devastation which are mighty in the demolishing of strongholds. In addition to this, as saved and sanctified sappers, by continual confession, repentance and forgiveness, we must forge on in the filling in of the many footholds we have also given to the enemy.

It is these footholds, in these places of unforgiveness and these places of festering hurt and lying agreement with the enemy, these strongholds, that will if left unattended, eat away a chasm of emptiness beneath the seeming settled surface of our lives. Unless we fight and fill, then one day the surface of our world will collapse beneath our feet and whooompeta! All above shall be swallowed into a giant hole of devastation.

We are involved in a spiritual war and it rages over and around our hearts and minds and bodies every single day.

Dear friend, demons assail you and their intent is your fall, destruction, and the devastation of all God and all good that is connected to you. They seek a hole-iness in your life, of the collapsing kind. Today, may I suggest that if you feel the ground beginning to give way beneath your feet, then there are probably some strongholds and footholds to be dealt with, for friends, there are fighting's and fillings that we all must attend to and until we do this, we shall all continue to be demonized at some level and in some dark way that makes the ground seem to quiver beneath our steadfast feet.

Listen: *"No weapon formed against you shall prosper, and every tongue which rises against you in judgment You shall condemn. This is the heritage of the servants of the LORD, And their righteousness is from Me," says the LORD. Isaiah 54:17*

Pray: Our Father in heaven, Hallowed be Your name. Your kingdom come. Your will be done On earth as it is in heaven. Give us this day our daily bread. And forgive us our debts, as we forgive our debtors. And do not lead us into temptation, but deliver us from the evil one. For Yours is the kingdom and the power and the glory forever. Amen and let it be so. (Matthew 6:9-13)

Night-Whisper | **WITNESS**

God's IP address

"Cyberspace exists within a worldwide network of computer networks that use TCP/IP network protocols to facilitate data transmission and exchange." As we are on-line, searching for the nearest place to order pizza from, or looking up directions to get to the cinema, such a technical description of the space that the information we are looking at is perceived and received, falls far short of our experience within this humanly created metaphysical entity, doesn't it? How about this definition then: "Cyberspace has come to refer to the various information resources that are available through computer networks and the Internet, as well as to "communities" which have developed through their common use of such resources and also to the "culture" which is developing in such electronically connected communities. Cyberspace then distinguishes the physical world from the digital, or computer-based world." Yes, that's a little better, but not too much!

John 15:27

And you also will bear witness, because you have been with Me from the beginning. NKJV

It was William Gibson in his book '*Neuromancer*' that first coined the term, 'Cyberspace.' He describes it as "A consensual hallucination experienced daily by billions of legitimate operators, in every nation, by children being taught mathematical concept… a graphic representation of data abstracted from the banks of every computer in the human system, unthinkable complexity, lines of light ranged in the non-space of the mind, clusters and constellations of data, like city lights, receding." Now that, I like very much indeed!

We all are spending increasing hours each day functioning and communing in this seemingly man made and Godless cyberspace. Thomas L Friedman in his book *The Lexus and The Olive Tree* suggests to us that God is not in cyberspace unless we bring Him there! He further suggests that God wants to be there but cannot be there unless we bring Him there. Indeed, it is only our mouse clicks of free choice, that enable us to choose sanctity and morality and therefore bring the Lordship of God into a cyberspace He did not create! Hmmm. As Miss Marple would say, “How very interesting!”

Now, before I go further, you need to know that every wanderer and worker in cyberspace makes use of the TCP/IP system and is assigned a unique identifier when on and in cyberspace, called an IP address. The vast, yet limited number of IP addresses means they are mostly intermittently and randomly assigned from country permitted pools. This is known as dynamic IP addressing. (Oh by the way, Cisco, the routing company, do have IP addresses reserved for aliens, but that’s another story for another day).

God’s IP address is not permanent but dynamic and may I say, that if you are a Christian then God’s IP address is the one you are using right now.

Now Friedman obviously does not think that God has His very own IP address and also that He never logs on Himself! However, it seems to me that God’s IP address is not permanent but dynamic and may I say, that if you are a Christian then God’s IP address is the one you are using right now. Freidman is correct in that it is we who take God into cyberspace. Imagine that.

Unlike Friedman however, I do believe there is of course nowhere where that God in His fullness is not present. So of course, I also believe that God is in cyberspace without us. However, I do concur that cyberspace does not have the primary testimonies of “creation” and “conscience” that we have in the physical world. So, maybe Friedman is partly correct by observing that God is seen to be in cyberspace only, I mean only, by the choices we make in it and the way we use it. So friend let me ask you today. Who are you in cyberspace? Where do you go? What do you do? How do you manifest the testimony of God, the Lordship of Christ and the look of His face to the barren creation of man’s cyberspace.

Listen: *“‘You are My witnesses,’ says the LORD, ‘and My servant whom I have chosen, that you may know and believe Me, and understand that I am He. Before Me there was no God formed, nor shall there be after Me. I, even I, am the LORD, and besides Me there is no Savior. I have declared and saved, I have proclaimed, and there was no foreign God* *among you; therefore you are My witnesses,' Says the LORD, 'that I am God.'*

Pray: O Sacred King, O Holy King, how can I honor You rightly, honor that's fit for Your name? In every space Jesus, be my Lord, amen and let it be so.

| Vol 02 | Q3 | NW00594 | August 15th |

Night-Whisper | **FELLOWSHIP**

Solitude and the solace of the Son.

John Eldridge writes from the heart, about the heart. He sees the absolute necessity of small communities living and fighting for one another's hearts. From his book *Waking the Dead* I have pulled just two comments referring to small community and what is necessary for them to work. Here is the first: "Most churches survive because everyone keeps a polite distance from the others". And secondly: "Community cannot live without solitude".

John 6:15b

He departed again to the mountain by Himself alone. NKJV

These two statements describe the two extremities of community. The first being the "toe dip". The toe dip is like getting all dressed down to go swimming, then wrapping the thickest towel around you whilst tentatively dipping your toe into the waters in front of everyone who's urging you to come right on in but in response you simply smile politely, saying "Ooh it's freezing, I'll just wait a while." You are there but you are not there and truth is, you have no intention of fully going there. It might be bad English but it's the truth and most of us are like that.

The second statement describes the "dive bomb". You've gone and got yourself naked and then ran screaming with joyful expectation, leaping into community from the side of the pool with a giant "I'm here!" explosion of a splash, only to find people wished you would have least put some bathing attire on and actually they can't look at you properly anyway now because they are rubbing the chlorine water splash that you made, out from underneath their eye lids and the waves of that same splash, are lifting them up from their own grounded bottom and bouncing them up and then thumping them down again. This community cannot cope with your naked and needy, naughty and noisy, dishonorable and disrespectful arrival. Stop doing that! No community can meet your every naked need.

The church is an organism not an organization. The church is a community not a convocation. The church is a body of mutual ministry. These three good statements that the church is an organism, a community and a body of mutual ministry may be true but can also lead us to a thoroughly unwarranted belief that the church is a community where everything that is lacking and needful for us to glorify God is in fact most wonderfully provided for. For after all, the church is a community where we get every need met and every hurt healed! You know, church community is fun, fodder, fellowship and fixing! Ha! If only it were so.

With such unrealistic expectations in our hearts, community can move from the place of encounter with God to the place of replacement for God! The church community however is not a replacement for God because the church community, even when it is at it's best in being powerful and spiritually productive, cannot fix everything!

Eldridge has it then! "Community cannot live without solitude." In other words, total reliance on others, whether in community, single friendships, marriage or even children, to come and meet our deepest need is simply an unrealistic madness. No one, no matter how lovely, can meet the deep needs of our heart. We need to get alone with God friends. We need some solitude with our Lord.

"Community cannot live without solitude." In other words, total reliance on others, whether in community, single friendships, marriage or even children, to come and meet our deepest need is simply an unrealistic madness. No one, no matter how lovely, can meet the deep needs of our heart. We need to get alone with God friends. We need some solitude with our Lord.

You see the solitude I speak of is actually the company of Jesus. We need to get alone with Him. Now, for most of us, this is a challenge of gigantic proportion. We fear being alone with ourselves, for we do not truly know (or like) ourselves and are uncomfortable in even our own presence. We fear being alone with ourselves for we do not truly know ourselves. In the same way, we fear being alone with God, for we do not intimately know Him (or really trust Him) and so are also uncomfortable in His presence. Yet being alone with God is absolutely vital to our own health and healing and consequently it is directly related to the blessing, or lack thereof, that we bring to community. Do you see that?

Solitude is to be with oneself and with God and solitude is the only place where we can receive the intimate solace of the Son. So despite our fear, despite our manufactured business, we need to seek some solitude each and every single day. It is only when we get naked with God that we can see ourselves for who we are. It is only then, that we can accept, honor and help others in our Christ-like communities.

I remember a wreck of a woman, quickly and most fearfully finding herself naked, hurt, ashamed and alone with Jesus.

Listen: *"When Jesus had raised Himself up and saw no one but the woman, He said to her, 'Woman, where are those accusers of yours? Has no one condemned you?' She said, 'No one, Lord.' And Jesus said to her, 'Neither do I condemn you; go and sin no more.'" (John 8:10-11)*

Pray: Lord I have once again believed the lie that You do not care and that You do not speak and even if You do, it is but to pick and to condemn. I have believed the lie that You do not love me and are not good. Will You please seek my company again dear Lord. Draw close to me today, call my name, call me to You again dear Jesus in the quietness and the sometimes fearful solitude of my soul. Amen, and let it be so.

| Vol 02 | Q3 | NW00595 | August 16th |

Night-Whisper | **FELLOWSHIP**

Come O breath and breathe

We left another one of our favorite poetry groups to depart for new pastures. There amongst other poets, we had immensely enjoyed our fellowship around words and hearts; indeed, chiefly we had enjoyed hearing other people's voices, always distinct, often dancing and sometimes even, dangerous! For voices when released do cause revolutions. Selah!

Ezekiel 37:9,10

Also He said to me, "Prophesy to the breath, prophesy, son of man, and say to the breath, Thus says the Lord God: "Come from the four winds, O breath, and breathe on these slain, that they may live." So I prophesied as He commanded me, and breath came into them, and they lived, and stood upon their feet, an exceedingly great army." NKJV

One of the poets there, immense and intense, had written for us a going away poem entitled "A Song of the Four Winds". It's a treasured gift. It is beautiful and focuses around life, friendship and fellowship. Did you know that life comes from the four winds?

Ezekiel is not called to chant some strange incantation into thin air but as a prophet of God, as a "Lord" of the earth under the Lord of the earth he is commanded to speak words of power greater than any strange magic. We can summaries his prophetic command in a simple sentence; "Come O breath and breathe".

The four winds blow from the four corners of the earth. In other words they come from everywhere. They blow at different times of the year, with differing strength and carry with them distinct tools. In Israel the north wind brings substantial rain at just the right time to be favorable to vegetation and so, is indicative of growth. The east Wind comes from across the wilderness and brings with it enough violence to clear out every hidden cobweb of our life. It is a wind of cleansing, a wind of clearing. The west wind is of a lighter touch, bringing refreshing showers.

The south wind brings the heat. The close heat of communion and comfortableness.

Cleansing, refreshing, growth and communion are all marks of friendship and of fellowship; are all marks of life, if you will. Let me ask you today then, do you have these four winds blowing across the face of your soul? Let me ask you as a local church today, do you have these four winds caressing your tall colonnades? If not, then today maybe the Master asks you to stand on your feet and shout in prophetic command to the four winds to fall upon you with life and love and friendship and fellowship? Yes, O Christian, you ruler and reign with Him, maybe today God has put it in you, to call life into yourself and into your community and with prophetic and believing cry to also lift up your voice with Ezekiel of old and shout, "Come O breath and breathe!" Go on! Shout it to the four directions of the compass today, "Come O breath and breathe!" Do it. Keep doing it! And don't you dare go home until one of the good winds of God billows in your cheeks.

Cleansing, refreshing, growth and communion are all marks of friendship and of fellowship; are all marks of life,

Listen: *"And He rode upon a cherub, and flew; He flew upon the wings of the wind." (Psalm 18:10 NKJV)*

He causes the vapours to ascend from the ends of the earth; He makes lightning for the rain; He brings the wind out of His treasuries. (Psalm 135:7 NKJV)

Pray: Lord in Your Great Name and by Your sovereign and unassailable power I now stand and call to these four winds today and in believing words I cry "Come O breath and breathe!" Now O Lord, clothe these dry bones of ours in flesh, stand us on our feet and make us into a great army. O God! Send amongst your churches these four winds today. In Jesus mighty name I ask it, amen.

| Vol 02 | Q3 | NW00596 | August 17th |

Night-Whisper | **WITNESS**

Riveting reads

It was today in 1993 that Random House publishing agreed to pay General Colin Powell an advance of about $6 million for the rights to his autobiography, *My American Journey.* I bet you thought it was only sports people that got paid exorbitant fees!

Ecclesiastes 12:12

Of making many books there is no end, and much study is wearisome to the flesh. NKJV

Books continue to be big business and the electronic age has not diminished this but only intensified it. I am not a good reader and so I listen to many books. Log on, pay your money, down load, get on with some none mentally demanding chore, jog or paint or walk the dog and just listen! It's a great way to absorb I can tell you. Yup, I can in just a few seconds download a new book and throw it on my handheld or my iPod along with numerous other titles, slip it into my shirt pocket and whip it out whenever I need it. Amazing really! There is in fact so much information available now that you could drown in it. Indeed, there is so much information and so much accessibility to it that it's like putting your mouth around a fire hydrant and in the end it can indeed become very wearisome to your flesh.

I am a perpetual student and so know how wearisome study can get and so I am always gladdened and greatly encouraged when I come across a book that is hot in my heavy little hands. A book that speaks to me, encourages me, scratches where I itch and it brings out many an "Amen" and sometimes a "You've got to be kidding me!" This is the kind of book that for me is alive and speaking. I might not agree with it all but I cannot ignore it for it has a voice and it speaks.

The Church is like an old book to the world. On the whole, we are ignored. The world finds us often to be wearisome to them, indeed, we are to them just one big yawn! "There they go again, spouting their musty mantra, the tea at three brigade, religiously righteous, clothed in mediocrity, irrelevant sad and powerless. I mean look at them! Come on, why bother with such feeble voices."

Let's be honest, in the West the local churches have long since ceased to be a group of revolutionary world changing voices. Yet we should be banners of truth, bearers of burned and heartfelt words! We should be the books that are too hot to handle, the books demanding to be seen, read and heard, books that are seditious to the world the flesh and the devil, irregular, intriguing, intrusive, intrepid, irritating, irrefutable, and thoroughly inspired!

We should be banners of truth, bearers of burned and heartfelt words! We should be the books that are too hot to handle, the books demanding to be seen, read and heard, books that are seditious to the world the flesh and the devil, irregular, intriguing, intrusive, intrepid, irritating, irrefutable, and thoroughly inspired!

Friend, fellow book of God containing a story heard and written nowhere else in the universe, how are your pages today? Smudged? Closed? Torn, ripped, burned or stained or worse still, boring? Don't you know that Jesus makes great books! That He is the restorer of better dreams and far, far better stories. Maybe your story has yet to properly begin? So, why not today, ask Jesus to write you a story that you can be proud of; a story that the world just cannot ignore.

Listen: *"You are our epistle written in our hearts, known and read by all men; clearly you are an epistle of Christ, ministered by us, written not with ink but by the Spirit of the living God, not on tablets of stone but on tablets of flesh, that is, of the heart." (2 Corinthians 3:2-3 NKJV)*

Pray: Lord, take my Life and let it be, consecrated Lord to thee. Take my moments and my days and make them flow in ceaseless praise to You. Make me into a book whose pages drip with warm grace and rich red love. Make me an adventure that people want to join. Oh author of life, come sign Your name on me! Amen.

Evangellyfish

Recently I read an insignificant little paper written by a member of the American Humanist Society that had the audacity to quote just the first two lines of Emily Jane Bronte's poem, "No Coward Soul is Mine" to vainly try and bolster up the shattered dyke of the denial of the sense of the infinite and the knowledge of immortality, which is bound up in the heart of each one of us. It attempted to do this whilst spouting on about the glorious optimism and bravery of humanism within society at large. What humbug!

Ecclesiastes 3:11b

Also He has put eternity in their hearts. NKJV

Listen Friends to what Bronte really said beyond the first two lines of the poem! (This is, by the way, the last poem she ever wrote.)

No coward soul is mine,
No trembler in the world's storm-troubled sphere:
I see Heaven's glories shine,
And Faith shines equal, arming me from Fear.

O God within my breast,
Almighty, ever-present Deity!
Life, that in me has rest,
As I, undying Life, have power in Thee!.

Vain are the thousand creeds
That move men's hearts: unutterably vain;
Worthless as withered weeds,
Or idlest froth amid the boundless main,

To waken doubt in one
Holding so fast by Thy infinity,

So surely anchored on
The steadfast rock of Immortality.

With wide-embracing love
Thy Spirit animates eternal years,
Pervades and broods above,
Changes, sustains, dissolves, creates, and rears.

Though earth and moon were gone,
And suns and universes ceased to be,
And Thou wert left alone,
Every existence would exist in Thee.

There is not room for Death,
Nor atom that his might could render void:
Thou -Thou art Being and Breath,
And what Thou art may never be destroyed.

Emily became ill after attending the funeral of her brother Bramwell. Overcome by tuberculosis she died aged 30 refusing the help of the medical profession, which she distrusted greatly. An introvert with no real close friends, her world-famous novel *Wuthering Heights* brought the sceptics rebuff that "no woman of such a circumscribed life could have written such a passionate story." Again, what humbug!

Friends, passion is a misplaced, misunderstood and much maligned quality within the Church.

Friends, passion is a misplaced, misunderstood and much maligned quality within the Church. Gentleness, balance, wisdom, circumspection, have in our Evangelicalism been presented from such a high and calmed vantage point, that passion is attributed mainly to those ignorant youths, who bark and leap like little labrador puppies all over the great things of God! Our methods of discipleship and mediocre mentoring often result in training people and men especially, to be so quiet, so well bread, read and dead, that it is easy to hitch them to the white-sticked blind, that they, now also bound misled and scared to see, may be together led carefully, quietly and miserably along the safe pathways of the "agreed upon". So much so that are churches are more like Bruce Forsyth then Bruse Willis. What humbug!

Surely as those born again by the Eternal Spirit, who have enlivened eternity so bursting within our hearts that our chests expand big with the eager expectancy of heaven, breathing out gregarious groaning's, hyper ventilating our dizzy little heads with visions of the New Jerusalem, if we who are gagging for God and a better world to come, if we cannot be a people of passionate bravery, treading down the waves of fear and crying "Charge!" and "Onward!" "Farther in!" and "Higher up!" to one another, then who can?

Out of so many millions of men in the church, I could not tell you of any current heroes that I can count on but one hand that has the audacity to shout, "Follow me even as I follow Christ!"

Out of so many millions of men in the church, I could not tell you of any current heroes that I can count on but one hand that has the audacity to shout, "Follow me even as I follow Christ!" All of our boys have for years been told to make nice and keep taking the estrogen and yet we wonder why we are so limp and insipid! Passion! It might get in you trouble sometimes but there is no life without it!

Bronte, a 30-year-old isolated introvert put burning passion down on a page, looked into death and eternity and cried "No Coward Soul is Mine!" What about you pussycat?

Listen: *"Then He appointed twelve, that they might be with Him and that He might send them out to preach, and to have power to heal sicknesses and to cast out demons: Simon, to whom He gave the name Peter; James the son of Zebedee and John the brother of James, to whom He gave the name Boanerges, that is, 'Sons of Thunder'." (Mark 3:14-17 NKJV)*

Pray: Lord, when we together write Your story in my life, let it be one of felt pleasure and of pulsating passion. God! Help us to burn the pink plastic molds that have produced wet Evangellyfish for far too many years! Amen, and let it be so.

| Vol 02 | Q3 | NW00598 | August 19th |

Night-Whisper | **PERSEVERANCE**

From backside to flipside

Along with thousands of others today and in the future, I will be writing of the extraordinary scenes in the Athens 2004 Olympics concerning the young American, Mr. Paul Hamm and his amazing achievement of being the first American to win the all-round gymnastics gold medal. How he did it, was high drama indeed!

2 Peter 1:5b-8

Add to your faith virtue, to virtue knowledge, to knowledge self-control, to self-control perseverance, to perseverance Godliness, to Godliness brotherly kindness, and to brotherly kindness love. For if these things are yours and abound, you will be neither barren nor unfruitful in the knowledge of our Lord Jesus Christ. NKJV

I can't imagine the years of training that go into preparing for such an event. Out of six disciplines, after the third one Hamm was on the top of the leader board. A gold medal was expected of him and was in his grasp. Disaster struck in his fourth discipline of the Vault. Failing to rotate well enough, he landed to the side, the impact causing him to topple off the mat and land flat on his bottom right in front of the shaken judges and unbelieving crowd! Hamm, in an instant plummeted from 1st to 12th place. At this point if he could summon the wherewithal to exceed expectations in his performance on the final two disciplines, then maybe, with a miracle, just maybe, he might achieve a bronze medal. That alone would be quite a comeback.

Whilst sitting flat on his bottom, cameras and commentators zoomed into the blank and staring eyes of Hamm, speculating on the raging storm of doubt disbelief and shocking disappointment that must have been wreaking havoc along the coastlands of his soul and even laying waist to the inlands of his spirit. It was cataclysmic, it was catastrophic, it was awful.

Somehow and I don't how, Hamm managed to attack the final two events of parallel and high bars with such glorious and determined precision, that onlookers were shocked that such audacity and determination should come from someone who just earlier had landed on their embarrassed backsides before the judges and the watching world. The near perfection of his final performances meant that Hamm shot from 12th to 1st place winning gold by the slimmest of recorded margins, 0.012. Now, just how utterly amazing is that!

One hour after being crowned Olympic champion Hamm made the following remarks. "I'm very happy right now, I was so angry at myself after I'd missed the vault. I had worked years for that moment, and it all went down the drain. And then I had the best performance of my life on high bar. I'm proud of myself. I realized my dream. And I never, never, never gave up."

Friend, don't give up! Skin that cat a different way maybe but don't give up. Find a different angle of attack maybe, but don't give up! Cast your net on the other side of the boat maybe but don't give up.

Friend, don't give up! Skin that cat a different way maybe but don't give up. Find a different angle of attack maybe, but don't give up! Cast your net on the other side of the boat maybe but don't give up. The gold medal is always possible even if it's by the slimmest of margins, even if it's by the skin of your teeth, so today; don't give up! Go Hamm it up! Yes, be determined to find the perfect better way.

Listen: *"And let us not grow weary while doing good, for in due season we shall reap if we do not lose heart." (Galatians 6:9 NKJV)*

Pray: Lord, I am more than an Olympian, for You have made me more than a conqueror through Your love and Your sacrifice. How then can I not persevere? So heal me, so help me, so infuse me, so empower me, so change me that I would indeed persevere to the final victory. In Jesus name I pray, amen, and let it be so.

| Vol 02 | Q3 | NW00599 | August 20th |

Night-Whisper | **PERSEVERANCE**

Waiting with names!

A month after war broke out with Britain, on July 16th the USS Constitution, encountered a squadron of five British ships off Egg Harbor, New Jersey. The constitution was surrounded and preparing to escape when the wind suddenly died. Out of gunnery range and both sides now dead in the water, for 36 hours the Constitution's crew kept their ship just ahead of the slowly pursuing British by towing the frigate with rowboats and by tossing the ship's anchor ahead of the ship and then reeling it in. Later when the wind came up, the Constitution was far enough ahead of the British warships to then make her escape by sail. She was running rather than fighting, a wise move for the day.

Genesis 32:27-28

So He said to him, "What is your name?" He said, "Jacob." And He said, "Your name shall no longer be called Jacob, but Israel; for you have struggled with God and with men, and have prevailed." NKJV

It was actually yesterday, August 19th in 1812 that the USS Constitution earned its battle name of "Old Ironsides". During a ferocious engagement off the coast of Nova Scotia resulting in the sinking of the British frigate Guerriýre, witnesses to the crash of cannon balls claimed that the British shot "merely bounced off the Constitution's sides, as if the ship were made of iron rather than wood".

The wisdom, courage and tenacity of the crew of Constitution seen in these two incidents fire my blood for I am increasingly convinced that perseverance cannot exist without passion and passion cannot succeed without focus and dedication. The crew of the Constitution showed such tenacity and bravery that they were attributed a name far beyond their design and capability. A ship that seemed so unsinkable that it was attributed with both hidden design and secret properties. A wooden ship with iron sides even.

I am equally convinced that the Sovereign Lord awaits with names to knight in the field those with a constitution sturdy enough to turn to flight armies of demons, be valiant in battle, bring forth strength from weakness, escape the edge of the enemy sword, quench violent burning, stop the mouths of lions, obtain promises, work righteousness and by faith subdue kingdoms! O brave hearted friends, step up, step out, tread down, trample and be victorious in the fight, for He is waiting with names!

Listen: *"To whom He gave the name Boanerges, that is, 'Sons of Thunder'." (Mark 3:17b NKJV)*

Pray: I hurt O Lord and my day breaks upon me but I will not let You go, until you give me a prevailing name O my Jesus. Amen and let it be so.

| Vol 02 | Q3 | NW00600 | August 21st |

Night-Whisper | **FELLOWSHIP**

Kisses and whispers

Love song lyrics can be both banal and cringeworthy! Yet an examination of cultural musical trends can give us indications of social anxieties, structure and even some prevailing problems. I suppose gangsta rap being one example in the US and punk another example in the UK. These two genres of music can be viewed as dangerous, anarchistic and violent, whilst the only damage a simple love song lyric can do is maybe mislead some silly women and sad men into stupid affairs. Yes, musical genres do say something and unfortunately, even if be it ever so nice, all cultural expression rooted primarily in a fallen world always carries with it a duplicitous danger and seduction to sinfulness that we would do well to be aware of.

Romans 16:16a

Greet one another with a holy kiss. NKJV

Yet friends, we must also be aware that singing rises from the soul, even from the depths of our being and so may bring to the surface some of the lost jewels of our deepest desire, even some of the hidden things of God? For if eternity is indeed laid up in our hearts, then as we open our souls, maybe some of the bright sands of that lost shore will sparkle sometimes in the words we sing and in even the way we sing them? So then, to my fascination with love songs, for my observed premise is that everything that is true of love as expressed in various songs, everything, is in the end talking about Jesus, who is, love incarnate!

It seems to me then, that two noticed and ever present themes in successful love songs, keywords if you will, are "kissing" and "whispers". I want to suggest that the kisses and whispers of love songs are in fact, reflections of some deep spiritual issues, for whilst kissing is the sign of deepest intimacy, of connectivity and Holy knowing, whispers are the private caressing of the kind and delicately used keys of unlocking words to a person's most innermost being. Maybe even here then in seemingly banal loves songs lies some of the secret evangelism of God?

For example, Lonestar, in their song "Softly" (Annie Roboff/Holly Lamar) sing:

Baby, with the sweetest kiss
You came along and stole my breath
Tore down my defences with a whisper
Oh you showed me how love can be
You broke through to my heart
Softly, baby softly

In my long examining of love song lyrics it is obvious that our chief and deep desire, is to be embraced and held close. I would suggest this desire is a metaphysical echo of the deepest need of ours to be embraced intimately by God, to be held softly by Him. This is at least one answer to the unusual scenes surrounding the Hindu Guru, "Mata Amritanandamayi Devi" (mother of absolute bliss), who at the beginning of the 21st century is reported to have divinely "hugged" over 30 million people in the prior 30 years? Imagine that! People do need embracing you see. That shake of a hand on Sunday morning, that moment of manly hugging, is for many sometimes the only intimate human contact people will get all week. Think about that. Embracing one another is very important for the soul.

Second then, love song lyrics indicate that our own soul's longing is to hear unlocking whispers, and in particular I would say, His unlocking words, even His whispers to our own lost and hurting hearts. Is this why so many desperate Christians run to every prophet, approved or otherwise, every seemingly wise whacko even, with the hope of hearing but one word directed especially to them, just for them, from Him, just once? People are longing for a personal whisper from the Lord. Aren't you?

People are longing for a personal whisper from the Lord. Aren't you?

Friends, let us the church, at least learn to embrace one another in Holy intimacy and Godly gentleness and then to speak to one another from the depths of who we are to the depths of who they are, with tender and touching tenderness. I wonder if then and only then, we shall begin to truly be the body of Christ engaged in singing His eternal love song over one another? Those who have ears to hear, let them hear and those who have arms to hold, let them embrace!

Listen: *"And after the earthquake a fire, but the LORD was not in the fire; and after the fire a still small voice. So it was, when Elijah heard it, that he wrapped his face in his mantle and went out and stood in the entrance of the cave. Suddenly a voice came to him, and said" (1 Kings 19:12b-13a NKJV)*

"Do not fear; Zion, let not your hands be weak. The LORD your God in your midst, The Mighty One, will save; He will rejoice over you with gladness, He will quiet you with His love, He will rejoice over you with singing." (Zephaniah 3:16-17 NKJV)

Pray: My God, my Father of absolute bliss, embrace me today. Do not leave me without a whisper from Your mouth, for as the deer pants for the water brooks, so pants my soul for You, O God. My soul thirsts for God, for the living God. Kiss me with the kisses of your mouth for your love is sweeter than wine. Come close dear Savior, come close. Amen and let it be so.

| Vol 02 | Q3 | NW00601 | August 22nd |

Night-Whisper | **WITNESS**

Eden and evangelism

I have a ministered in a few homes for the elderly, visiting the sick and aged and conducting church services. Christian or otherwise and despite the care and attention of staff, these "homes" have often been difficult and unpleasant smelling institutions. Helplessness, hopelessness, boredom and loneliness seemed to be the norm but no more! The "Eden Alternative"™ is an organization that seems to be remaking the experience of aging, dementia and disability. It seeks to improve people's quality of life by forming coalitions committed to creating better social, physical and enlivened environments that minister to the whole person.

Isaiah 62:1-4a

"The Spirit of the Lord GOD is upon Me, because the LORD has anointed Me to preach good tidings to the poor; He has sent Me to heal the broken hearted, to proclaim liberty to the captives, and the opening of the prison to those who are bound; to proclaim the acceptable year of the LORD, and the day of vengeance of our God; to comfort all who mourn, to console those who mourn in Zion, to give them beauty for ashes, the oil of joy for mourning, the garment of praise for the spirit of heaviness; that they may be called trees of righteousness, the planting of the LORD, that He may be glorified." And they shall rebuild the old ruins. NKJV

I visited an Episcopalian memory care center for those with differing levels of Alzheimer's and dementia, which was applying these Eden Alternative principles. The magnificent and spacious buildings, the kind, caring and positive staff, beauty salon, gift and flower shop, spa, indoor aviaries, cats, dogs, visiting children, ice cream soda fountain shop, self service kitchens, restaurant areas, themed areas, pictures, front porches, gardens, and a whole lot more besides, made this secure unit a most welcoming little town! For that is what it was. The unit itself is divided into neighborhoods where the residents at different stages of dementia live, grow, and are cared for. The quality of care and life is substantial. The smell was gone! I was told of one lady, who as her dementia progressed did not like to bathe, as she needed help and found it embarrassing. They enticed her into cleanliness by laying out alongside the beautiful bath, candles, crackers cheese and wine; all her favorite foods. It worked!

Proclamation is not dead, neither is it an old tool to be laid aside but rather, it remains God's means of declaring good news! However, proclamation must recover the full power of its all-encompassing voice and speak to the body the soul and the spirit, to communities, to social justice, to poverty, to environment, to care, to art and even to the animal kingdom. Proclamation must learn how to be enticing wine, cheese and crackers, laid out alongside a sparkling bath, to a desperate lost and lonely, unclean smelly old insane and demented world.

Proclamation is not dead, neither is it an old tool to be laid aside but rather, it remains God's means of declaring good news!

Friends, let us the church, learn to embrace those created in God's image in winsomely deep, new and innovative, touching ways, gently speaking to people with consistent care and felt tenderness. So shall we begin to be the body of Christ in this poor world. So shall we begin to truly proclaim the Gospel.

Listen: *"She is like the merchant ships, She brings her food from afar. She also rises while it is yet night, and provides food for her household, and a portion for her maidservants. She considers a field and buys it; from her profits she plants a vineyard. She girds herself with strength, and strengthens her arms. She perceives that her merchandise is good, and her lamp does not go out by night. She stretches out her hands to the distaff, and her hand holds the spindle. She extends her hand to the poor." (Proverbs 31:14-20a NKJV)*

Pray: Full voices Lord, full and strong. Grant to Your church full and strong voices today, amen and let it be so.

| Vol 02 | Q3 | NW00602 | August 23rd |

Night-Whisper | **PROSPERITY**

Heads or tails?

Deuteronomy 28:33

And you shall be only oppressed and crushed continually. NKJV

Mount Gerizim and Ebal are two mountains of Samaria, which form the opposite sides of the valley which contained the ancient town of Shechem. The valley, which these mountains enclose is about 200 or 300 yards wide and over three miles long. These two mountains were the scene of the great declaration of interdependence of which our text today is but a very small part. Here, God lays out His covenant and the blessings of obedience and the cursing of disobedience before the brand new and tippy toed listening Israelite nation. It is a terrible covenant! As the millions of people stood in the valley, the consequence of disobedience thundered forth from the tops of Ebal and fell like fierce lightning upon the people's hearts. From the tops of Gerizim however, words of the blessings of obedience rained down upon their same sorry heads. In awesome high fidelity, a terrible stereophonic declaration of the old covenant was given to the new and waiting nation.

Our verse today sums up the consequences of the cursings of Ebal and to live continually oppressed and crushed is indeed, a very bitter curse. Now here is a big problem friends, for far too many children of God could use this wee verse as a summary of their own lives and as a testimony to how they feel in their innermost being or as a true statement of their daily accounting. It's pitiful, it's horrible and it's not right. Why then do too many Christians seem to live then under the shadow of Ebal?

This is a problem of four parts. Generational sin and its consequences no doubt play a part. Demonic oppression, thieving killing and destroying, no doubt have another part. Christians living in subjection to their own sin nature no doubt plays the third part. Yet I believe that it is ignorance that plays the biggest part. Ignorance of where we stand in Jesus.

Friends, those who have put their trust in the shed blood of Jesus Christ are called the sons of the Most High God and they are blessed! So, we no longer stand in the shadow of Ebal. Truth is neither do we stand in the shadow of Gerizim, that is, we do not stand in the shadow of cursing or blessing! We stand in the shadow of no mountain now but rather we are in mount Gerizim and so much so that it could be said that Christians are Gerizim. Yes, we are the blessed mountain itself! We are blessed, we are blessing, we are in its own remarkable summary, made to be the "head and not the tail; above and not beneath!" (Deut 28:13)

Christians are the blessed mountain itself! We are blessed, we are blessing, we are in its own remarkable summary, made to be the "head and not the tail; above and not beneath!"

As God reveals them to you, repent of the sins of your fathers. Resist the Devil and do not believe His lies. Yield to the Holy Spirit, bow down and humble yourself under the mighty Hand of God and listen to His good news, His glorious truth, and His tremendous testimony. For He has done us great good, far and above and way, way beyond all that we might ask or think.

Listen: *"Grace to you and peace from God our Father and the Lord Jesus Christ. Blessed be the God and Father of our Lord Jesus Christ, who has blessed us with every spiritual blessing in the heavenly places in Christ, just as He chose us in Him before the foundation of the world, that we should be holy and without blame before Him in love, having predestined us to adoption as sons by Jesus Christ to Himself, according to the good pleasure of His will, to the praise of the glory of His grace, by which He made us accepted in the Beloved." (Ephesians 1:2-6 NKJV)*

Pray: Lord, I am blessed in You. Lord in You I am made the head and not the tail, I am above and not beneath. Lord deliver me today from every evil, from every darkness, from every falsehood I have believed about myself and replace these four debilitating issues with the mounts of Zion, Moriah, Gerizim and Calvary. Surround me then O God, and marry me to these four great peaks today, in Jesus name I ask it, Amen, and let it be so.

Disinterested, disengaged and ultimately disenfranchised

In our text for today, "To speak evil of" is a translation of the Greek word: "Blasfeemein". That's right, blaspheming! It is possible to curse, swear, and use foul and odorous language against other people. It is possible to blaspheme other people, especially if they are politicians! I think that this is the context of the admonition related to this kind of "speaking evil against". The text for today appears to be saying: ***"Obey your rulers and authorities, your politicians and don't blaspheme them."*** Now there's a challenge! No really, it is a challenge! Especially within free and democratic societies. Especially when they've all been on the fiddle. Well, nearly all.

Titus 3:1,2

Remind them to be subject to rulers and authorities, to obey, to be ready for every good work, to speak evil of no one, to be peaceable, gentle, showing all humility to all men. NKJV

In my home country, our form over the years of political debate has always been adversarial. In England, the floor of the House of Commons has two drawn swords facing one another. The government and the opposition in their opposing benches often going beyond probing and testing, to verbal prodding and tearing, ripping and ridiculing the other member to shreds. Always in the most polite and "Speaker" guided way of course. Indeed, prefix any statement with "The right honorable member" and you can carry on to kindly gut anyone you do not agree with. This kind of a verbally vicious environment is the stuff of present day politics, ask any "shock jock".

In addition to this, some Presidents and Prime Ministers have ensured by their double-dealing, dirty living and foul and odorous actions, to bring curses upon themselves and the countries they represent. It's hard not to speak evil of such people isn't it? But let's ramp it up a little further. How about not speaking evil of such leaders as Hitler, Nicolae Ceausescu, Stalin, Idi Amin, Pohl Pot, Saddam Hussein and the list goes on. Let me ask you, was it OK to speak evil of them?

The church and its members are to be the bulwarks of any community, acknowledging the sovereignty of God and His administration of protecting the good and punishing the evil. However, we are called to discern when Government's protect evil and punish good. When this happens, that is when evil is rewarded and good is punished, our response to such calamity as individuals, communities and nations will be difficult, disconcerting and somewhat divisive, especially within our own communities of faith. History has at least taught us this! Nevertheless, in the face of such a sickness in social order, if we as Christians go on to merely adopt an attitude of head in the sand spiritual other worldliness, we shall appear to be so disinterested that we will certainly be ridden over by the opponents of truth and good! We shall also be seen to be totally disengaged from the real world and therefore amongst our neighbors, we shall be powerless, disenfranchised and therefore ineffective for any good work whatsoever.

"Evil shall triumph when good men do nothing." With truth, goodness and honor, let us then fully engage the political world at community, local and national level

Every committee, community board, political party and neighborhood scheme of every kind needs to have powerfully gentle, honorable and humble, truth talking, good working Christians involved with them for we can be sure of this, if we don't: "Evil shall triumph when good men do nothing." With truth, goodness and honor, let us then fully engage the political world at community, local and national level.

Listen: *"Of the sons of Issachar who had understanding of the times, to know what Israel ought to do, their chiefs were two hundred; and all their brethren were at their command." (1 Chronicles 12:32-33 NKJV)*

Pray: Lord in all areas of our life, from local communities to national and international politics we cry out for the raising up and revelation of the men of Issachar; anointed ones who understand the many types of hurricanes and tornadoes that the end of days shall bring upon us. Lord, help us to engage in prophetic power. Amen, and let it be so.

| Vol 02 | Q3 | NW00604 | August 25th |

Night-Whisper | **TRUST**

Planes, trains and automobiles

1 Thessalonians 2:1,18

But we, brethren, having been taken away from you for a short time in presence, not in heart, endeavoured more eagerly to see your face with great desire. Therefore we wanted to come to you - even I, Paul, time and again - but Satan hindered us. NKJV

"What he really wanted was to spend Thanksgiving with his family. What he got was three days with the turkey." So goes the tag line of this comedy made in 1987 starring John Candy, an obnoxious slob of a travelling shower ring salesman and Steve Martin, a pristine and uptight advertising executive. This story uses the horrors of travel to reveal how circumstances can link two lonely souls. One so uptight that he can't see his loneliness through the narrow controlling slits of his soul and one so hurt and in denial, that it pains him to acknowledge it.

The two main characters in this film are more alike than they think and providentially are thrust together so they might learn to see more deeply and in so doing, be released, healed, be helped and be eventually, bonded together. I do believe that this is what God is about. You know? Using all things, including planes, trains and (in my life especially) automobiles, to accomplish His purpose. For I hate being helped by other people and God both knows it and arranges my circumstances so I have to be helped by other people! Why do I have this preclusion to the help of others? Well, it's because I feel so vulnerable you see and also so in debt to the helper, and so annoyed at being helpless yet again. However, God always seems to override and dismiss these feelings of mine, not really even taking them into account even! "How does He do this?" You may ask and I would reply: "He does this by allowing me to purchase cars that publicly drop their pants at the most inconvenient of times." Now how's that for blaming God!

The Greek word for "hindered" in our text today is from the Greek word "enkopto," literally meaning, "to cut into" and was used of "impeding" persons by "breaking up the road" and therefore "detaining" a person unnecessarily. So if the winds are not blowing and the ships are not going; or if the car won't start and it's breaking your heart; or if the planes are a pain and the your flight's down the drain and concerning the train, well it's all just the same… then maybe dear friend, just maybe, Satan is breaking up the road before you? He's cutting into your schedule and your plans. This time it's not God that's restricting you, retracting you, oh no, it's the enemy that is trying to restrain you!

God is still in control and working out His supreme purposes of love. Love for you and love for others. Satan may seem to be pulling your travelling plans apart but God is pulling them all together for good! Believe that.

We are in a battle and we do face felt resistance time and time again, yet no matter friend! Yes when this happens, no matter I say and don't worry! For even if your alternator is demon possessed or your mechanic is mathematically challenged, God is still in control and working out His supreme purposes of love. Love for you and love for others. Satan may seem to be pulling your travelling plans apart but God is pulling them all together for good! Believe that.

So if the road you are travelling this morning is broke up before you and you can see Satan with a hard hat on and a pick and shovel in his hand, sneering at you as you bang your fists on the wheel, be not dismayed. Look at God as He nonchalantly steps out onto your highway and puts up His very own sign saying, "Walk carefully, for in truth, it is your Sovereign Father who is actually about His business here!"

Listen: *"And we know that all things work together for good to those who love God, to those who are the called according to His purpose." (Romans 8:28 NKJV)*

Pray: Unstoppable, Almighty ever loving Father. Even if there's only one wheel on my wagon, You O Lord will get me where You want me to be. So calm me, so teach me, and so help me today, in Jesus name I pray, Amen, and let it be so.

Night-Whisper | **PERSEVERANCE**

Hold fast

Corporal Jones, the calmest platoon leader who ever lived and veteran of the Crimea War, knew the enemy "Did not like it up 'em!" and we can all say an Amen to that! The highly decorated and very vocal (once he had permission to speak) Corporal Jones, would have had great empathy with this following poem by Rudyard Kipling entitled, "Infantry Columns".

Revelation 3:8

For you have a little strength, have kept My word, and have not denied My name. NKJV

So, today I dedicate this poem to the millions of faithful men and women, who get up at the same time each morning and travel to the same job every single day and who by their faithful and consistent lives, give great testimony to Jesus, each and every day.

We're foot-slog-slog-slog-sloggin' over Africa -
Foot-foot-foot-foot-sloggin' over Africa -
(Boots-boots-boots-boots-movin' up an' down again!)
There's no discharge in the war!

Don't-don't-don't-don't-look at what's in front of you.
(Boots-boots-boots-boots-movin' up an' down again)
Men-men-men-men-men go mad with watchin' em,
An' there's no discharge in the war!

Try-try-try-try-to think o' something different -
Oh-my-God-keep-me from goin' lunatic!
(Boots-boots-boots-boots-movin' up an' down again!)
There's no discharge in the war!

Count-count-count-count-the bullets in the bandoliers.
If-your-eyes-drop-they will get atop o' you!
(Boots-boots-boots-boots-movin' up an' down again) -

There's no discharge in the war!

We-can-stick-out-'unger, thirst, an' weariness,
But-not-not-not-not the chronic sight of 'em -
Boot-boots-boots-boots-movin' up an' down again,
An' there's no discharge in the war!

'Taint-so-bad-by-day because o' company,
But night-brings-long-strings-o' forty thousand million
Boots-boots-boots-boots-movin' up an' down again.
There's no discharge in the war!

I-'ave-marched-six-weeks in 'Ell an' certify
It-is-not-fire-devils, dark, or anything,
But boots-boots-boots-boots-movin' up an' down again,
An' there's no discharge in the war!

Friends when your calling and your obedience to it, leads to the often boring predictability of the daily grind, know that despite the lack of excitement and terror, you are nevertheless in very known and demanding circumstances. Called repetition, consistent witness and careful treading, demand a dedicated and faithful perseverance that will not go unrewarded, for there is nothing more demanding than the daily grind. Keep on trudging on dear friends, keep on trudging!

Called repetition, consistent witness and careful treading, demand a dedicated and faithful perseverance that will not go unrewarded, for there is nothing more demanding than the daily grind.

Listen: *"Because you have kept My command to persevere, I also will keep you from the hour of trial which shall come upon the whole world, to test those who dwell on the earth. Behold, I am coming quickly! Hold fast what you have, that no one may take your crown." (Revelation 3:10-1 NKJV)*

Pray: O Lord, let me not hide myself in the mundane or allow my heart to die in the debilitating and seeming nothingness of my days that pass like infantry columns, going nowhere. Where You have called me to be persistently and constantly faithful in the daily grind, give me the power to persevere in pleasing You. Grant to me please, the warmth of Your pleasure on my back and the joy of Your presence in my front, for it is You who have called me here. Help me to hold fast. In Jesus name I ask this, Amen, and let it be so!

Night-Whisper | **FAITHFUL**

Creating kissable feet

Romans 10:15

"How beautiful are the feet of those who preach the Gospel of peace, who bring glad tidings of good things!" NKJV

"Walmington-on-Sea", an imaginary south-coast town not far from Eastbourne, was the setting for the Second World War adventures of a disparate group of men who prevented by age or some other disability from enlisting in the fighting services, enrolled as Local Defense Volunteers (LDV), forming part of Britain's last line of defense, a force which became known colloquially as "Dad's Army". Corporal Jones may have been the platoon leader on the ground, but the commander, par excellence, was one Captain Mainwaring. One of his many and thankfully, recorded speeches, refers to the awesome responsibility that any soldier of any age has of taking care of his feet. From the church hall of St. Aldhelm Walmington on sea, he is recorded addressing his troops on one occasion saying: "And so to sum up. Whatever mode of transport we use, be it bicycles or Jones Van or other forms of vehicular transport, in the end, it all boils down to one thing. Three Fs".

- ***Fast feet***
- ***Functional feet (and last but not least)***
- ***Fit feet***

A soldier without his feet is useless.

What incredibly inspiring true and insightful words flow forth from the mouth of this most intrepid and fictitious captain of men! A soldier without his feet is useless! Note well: Even a fool and a pompous ass, knows the importance of taking care of feet!

Are you taking care of your feet dear friend? Are they fast feet? Speedily obeying the Master, carrying out what He has told you to do. Are they functional feet? In other words, will they hold you up, keep you steadfast unmovable and always abounding in the work of the Lord? Are they fit feet? Free of disease, sweet smelling, healthy, not being eaten away?

Take care of your feet today. If bad feet exclude you from the good fight, then you are useless for frontline duties.

Take care of your feet today. If bad feet exclude you from the good fight, then you are useless for frontline duties.

Listen: *"And behold, a woman in the city who was a sinner, when she knew that Jesus sat at the table in the Pharisee's house, brought an alabaster flask of fragrant oil, and stood at His feet behind Him weeping; and she began to wash His feet with her tears, and wiped them with the hair of her head; and she kissed His feet and anointed them with the fragrant oil." (Luke 7:36-39 NKJV)*

Pray: Lord, my feet are in a "bit of a state", please heal them and teach me how to keep them fresh, washed, fragrant, attractive and kissable; that the message they carry may be a sweet smelling savour to those with needy noses! Amen, and let it be so.

| Vol 02 | Q3 | NW00607 | August 28th |

Night-Whisper | **LOVE**

The song of the Son

Our verse today comes from the last lines of a song entitled "The Song of the Bow". It was taught and well known throughout all of Judah as a lamentation of both King Saul and his son Jonathan. However, the title betrays its true focus and intent and that is the love of King David's heart, Jonathan.

2 Samuel 1:26

I am distressed for you, my brother Jonathan; You have been very pleasant to me; Your love to me was wonderful, surpassing the love of women. NKJV

David loved Jonathan and found his love for him to be constant, costly, faithful and true. Jonathan, which means "Jehovah has given," was a brave and resourceful commander in the Kings army. Jonathan was steadfast and of fearful resolve with incredible faith. For example, without anyone knowing and having only the help of his armor bearer, he attacked the oppressive Philistine garrison at Miscmash causing such a defeat to them, that it spread a panic throughout the whole Philistine occupying army. Israel was delivered.

Jonathan became bosom buddies with David after David had felled the giant, Goliath of Gath, and to ratify this covenant of friendship Jonathan gave David his robe, sword, bow and belt, and so it is written that: **"The soul of Jonathan was knit to the soul of David, and Jonathan loved him as his own soul." 1 Samuel 18:1** There is a picture here of the desire Christ has for His people, and the desire Christ wishes from His people. For those who can hear, this is a backing track to this "Song of the Bow," called the "Song of the Son". Do you hear it?

Jonathan was the bravest of fighters and so when out of all the thousands of Israel he found a fighter braver than himself in David, Jonathan literally fell in love with Him! I am convinced that when we Jonathans meet King Jesus the giant slayer and listen to Him, listen to Him singing His songs of love over us, that we too will fall head over heels in love with Him. Jonathan stripped himself of his finery and his armor and gave them to David. Saul's armor would not fit David but Jonathan's fit him perfectly. Do you see that? True love fits the Savior perfectly well indeed. May I say, "My son, the best you can do today is listen to the giant slayer, see Him, fall in love with Him, give Him your very all and follow Him in covenant love." Jonathan pleased David more than any other man on Earth. Tell me today, how hot is your love for Jesus, the greater David? Dearest friend, please Jesus more than any other man on earth today and for the rest of your life.

True love fits the Savior perfectly well indeed.

Listen: "*Then Jonathan and David made a covenant, because he loved him as his own soul.*"

Pray:
Fairest Lord Jesus, Ruler of all nature,
O Thou of God and man the Son,
Thee will I cherish, Thee will I honor,
Thou, my soul's glory, joy and crown.

Fair are the meadows, fairer still the woodlands,
Robed in the blooming garb of spring;
Jesus is fairer, Jesus is purer,
Who makes the woeful heart to sing.

Fair is the sunshine,
Fairer still the moonlight,
And all the twinkling starry host;
Jesus shines brighter, Jesus shines purer
Than all the angels heaven can boast.

All fairest beauty, heavenly and earthly,
Wondrously, Jesus, is found in Thee;
None can be nearer, fairer or dearer,
Than Thou, my Savior, art to me.

Beautiful Savior! Lord of all the nations!
Son of God and Son of Man!
Glory and honor, praise, adoration,
Now and forever more be Thine.

Translated from German by Joseph vcSeis

| Vol 02 | Q3 | NW00608 | August 29th |

Night-Whisper | **DIFFERENT**

Learning the lute

To be a poet in earlier centuries, one had also to be a musician. The Parish church of St. Aldhelms, Walmington on Sea, may have been fictitious, but the saint was not. Aldhelm was a pop idol of his own time, writing poetry in metrical Latin and in Anglo-Saxon as well, setting many of his own compositions to music. Despite the fact that none of his songs, which were apparently popular in the time of King Alfred the Great, have been preserved, nevertheless, his legend lives on!

Matthew 22:9

Therefore go into the highways, and as many as you find, invite to the wedding. NKJV

Aldhem's songs must have been good, for he used them as bait. History records that because he found the people of his care slow to come to church, he stood at the end of a bridge singing songs to collect a crowd and once he had them, then he would lay down the lute and take up exhorting them in eternal and sacred matters! I like this "whatever it takes" approach. I suppose St. Aldhelm was, dare I say it, a "seeker sensitive saint".

One of my dear friends and ancient mentors has been a missionary and open-air preacher for years. John Howarth however, if he started singing, would scare a crowd away before he had a chance to speak on the sacred and the Divine. No, his method and the method of the "open air campaigners" is to use a large sketch-board. Taking this and some paint, they set up in a shopping center or on a crowded street and begin to paint. They do not say a word. Believe it or not, such silent activity does begin to gather a crowd and so when sufficient people have gathered, they turn from the painting to preaching and with swift brush strokes, the listeners hear the Gospel and see it live before them on the canvas. Whatever it takes!

I know another man who used an amazing combination of miracles and storytelling to preach the good news. Incontestable miracle after miracle and story after story. It got him into trouble with all kinds of people, especially the religious folk but it worked. Whatever it takes!

Friends, we must gather a crowd before we can tell them about the eternal, the sacred and the Divine. This is our mission after all, to tell people about Jesus, for He will have His heaven full to overflowing. Maybe today then, we should begin to learn the lute? Whatever it takes!

Friends, we must gather a crowd before we can tell them about the eternal, the sacred and the Divine.

Listen: *"So those servants went out into the highways and gathered together all whom they found, both bad and good. And the wedding hall was filled with guests." (Matthew 22:10 NKJV)*

Pray: Lord, break me out of my box and squeeze me out of my small thinking! Come coax me from my corners and send me fishing on the other side of my boat so that my present nights of fruitless labour, would turn to mornings of abundance and of fullness. Teach me O God, to learn the lute. For Your glory Lord I ask it, Amen.

Night-Whisper | **PERSISTENCE**

Charging the church

Hussars were originally Hungarian mounted troops raised by Matthias Corvinus in 1458 to fight the Turks. The name Hussar, meaning 'twenty' indicated that one man in every twenty inhabitants was pressed into the service. Long ago, the demand in the British Army for light cavalry with greater mobility than the Dragoons led to the formation of several Hussar regiments. Today of course, all light Cavalry Regiments have been turned into armored Brigades.

Matthew 10:34

"Do not think that I came to bring peace on earth. I did not come to bring peace but a sword." NKJV

At their inception into European armies, Hussars became the incredibly brave and ferocious fighters that broke in waves upon the squares of marching pike men and musketeers. They had great success, their lances being lighter and longer than the average pike. Certainly, the Polish Hussars constantly defeated much larger forces with far fewer casualties than any other mounted force. The Hussars with frightening force advancing on the enemy, moving forward from a walk to a trot and then to a gallop. One writer records a charge of the Hussars as follows:

"We saw it… the hussars let loose their horses. God, what power! They ran through the smoke and the sound was like that of a thousand blacksmiths beating with a thousand hammers. We saw it… *!@$%! The elite's lances bent forward like stalks of rye, driven by a great storm, bent on glory! The fire of the guns before them glitters! They rush on to the Swedes! They crash into the Swedish riters… overwhelm them! They crash into the second regiment - overwhelmed! Resistance collapses, dissolves, they move forward as easily as if they were parading on a grand boulevard. They sliced without effort through the whole army already! Next target: the regiment of horse guards, where stands the Swede King Carol. And the guard already wavers!"

Calculated, repeated, fast and persistent bravery seem to sum up the success of a Hussar attack.

Now friends we know that God has many weapons in His armory. We know that He also has different types of soldiers. Right personal for the right job with the right weapons at the right time. I would assume that in the host of heaven there are not only charioteers but also companies of charging Hussars. It's also my opinion that in the church militant that there is need today of some charging Hussars to break upon the well organized and marching gates of Hell.

I would assume that in the host of heaven there are not only charioteers but also companies of charging Hussars. It's also my opinion that in the church militant that there is need today of some charging Hussars to break upon the well organized and marching gates of Hell.

The tenor of Scripture is clear. Persistence and bravery are the marks of the day. Maybe if just one in twenty of us were to take up some lighter and longer weapons and charged in persistent fierceness against the pike men and musketeers of the devil, the mangling of Michmash and the crash of Jericho would occur more frequently? Where are the Kings own Hussars today friends? Where are they?

Listen: *"Then he said, 'Take the arrows'; so he took them. And he said to the king of Israel, "Strike the ground"; so he struck three times, and stopped. And the man of God was angry with him, and said, 'You should have struck five or six times; then you would have struck Syria till you had destroyed it! But now you will strike Syria only three times.'" (2 Kings 13:18-19 NKJV)*

Pray: Lord, help me to be persistent in attacking the ranks of our advancing enemies, that they may be truly defeated and routed, for I believe that the gates of Hell shall not be victorious over your charging church. Amen, and let it be so.

| Vol 02 | Q3 | NW00610 | August 31st |

Night-Whisper | **ENDURE**

Singing songs at midnight

Paul had met the band of women alongside the river at Philippi. Lydia had received the message of salvation with joy and she and her whole household had been baptized. Paul having been invited to her house, encamped himself and the band of brothers with him, right there! Daily he proceeded to prayer at the synagogue and daily was accosted by a demon-possessed girl who loudly followed them proclaiming his mission his proclamation and his purpose. After many days, Paul must have judged that this was becoming "bad press". Turning around then and addressing the spirit of divination within her, he cast it out in the name of the Lord Jesus. The slave girl is now free but unable to fulfil her previous and profitable role; her owners therefore have lost a good earner and are not well pleased! In spiteful revenge, they stir up an angry mob, in the presence of the local magistrates who hearing only the accusations and not the defiance, publicly tear off the clothes of Paul and Silas and have them beaten with rods and thrown into prison.

Acts 16:37

But Paul said to them, "They have beaten us openly, innocent Romans, and have thrown us into prison. And now do they put us out secretly? No indeed! Let them come themselves and get us out." NKJV

Naked, badly bruised and beaten, their feet in stocks, Paul and Silas sing songs at midnight. By earthquakes without and earthquakes within, the watching jailor and his whole family are saved and baptized… all in one night.

Morning comes. The misuse and madness of the magistrates is now passed, the slave owner's revenge is satisfied and the crowd is dispersed. All is well in Philippi once more, except that the earthquake of the night, which had rocked the city and released the prisoners, had probably also been seen as an omen of judgment against the magistrates of Philippi.

Their conscience aroused, in the morning, as early as possible, the magistrates send word to the jailor to release Paul and Silas.

The new Christian, the saved jailor, is obviously delighted and says, "Now depart and go in peace." Paul of course before the new believer and above all wanting the keep the peace will set a good example and turn the other cheek and scurry off into the distance from whence he came. Not likely! Nope! Surprise, surprise, for with a flash of fire, "Paul the peeved" thoroughly rooted in the Scriptures says, "'Noah waya Hosea!' let them come and get us! Let them do the hurrying and scurrying, this is outrageous!" Paul was intent on the whole city seeing the mistaken magistrates humbled for their illegal proceedings and also seeing that they as innocent Christians, had been unjustly condemned.

Friends there are three things of note here:

First, that the battle we are engaged in is fierce. It is a battle that is waged on physical, material, magisterial, economic and spiritual levels. It is a pan-dimensional battlefront.

God expects His servants to endure hardship.

Secondly, that God expects His servants to endure hardship. It would appear that naked and scabby midnight singers that did not do a runner when they had the chance were the only people that could purchase an audience with this hardened individual of a jailor!

Lastly and most wonderfully, despite and because of all the ensuing drama, the purple house of Lydia is quickly becoming the peopled house of Lydia. Jesus is building His church through it all.

Listen: *"You therefore must endure hardship as a good soldier of Jesus Christ." (2 Tim 2:2-3 NKJV)*

Pray: Lord in all our endurance send us glimpses if gold, baskets of fruit and messages from heaven. Come and tread upon our obedient pathways, come and shake the earth before us O God. In Jesus name, Amen.

--------------------------*0*--------------------------

| Vol 02 | Q3 | NW00611 | September 01st |

Night-Whisper | **CHANGE**

The present pox on the vox populi!

I am amazed at the type of leaders the living church is calling to its banners today. Of course, I use the term *living* only of those churches that are top heavy with people from the emerging generations and culture and focusing on the future. Here is an advert for an early 21st century Pastoral position, posted on the internet of course, for this is where they would find the people they were after.

Exodus 3:14

"Thus you shall say to the children of Israel, 'I am' has sent me to you." NKJV

"If you've seen at least three or four of the latest movies, you're probably culturally relevant. If you keep NT Wright, Leonard Sweet, Bill Easum, Jim Collins, John Grisham, or Ernest Hemmingway on your bookshelf, you're probably well read. If Black-Eyed Peas, Hoobastunk, Moby, and Coldplay are part of your iPod playlist, you're probably well versed in musical culture. If you don't have to google to figure out who's who on this list, you probably understand the role of the emergent church. We are looking for a lead Pastor who can deliver a message Moses would envy, work with a team the way Larry Brown led the Pistons to an NBA victory this year, cast vision like Bill Strickland, and yet linger over a chai latte with friends/staff/acquaintances without worrying about the day's agenda. We'd also appreciate it if you have at least five years experience in an emergent church culture and a master's degree and/or seminary training. Please send a resume accompanied with a DVD of a recent speaking engagement to…" And so it continued.

So distilling the advert, the lead Pastor must have high academic training, have been living and communicating with the emerging generation for five years, be visually and musically "well versed" and more especially "current," also having a hand on what is "today," the latest technology. Now if you are reading this in the near future and wonder what an iPod or DVD is, then you are the emergent of the future, so take note of what I am about to say for no doubt culture continues to maintain its ever-forward mega-shift as we reach the time of the end.

Since WW11 take a look at any 25-year block of time, indeed, take a look at even the last quarter of the last century and examine how the church handled change? How resourceful was the church in reaching people? Has defeat led it to the cowering guerrilla tactics of the old underground movement, or is it vocal, relevant and powerful in spiritual terms? Is it influencing the present culture in revolutionary expressions? Is the Gospel reaching even your contemporaries at work? Or is the Israel of God weeping and praying for the any right-handed or left-handed judge, to lead them out from oppression? Wherever you may be in time right now, I pray that the land is awash with men like Moses, brothers like Joshua and sisters of the stature of Deborah and the strength of Jael! But I doubt it.

Is the Israel of God weeping and praying for the any right-handed or left-handed judge, to lead them out from oppression? Wherever you may be in time right now, I pray that the land is awash with men like Moses, brothers like Joshua and sisters of the stature of Deborah and the strength of Jael! But I doubt it.

Mostly we are of the many thousands dismissed from Gideon's army for laying down our weapons, getting on our knees like dogs and lapping the milky water like so many sad little pussy cats. Yes we are. It seems the culturally absent church has left a pox in the "vox populi". A pox of vacuous blisters empty of absolute and powerful truth. God help us.

If you are reading this in the future, doing some historical investigation maybe of these generations that lapped the water at the beginning of the 21st century, then learn from us and maybe even pity us? God help us if from heaven you should hear the echoes of our feeble voice speaking to you saying, "Learn from the gross misfortunes of our terrible and petty blindness. If we have left you in a land of giants and high walled strongholds, then please forgive us and learn from our mistakes. Do not repeat our wrong doings."

Finally, right now though, what about you my friend and what about your church? Are you growing, prospering, prowling the outskirts of emergent culture and leaping in love right into the center of darkness, sword brandished high, challenging and changing the ruined heart in the swirling vortex of the vox populi? Or are you like some caged and hairy old beast, wandering around your feeble little confines in sorry and sick repetition.

God is the I am, He is the God of the ever present, of the living and not the dead, of the now and not the past. So, church of God, upgrade your thoughts and upgrade your outlook today. Change or die.

Listen: *"You stiff-necked and uncircumcised in heart and ears! You always resist the Holy Spirit." (Acts 7:51 NKJV)*

Pray: O Great I am, O Lord of all, O Holy Jesus, let me not be accountable for the blood of this generation because I have failed to heed Your ever present Voice. Have mercy on us Your church today O God. In Jesus name, Amen.

| Vol 02 | Q3 | NW00612 | September 02nd |

Night-Whisper | **WATCH**

The rock

"The gas station next to the coffee shop I am presently sat in, has just roped off its forecourts. They have sold out of gas. All the big named stores around about me have sold out of water. A young couple in front of me, this early in the morning are on their way to the opposite side of the East Florida coastline. "We're not staying for this one," they say. "It appears that Francis may be far worse than Andrew."

Judges 17:6

In those days there was no king in Israel; everyone did what was right in his own eyes. NKJV

I wrote this opening statement in 2004. Today even the catastrophe of Katrina and the Atlantis of New Orleans, still tottering in the possibility of falling beneath the waves, is now simply old news. The Army Core of Engineers is still not guaranteeing the invulnerability of the rebuilt and strengthened levies, and so new hurricanes, shall emerge now and in the coming seasons to worry us all once more.

I have now been through many hurricane warnings, watches and near misses. Truth is though, I slept through my first hurricane and believe it or not, it actually landed on the South coast of England in 1987. The "Great Storm" as it came to be known changed much of the landscape of south-east England for a long, long time. Katrina, initially classed as a category one hurricane, came ashore in South Florida just a couple of miles South of where we were living and robbed us of just a few trees and a few hours of electricity. I went to bed and slept through that one as well! She fooled us as just a short time later, Katrina gathered her strength and let rip her fury upon thousands and thousands in Mississippi and Louisiana. Those States and the people living in them were and will for a long time to come, never to be the same again.

Convective instability of the second kind, is a popular theory that explains how thunderstorms can evolve and organize into hurricanes. CISK is a positive feedback mechanism, meaning that once a process starts, it causes events which enhance the original process, and the whole cycle repeats itself over and over. So reports the University of Illinois.

Such a description of Hurricane formation sounds very much to me like the cyclical storms of judgement and redemption found in the book of judges. The prefix to such continuous and cyclical falling away, judgement and pain, crying to God, and His gracious redemption was our verse for today in that "Everyone doing what was right in their own eyes". Did you get that? The prefix to the storms of judgement was, "Everyone doing what was right in their own eyes." If there was ever a verse that sums up the state of our society in this generation it is this very verse. May God help us.

We all have our own individual hurricanes breaking upon our soul's shoreline but it is also a global and worldwide phenomenon. In the United Kingdom, every village, town and city holds at its heart a memorial to those slain in the Great War and the Second World War. WWI, supposedly the war to end all wars, brought only a twenty year span of reconstruction before the onset of WWII which itself culminated with the introduction of the nuclear age with all its attendant horrors. Since 1945, the whole world has been beset with rising and continuous conflict. We have sought peace and found war. Maybe we need to recognize that the whole world, all of us, are fraught with the numerous thunderstorms of sin and are now in fact caught in a convective instability of the second kind?

Since 1945, the whole world has been beset with rising and continuous conflict. We have sought peace and found war. Maybe we need to recognize that the whole world, all of us, are fraught with the numerous thunderstorms of sin and are now in fact caught in a convective instability of the second kind?

Prior to hurricanes, I have wandered the aisles in local shops. The shelves were sparse, the pumps were empty and yet, the sky seemed always blue and the wind, light and comfortable was ever only gently shaking the tropical leaves of the Royal Palms. It was the same deception with Katrina, only the outcome was far, far worse. That year a city was disappearing, dissolving in the toxic sludge of man-made waste. Yet the sun shone, the wind blew and the sky was blue before the onset of destruction. Despite all evidence to the contrary, the weather service at that time and even now is still today telling of more convective instability of the second kind building up in the tropics are storms which will form into waves of tropical depressions, some of which will in turn spin into wall eyed hurricanes rolling towards the same battered coasts already drowning in devastation. What shall we make of these things?

First, don't be fooled by blue skies! Don't kid yourselves that all is well when it patently isn't. Don't let a seasonal lull fool you into living in blind stupidity.

Second, look in! Recognize the seasonal storms that have broken upon the shores of your personal life over all these years. Some of this cyclical instability in your life needs breaking. They can be you know? You can break the cycles.

Recognize the seasonal storms that have broken upon the shores of your personal life over all these years. Some of this cyclical instability in your life needs breaking. They can be you know? You can break the cycles.

Thirdly look out! Humanity has set its own cyclical instability that will lead to its own ultimate demise. There is only one place of safety for the coming great storm. The "Rock of Ages" is only place to hide.

Listen: *"For you yourselves know perfectly that the day of the Lord so comes as a thief in the night. For when they say, "Peace and safety!" then sudden destruction comes upon them, as labor pains upon a pregnant woman. And they shall not escape. But you, brethren, are not in darkness, so that this Day should overtake you as a thief. You are all sons of light and sons of the day. We are not of the night nor of darkness. Therefore let us not sleep, as others do, but let us watch and be sober. For those who sleep, sleep at night, and those who get drunk are drunk at night. But let us who are of the day be sober, putting on the breastplate of faith and love, and as a helmet the hope of salvation. For God did not appoint us to wrath, but to obtain salvation through our Lord Jesus Christ, who died for us, that whether we wake or sleep, we should live together with Him. Therefore comfort each other and edify one another, just as you also are doing." (1 Thess 5:2-11 NKJV)*

Pray: Lord, we have something surer than science, your very Word. As former sleepers, we who are now awake, begin our hurricane watch for your coming and that terrible day.

| Vol 02 | Q3 | NW00613 | September 03rd |

Night-Whisper | **GO**

Storming Starbucks

A long time ago, when I was a mere trainee several hundred feet underneath the "oggin" I did not have my own bed! It was either an hammock strung adjacent to a couple of intercontinental ballistic missile tubes or I "hot bunked" it, climbing into whatever pit was available after the previous occupant had left it warm and invariably smelly, to take up his duties elsewhere on that long black sewer pipe of a submarine.

Isaiah 55:1

Ho! Everyone who thirsts, come to the waters; and you who have no money, come, buy and eat. Yes, come, buy wine and milk without money without price. NKJV

Later, my time in the corporate world saw the same idea - riding on the back of downsizing. If you once had an office, it was gone! If you had a desk and God forbid your own drawers, they too had been plundered and pulled down to the depths of rampant restructure. A person should never be without their drawers! Instead, a company laptop a large hard drive and abundant connectivity meant that when you arrived in the office, wherever it was, you found the first vacant desk, sat down, plugged in, pulled up your virtual drawers to gain at least the similitude of respectability and got on with it.

For a long time, my second office has been a bakery and coffee shop, offering comfortable seats, abundant and free liquid refills and most importantly, free WiFi. In other words, I now have an office in the public market place.

Interestingly, once people begin to see you there amongst them on a regular basis, working away, pounding the keys before the portable plasma playground, they become intrigued at what you are doing. "Where did you get your laptop?" "Can you help me get connected?" "What are you doing?" "You're a minister? Really? Where? Why? What do you think about this?" " Why does God? Why doesn't God?" and so on and so forth. It's amazing really. To put it in fishing terms, it's like having the having the fish swim right up to the boat and ask, "Hey what are you doing with that hook?"

I wonder if we need to get the ministers of the Gospel off campus and into the coffee shops. Imagine that. Our tendency has been to put everything on campus. Day care, dining, counselling, publishing, marketing, teaching, gathering, indeed you name it! Instead of going into the world, we have endeavored to create a pleasant and plastic utopia and bring them into it, all safe and seemingly sanitized. Problem is, they rarely come into this culturally strange Christian world and when they do they find it's not all it's cracked up to be and they prefer the reality of jagged metal to plied on and dried on fantastic plastic smiles.

Non-Christians rarely come into this culturally strange Christian world and when they do they find it's not all it's cracked up to be and they prefer the reality of jagged metal to plied on and dried on fantastic plastic smiles.

Meanwhile places like Starbucks are selling more than chic coffee; they are selling an ambience, a memory, a dream, a community, a safe gathering place of mutually minded people and maybe, in just ten years or so, they have achieved more in their own great commission, of building a global empire on the backs of people's personal relationships, than the church has been able to do in that same period and that on the back of more than 2,000 years of practice! I know it's a case of comparing apples and oranges but nevertheless it's a bit embarrassing don't you think?

Christian friend, set fire to your pew-like mentality today, remove those rattling shackles of religious restraint and stride out into the market place of religion shouting out the beckoning invitation of our Lord Jesus. The church needs to get itself off campus and back rooted in the community, fully integrating itself into the existing networks of connectivity and communication, that are now sick of mocking 'crapachino' and longing for bright and bubbly multi-colored, fragrantly fascinating and sparklingly faceted, truth. We've got the goods! We've got the market place! So let's go and do some business!

Listen: *For I will pour water on him who is thirsty, and floods on the dry ground; I will pour My Spirit on your descendants, and My blessing on your offspring; They will spring up among the grass like willows by the* *watercourses. One will say, "I am the LORD's." Another will call himself by the name of Jacob; Another will write with his hand, "The LORD's," and name himself by the name of Israel. (Isaiah 44:3-5 NKJV)*

Pray: Lord, put your logo, your brand name upon my coffee cup, my brown paper bag and my bared arm. Lord, be my tempting tattoo, my market cry; be my splendid and by my "Mr. Magnificent" in the milling market place of lost souls. Lord come and burn my campus down. Amen, and let it be so.

| Vol 02 | Q3 | NW00614 | September 04th |

Night-Whisper | **LEARN**

Personal training

Among the multitude of ostentatious observations attributed to Mark Twain, this time of year when students return to their places of education, prompts the remembrance of one of his most quotable of quotes: "I have never let my schooling interfere with my education." With nodding head and shaking smiles I have tell you today, that God will not allow your schooling to interfere with His education of you either!

2 Timothy 3:7,8

Always learning and never able to come to the knowledge of the truth. NKJV

The continuance of rapacious and rampant change in our society forces us to always be "in school". As we proceed towards the end of the age, we shall be ever learning, and for millions, we shall still be never able to come to a real knowledge of the truth. Our text today may have been written hundreds of years ago, but it's roots are in tomorrow and maybe as you read this, are now even in your perilous today, for our secular schooling system is now indeed anti-God, it is anti-Christian, it is anti-Christ! For the moment, it is still OK to say that out loud! We worry and rightly so, about the dreadful influence that such a philosophy of education has on our children. How can God ever work amongst so much anti-Christian propaganda?

Well the truth for all of us is that unless God comes and opens our eyes, unless God comes and uncorks our ears, those that are lost can never learn enough to know the truth. Never! We need to see the simple and horrific fact of this. God must act to open hearts before any knowing can be accomplished. Got it? God must act to open hearts before *any* knowing can be accomplished. Selah.

Child of God, let me tell you this: no form of indoctrination or deceit, no choice of education and direction will stop Him learning His elect. Those chosen to know the Lord, shall know the Lord. In any age and especially at the end of the age, God will not allow schooling to interfere with the education of His children.

No form of indoctrination or deceit, no choice of education and direction will stop Him learning His elect.

Listen: *"But know this, that in the last days perilous times will come: For men will be lovers of themselves, lovers of money, boasters, proud, blasphemers, disobedient to parents, unthankful, unholy, unloving, unforgiving, slanderers, without self-control, brutal, despisers of good, traitors, headstrong, haughty, lovers of pleasure rather than lovers of God, having a form of Godliness but denying its power. And from such people turn away! For of this sort are those who creep into households and make captives of gullible women loaded down with sins, led away by various lusts, always learning and never able to come to the knowledge of the truth." 2 Timothy 3:1-7*

"For consider Him who endured such hostility from sinners against Himself, lest you become weary and discouraged in your souls. You have not yet resisted to bloodshed, striving against sin. And you have forgotten the exhortation which speaks to you as to sons: 'My son, do not despise the chastening of the LORD, nor be discouraged when you are rebuked by Him; For whom the LORD loves He chastens, and scourges every son whom He receives.' If you endure chastening, God deals with you as with sons; for what son is there whom a father does not chasten? But if you are without chastening, of which all have become partakers, then you are illegitimate and not sons." (Hebrews 12:3-8 NKJV)

Pray: Lord. Teacher. I am enrolled in Your school and my colors are black and blue. Please dear Jesus, let nothing be wasted in my pursuit of knowing You and in Your pursuit of knowing me. Amen.and let it be so.

Kill the camel

In this world, money counts itself as all mighty and is both vocal and voluptuous in its lying intent and presentation. The problem is, that we believe it and our actions are clear evidence of our adherence to this vile lie dressed as virtue and our fat bellies and fat wallets, are heavy judges to our adulterous embracing of this big money mouth, which speaks great, great things! Money has become our desire, money has become our hope, money has become our provider, money has become our rock of refuge, and money has become our God!

1 Timothy 6:10

For the love of money is a root of all kinds of evil, for which some have strayed from the faith in their greediness, and pierced themselves through with many sorrows. NKJV

The fragrant flower of triumphant capitalism is a particularly thorny one for the Christian in this new century, yet the conservative church seems to have ignored this flower festooned mastodon of more, sitting fat and pompously upright in her pews. Indeed, the keepers of many pulpits have simply become popular zookeepers of this elephantine and ancient seduction! Whatever your political persuasion, rightly or wrongly the popular mind has portrayed and personified the rise of personal possession and individual prosperity with "avarice riding a camel laden with gold," which by the way, still won't fit through the eye of any needle! Why then are we in the Western church still trying to squeeze it on through? How has this dire and gigantic disease of eating avarice, seemingly and amazingly hidden itself among the Western community of the saints?

The answer is by flaunting itself as a sign of God's blessing, of Christian prudence and loving wisdom that provides for its own. All very Biblical it would appear. Yet I wonder if our in fact only part-Biblical presentation is in fact two signs of a growing fear of financial failure and a frightening fear of soul gnawing need? If so, then this is a wide spread faithless disorder and such a faithless disorder presents the local spiritual medical practitioners, those real curer of souls, those Pastors of old, with three seeping symptoms.:

First within the worshippers of the money God is a real need for power. That is, the need to possess and to influence; to impress, to flaunt and control; to direct and to manipulate for the purpose of self-protection and self-propagation. Watch out for this power mad symptom.

Secondly, within the worshippers of the money God is a festering fear: that is the driving fear that needs to provide against future disaster. The need to make safe our own vast bastions of full and fat forgetfulness. Watch out for this symptom of fat and future provision.

Thirdly, within the worshippers of the money God, is the need to possess, simply for possessions sake.

Watch out for control via the power of wealth, watch out for personal over provision, watch out for the gathering of more and more toys and trinkets to be used as badges of blessing. When you find these three symptoms manifested in your church, then a plague has broken out amongst you. Get rid of the stuff and you shall get rid of the plague.

Watch out for control via the power of wealth, watch out for personal over provision, watch out for the gathering of more and more toys and trinkets to be used as badges of blessing. When you find these three symptoms manifested in your church, then a plague has broken out amongst you. Get rid of the stuff and you shall get rid of the plague.

In olden times such symptoms and enslavement to the objects of our own making was called idolatry, and those marked with such calamity were placed outside of the camp and pronounced “unclean”! Today it would appear they dress in smart whistles and fine Armani flutes and take the lead in a drooling dance of avarice, banging the drums of abundance all the way into the side of the dark mountains of more. Today we idolise the idolaters.

Is it too much to say that the only way to deal with avarice is to give away all we have? I wonder? If you will excuse my mix of metaphors, may I say that it is time to look down and discover if we are sat on golden camels or fat brown elephants and then change horses!

Listen: *"Then Jesus, looking at him, loved him, and said to him, 'One thing you lack: Go your way, sell whatever you have and give to the poor, and you will have treasure in heaven; and come, take up the cross, and follow Me.' But he was sad at this word, and went away sorrowful, for he had great possessions." (Mark 10:21-22 NKJV)*

Pray: Two things I request of You (deprive me not before I die): Remove falsehood and lies far from me; Give me neither poverty nor riches - feed me with the food allotted to me; Lest I be full and deny You, and say, "Who is the LORD?" Or lest I be poor and steal, and profane the name of my God. (Proverbs 30:7-9)

| Vol 02 | Q3 | NW00616 | September 06th |

Night-Whisper | **HOPE**

But one word

Sin and Satan have performed a terrible work of destruction upon mankind. Poverty, disease, despondency, desperateness, deviation, devastation and before I distress us any further, I had just better stop. The world's a mess and everyone in it.

Genesis 1:1,2

In the beginning God created the heavens and the earth. The earth was without form, and void; and darkness was on the face of the deep. And the Spirit of God was hovering over the face of the waters. NKJV

A wee while ago a couple of us went out just hours before the landfall of a large Hurricane distributing leaflets that announced the church would be open for shelter. A very thin and very dark African woman stood alone in a small shopping complex. She carried with her a clear trash bag full of her belongings. She spoke little English and it was hard to communicate as she nonchalantly pulled on a cigarette in her mouth. I don't know if she was an addict or a prostitute but having left her with some instructions on how to find us, I walked away from her touched by a sense of loneliness, uselessness, formlessness even, as though I had just left the gravitational pull of a spiritual void, a place of pleading darkness.

It is particularly hard for those of us who have family, maybe even sons and daughters who carry that same darkness that same seeming sucking void that daily appears and fades them way before our very eyes. It's hard but remember dear friends that God understands our hurting hearts in this and how difficult it is for us to enjoy the warmth of the Daysprings light whilst those we love burn away like imploding stars in the high hopes of your own crashing heavens.

Today, I would point us to the Mighty Creator. Look at our verse; God's Spirit even now, even in answer to our daily prayers, is hovering over the faces of the formless void and the deep, deep darkness of those we love. That word "hover" is not like a news crew would just look out of a watching helicopter to simply report the devastation, no, it's not simply to hover as an information gathering exercise, neither is it to hover like some search and rescue helicopter throwing down a ladder or a life raft and pleading for the survivor to grab hold. Oh if only they would lay hold! But no it's not that either. It's not that kind of chancy and powerless hope-fullness.

This hovering is not panicked either. It is an at ease brooding. It is an expectant fluttering; it is almost a cherishing caressing, a moving, an incubating, an enticing, a watching with purpose, a fluttering upon, like that of a mother hen over her soon to be hatched eggs. There is a sense of both care and communication in this word hover, for God, when He is ready, is about to speak and when God speaks friends, the universe is both changed and then sustained forever.

Wherever you see darkness, deeps and devastation, then with your eyes of faith, see also the Mighty Creating Spirit of God hovering in expectant fluttering around the lost, even our own lost loved ones.

Wherever you see darkness, deeps and devastation, then with your eyes of faith, see also the Mighty Creating Spirit of God hovering in expectant fluttering around the lost, even our own lost loved ones. They are but one word from deliverance, but one word from blessing, but one word from change, but one word from salvation, but one word from life, but one word, that's all friends, just one word! Remember that today, and take great hope in our great Creator God.

Listen: *"Therefore I did not even think myself worthy to come to You. But say the word, and my servant will be healed." (Luke 7:7 NKJV)*

Pray: Blessed are you O Lord, King of all creation, Lord of heaven and earth. Creator God, loving Father, hear our prayer and deliver those in deep darkness and formless voids, into light and change and purpose. For Your everlasting glory and for our eternal comfort we ask this: "Father just say the Word and they shall live." Amen, and let it be so.

| Vol 02 | Q3 | NW00617 | September 07th |

Night-Whisper | **REST**

R and R and R

Rest and relaxation are two of the most basic requirements of physical and spiritual health. Indeed growth is dependent upon it. Ask any body builder and they shall tell you that one of the chief components of building muscle mass is, believe it or not, rest! Pump iron, rip those muscles, and eat the right fuel and then, rest.

1 Corinthians 15:9,10

For I am the least of the apostles, who am not worthy to be called an apostle, because I persecuted the church of God. But by the grace of God I am what I am, and His grace toward me was not in vain; but I laboured more abundantly than they all, yet not I, but the grace of God which was with me. NKJV

One look at the life of the apostle Paul, who it seems is often a far more attractive role model for the driven evangelical than Jesus, presents us with what us "people of the pew" would often regard as a superhuman saint. The great apostle, suffering ferociously for the cause of Christ, is always it seems, like some incessant and pounding wave is constantly throwing himself with holy abandon, again and again, against the gates of hell. It is a hard act to follow. Believe me!

Now without question, lest I offend some of you, I do regard my brother Paul, the least of all the apostles, to be the greatest of them all in both in word and deed. I wonder if a part of Paul also felt the same? Anyhow, I would not even consider measuring myself against his stature in any way. Paul is most certainly one of life's awesome individuals, totally dedicated and driven mostly and magnificently by the grace of God in the face of Christ Jesus. I do not say this in any secret cynicism or hidden criticism; on the contrary, the measure of anointing and grace upon Paul was awesome! He knew his calling, his destiny and with confidence could say, "I have fought the good fight, I have finished the race, I have kept the faith. Finally, there is laid up for me the crown of righteousness, which the Lord, the righteous Judge, will give to me on that day, and not to me only but also to all who have loved His appearing." 2 Timothy 4:7-8. Friends, that is incredible. I hope to have that knowledge one day.

I refuse to listen to Pastors with pension plans, plump Pastoriums and packed wallets, who whilst dripping with gold and stylish suits, exhort the faithful to follow the sacrificial example of Paul. When they start to follow the great pull of Paul, and bear his scars and wear his torn clothes and stinky sandals, then in of my most insane moments, I might just consider doing likewise. Maybe. Until then fine Pastor, please, just keep it shut!

Yet I tell you, despite Paul's sacrificial life, I refuse to listen to Pastors with pension plans, plump Pastoriums and packed wallets, who whilst dripping with gold and stylish suits, exhort the faithful to follow the sacrificial example of Paul. When they start to follow the great pull of Paul, and bear his scars and wear his torn clothes and stinky sandals, then in of my most insane moments, I might just consider doing likewise. Maybe. Until then fine Pastor, please, just keep it shut!

Now to you my dedicated and tired Pauline-like brethren. Do you know your calling and your destiny? Do you know the measure of your gifting and of your anointing? Do you know where you stand in the battle line of Jesus? Do you know your orders? I suspect the answer for many of you is, probably, "No, not really."

I ask these questions of you today because it has been my observation that the majority of the saints do not have a clue about these vital things, not a clue! Sadly, one of the reasons why they don't, is that their local church has robbed them of the three Rs; that is, rest, relaxation and reflection. To find out the answer for yourself to my important questions of today, you really need to get off that guilty treadmill, maybe to forego the weekly whip of words that bleeds your tired back once more, forcing you to walk in ways you are not called! Finding the answers to my questions of you today, takes prayerful quiet and reflective listening and I tell you the truth; you will not reflect without rest and relaxation. Indeed without all of these three Rs in your life, whilst either working on the Master's vine or more likely slaving in the vineyard of some Pastor's own making, you shall most certainly wither and waste away.

On the other hand, my esteemed brethren, If Paul's mantle has become yours then may God help you, anoint you and enable you, just like He did for the great apostle himself. However, if Paul's mantle has not fallen from heaven upon your quaking shoulders, then don't you dare try and take it up and don't let any leader intent on his own glory try and lay it on you. You can't do what Paul did! Instead, today, tomorrow and for the rest of your days, get with God and find out your own duty, your own destiny and your very own place in the battle line of Jesus. Today be Holy. Rest, relax and reflect!

Listen: *"Then the apostles gathered to Jesus and told Him all things, both what they had done and what they had taught. And He said to them, 'Come aside by yourselves to a deserted place and rest a while.' For there were many coming and going, and they did not even have time to eat. So they departed to a deserted place in the boat by themselves." (Mark 6:30-32 NKJV)*

Pray: Lord, I want to be like Paul in knowing that I have completed the orders You have for me and have been found both faithful and fruitful. Help me to make time to find my destiny and so be renewed and rightly refreshed, for the work You have for me in the Holy Spirit. In Jesus name I pray, Amen.

| Vol 02 | Q3 | NW00618 | September 08th |

Night-Whisper | **GRACE**

Desperate defilement

Spurgeon the "Prince of Preachers" makes a wonderful devotional observation on today's text. He says, "This unclean person had broken through the regulations of the ceremonial law and pressed into the house, but Jesus so far from chiding him broke through the law Himself in order to meet him."

Mark 1:40,41

Now a leper came to Him, imploring Him, kneeling down to Him and saying to Him, "If You are willing, You can make me clean." Then Jesus, moved with compassion, stretched out His hand and touched him, and said to him, "I am willing; be cleansed." NKJV

Two lawbreakers touch and one is delightfully delivered of his desperate defilement. Now isn't this interesting? Jesus broke the ceremonial law. ***"Command the children of Israel that they put out of the camp every leper." Numbers 5:1***

This leprous man is desperate in his faith. He breaks all social and ceremonial boundaries to get to the Savior. Friends today, even today if we let Him, Jesus will still break all social and ceremonial boundaries in receiving those "desperate in faith".

Unfortunately, there are still those amongst us so settled and seemingly untouched and untroubled by sin and the conquest of the same, that they are "sleepy stories" once told a long time ago, who to remain undisturbed, ensure that they posses their Christianity in the far right, separatist colors of black and white.

I wonder if the increasing defilement of sin, amongst the desperate dwellers in this dark-age will once again drive such folk to daring believing faith? When they hear of Jesus will they come running to Him, and when they do, will they break our "ceremonial rules" of black and white?

I remember, many years ago, once seeing a young Brazilian woman stand at the end of a sermon in the church I attended (the Pastor later related to me that her face "seemed to shine like the face of an angel") and publicly, pouring out her heart with such thankfulness and tears she was heard to say, "Pastor O Pastor, I believe God has called me to be a missionary." A long-standing member stood up and with grumbling thunder forming on his brow, took himself and his family striding out of the church because the service had been interrupted and the Pastor, rather than admonishing the outburst, had publicly thanked the young woman for sharing her heart! Like Jesus, the Pastor was moved with compassion. Like the Pharisee, the member stoned her with his silence and wounded her with his walking. A woman interrupting the service, a non-member, unchecked and unchided in her misled call to ministry. What was the church coming to!

Maybe when our bloody feet stand amongst the irrelevant shards of our man made rules, then those desperate with defilement, will see the blood and bear witness to our brokenness and then more easily to theirs and finally, may dare to approach the reaching hands of the compassionate "Christ in us, the hope of glory"

Friends, many of us still have such 'iconic like' rules and laws in our assemblies, that God needs to be compassionate toward us and coming with iconoclastic passion, wielding His hammer of grace, He needs to smash them all to pieces! Maybe when our bloody feet stand amongst the irrelevant shards of our man made rules, then those desperate with defilement, will see the blood and bear witness to our brokenness and then more easily to theirs and finally, may dare to approach the reaching hands of the compassionate "Christ in us, the hope of glory."

Listen: *"For we do not have a High Priest who cannot sympathise with our weaknesses, but was in all points tempted as we are, yet without sin. Let us therefore come boldly to the throne of grace, that we may obtain mercy and find grace to help in time of need." (Hebrews 4:14-16 NKJV)*

Pray: Compassionate Savior, rid us of the irrelevant, that reaching grace may reach out through us. O Lord, stretch out Your hand and clean Your church. Amen and let it be so.

| Vol 02 | Q3 | NW00619| September 9th |

Night-Whisper | **SMELL**

Adam's nostrils

No doubt, you will have heard the old, old joke:

Statement: "My dog has no nose!"
Question: "Well how does he smell?"
Answer: "Awful!"

It's not funny, I know. Awful is often the way the interior of our cars smell sometimes when we leave them standing awhile. We need to open the windows put the AC on, clean the rubbish from under the seats and door compartments and probably get a new dangly air freshener!

> ***1 Corinthians 12:17***
>
> *If the whole body were an eye, where would be the hearing? If the whole were hearing, where would be the smelling? NKJV*

Sadly, my mother-in-law had no sense of smell. No, honest! As a youngster, she befriended an outcast at school simply because she was the only one who could not smell the awful body odor the poor unwashed person exuded. It's true! When everyone moved away in sickening disgust, her lack of smell allowed her to be kind without being offended. Now there's a thought.

Our sense of smell is one of our two chemical senses, the other being, the sense of taste. However, the sense of smell is the dominant one and the sense of taste is always subject to it. Get a bad cold, block up your sniffing ability, your smelling ability, and you know how bland good food then appears to taste.

Our sense of smell is so powerful that when you smell skunk, you are only smelling 0.000,000,000,000,071 of an ounce of its scent! Maybe it's the skunk's scent that's so powerful! Ha! Yet no matter how powerful our sense of smell might be, no two people can experience the same smell in precisely the same way. A rose may smell far sweeter to you than to other people you see. Indeed, even our ability to detect odors changes throughout the day and a woman's sense of smell is much keener than a man's (tell me about it) and is related to her cyclical levels of estrogen. Yup, smell is relational, directional and even works when we are asleep! Did you know there are smell alarm clocks that can wake you in the morning silently and they do this by emitting a known smell that says to you "wake up"? The smell of percolated coffee or fresh bread maybe? Amazing!

Ahhh smell. Isn't it wonderful? Yet, have you noticed that although we can differentiate between over 10,000 different odors, our vocabulary is so very limited in its descriptive ability to painting and picturing these odorous qualities to one another? Watch any wine tasting event and you will be amazed at the adeptness of choosing other smell descriptions to describe a wines particular aroma.

Ah smells and noses! I find it very interesting that God breathed life/lives into Adam's nostrils. This wasn't mouth-to-mouth resuscitation as we know it, this was not a holy kissing, no! This was the breathed infusion of immortality and mark you well now, this infusion of life came through the nostrils! Some say this is indicative of the activation of the conscious mind, others that the spirit of man resides in the head of man, after all, to be thoroughly dead is to be brain dead. Well, I shall leave those discussions and musing for your consideration, my point however, is this: God breathed life into the first man through his nose, yes, God made noses and odors and God delights in sweet savory smells. So let me ask you, "How do you smell to God? How do you smell to other people? Are you sweet and savory or are you odorously foul?"

When the Holy Spirit unlocks the spiritual olfactory membranes in another person's heart, we who possess Christ become to them, attractive, sweet smelling and even odorously intriguing.

When the Holy Spirit unlocks the spiritual olfactory membranes in another person's heart, we who possess Christ become to them, attractive, sweet smelling and even odorously intriguing. For us who become Christians, everyone else we know, every other non-Christian if you will, somehow does not smell right to us! Think about that. Apparently, this bad odor is even worse for the non-Christian when they spiritually smell the Christian, for interestingly enough, we Christians are said by God to be a foul stench to those who have yet to have the Holy Spirit activate the sweet membrane of heaven lying dormant within them. Oh yes, in the unsaved and unregenerate, unrepentant and death-fixated nose of the non-Christian, we followers of Jesus, well and truly stink!

Watch and pray friends, watch and pray for salvation and life, one way or another, leaves its mark around the nostrils of men.

Listen: *"Now thanks be to God who always leads us in triumph in Christ, and through us diffuses the fragrance of His knowledge in every place. For we are to God the fragrance of Christ among those who are being saved and among those who are perishing. To the one we are the aroma of death leading to death, and to the other the aroma of life leading to life. And who is sufficient for these things?" (2 Corinthians 2:14-16 KJV)*

Pray: Father thank you for the soothing and sweet smelling aroma that the sacrifice of your Son, Jesus Christ our Lord, is to You, once and for all, forever and ever, Amen. Now Father God, may all our sacrifices to You be sweet smelling and may we also become the stronger attractive aroma of life to those who would be saved and the dangerous and pungent stink of death to those who presently will not, that they, even they, may be "disgusted" into life. In Jesus name we pray, Amen**, AND LET IT BE SO.**

Stinky's house of shame

Jericho of course was rebuilt under a curse. Indeed, it was General Joshua who pronounced, ***"Cursed be the man before the LORD who rises up and builds this city Jericho; he shall lay its foundation with his firstborn, and with his youngest he shall set up its gates." Joshua 6:26.***

Luke 19:1,2

Then Jesus entered and passed through Jericho. Now behold, there was a man named Zacchaeus who was a chief tax collector, and he was rich. NKJV

The Scripture later records that it was Hiel of Bethel that did just that. He did not rebuild Jericho in the exact same location but he did establish a city of the same type, purpose and name. In doing so, Hiel sacrificed Abiram his firstborn at the laying of its foundations and setup its gates over the sacrifice of his youngest son, Sergub. Jesus entered this same Jericho through those same cursed gates and passed over those same cursed foundations. Truly, Christ honored it the accursed city with His presence and continues to do the same today for many cities, for He has come to take away the curse of sin.

Here in accursed Jericho, Zacchaeus was the chief of tax collectors, the chief of publicans, the "head honcho," the "big boss" and in the nose of his fellow Jews was no doubt, "the littlest biggest stinker" in Jericho. So, this sick and culturally rejected and ejected little man with foul-fame-filled ears, is found atop a sycamore tree trying to catch a glimpse of Him of whom he has heard so very much. Note that even the stinkiest of sinners are intrigued by the real Jesus, "And when Jesus came to the place, He looked up and saw him, and said to him, 'Zacchaeus, make haste and come down, for today I must stay at your house.' So he made haste and came down, and received Him joyfully." Luke 19:3-6

So the little stink sets his sights on Jesus and Jesus, knowing His name, encourages this seemingly simple and curious beginning, by inviting Himself to tea! In the accursed city, Jesus now enters the accursed house only to be squashed in even tighter by the angry presence of some of those slit sphincter like souls, those sorry religious hypocrites, who at the same time were murmuring in unison together, their same sad little mantra. Will you listen: "they all complained, saying, 'He has gone to be a guest with a man who is a sinner'." Luke 19:7

If your face looks like a pompous little pussy cat's rear end, whenever Jesus enters Stinky's house of shame, then maybe, just maybe, you are on the wrong team my dear friend?

Friends we don't know what went on at Stinky's house that hot afternoon but we do know that the spiritual olfactory membranes of Zacchaeus were activated to smell something sweet and something wholesome in the glorious graciousness of King Jesus. So much so that the only recorded words of Jesus after inviting himself to tea, is in response to the interesting declaration of faith made by Zacchaeus: "Look, Lord, I give half of my goods to the poor; and if I have taken anything from anyone by false accusation, I restore fourfold." And Jesus said to him, "Today salvation has come to this house, because he also is a son of Abraham; for the Son of Man has come to seek and to save that which was lost." Ahhhh wonderful. Look at the faces of the Pharisees now, they've sucked in air so quickly, you know longer know which tight end is which!

Now friends the "just saved" will no doubt cause some consternation in the house of the "righteous redeemed," they always will but what a glorious mess to begin clearing up eh? What an utterly glorious mess! And I tell you what, when Stinky starts getting cleaned up, I hear singing friends, I hear happy songs from heaven, even from the throne. Do you?

If your face looks like a pompous little pussy cat's rear end, whenever Jesus enters Stinky's house of shame, then maybe, just maybe, you are on the wrong team my dear friend?

Listen: *"What man of you, having a hundred sheep, if he loses one of them, does not leave the ninety-nine in the wilderness, and go after the one which is lost until he finds it? And when he has found it, he lays it on his shoulders, rejoicing. And when he comes home, he calls together his friends and neighbours, saying to them, 'Rejoice with me, for I have found my sheep which was lost!' I say to you that likewise there will be more joy in heaven over one sinner who repents than over ninety-nine just persons who need no repentance." (Luke 15:4-7 NKJV)*

Pray: Lord in all my hymns of praise and adoration, in all my hymns of declaration and dedication, let them never drown out Your songs of joy over stinking sinners now saved. Teach me to listen to Your singing, to learn Your tune, and to sing along with Your joy. Teach me to rejoice with You O Lord, over the arrival of Your salvation at every foul smelling, stinking house of shame. Amen Lord and Amen!

Night-Whisper | **REAL**

Snake oil and new t-shirts

The shop window was a dumping ground. Everything you could imagine was packed into the display section and I mean everything! It was only through the smallest crack in the display that you could actually see inside the store and sure enough that too was packed to the gunnels. The large sign on the window seemed to ring true, "If we don't have it, you don't need it!"

Romans 3:1-6

Concerning His Son Jesus Christ our Lord, who was born of the seed of David according to the flesh, and declared to be the Son of God with power according to the Spirit of holiness, by the resurrection from the dead. Through Him we have received grace and apostleship for obedience to the faith among all nations for His name, among whom you also are the called of Jesus Christ. NKJV

In the West, Christianity is once again having to compete in the market place of religion and that, not only when it "Super Wal-Mart's" itself and competes against other large churches in the same area! No, postmodernism and post-Christendom seem to walk hand in hand and so a spiritual vacuum has been left and "hucksters" and "snake oil sellers" of every kind and description are on the rise and faring very well indeed. The disadvantage for the pseudo church, for that is what they are, is that their very own snake oil sellers, those heavily involved in the religious industry, will have to work that much harder. However, I do believe that time will show that Christian snake oil does not compare to that which other religions sell for in the end, frankly, Christian snake oil is just not that good, no, it's just not efficious enough to do everything it says on the bottle. It's a con. It's health wealth and prosperity seeker sensitive con!

Now friends be encouraged, for the advantage for the real church in such a religious and competitive market place, is that we shall have to at last, come up with the real goods. It's becoming a worn out word I know but we shall have to prove ourselves, especially for these last generations, to be the actual authentic article. That takes integrity and in the market place of religion, we had better make sure our bottle contains what it says on the label.

What is 'Christian authenticity' and how shall we know when we possess it? Well, may I say that to be an authentic Christian we need to manifest grace, truth, faith and power in the real world, rather than behind the closed doors of the sanctuary. Mind you, even the sanctuary would be a good place to start with those four fellas! Well, wouldn't it?

An authentic Christian we need to manifest grace, truth, faith and power in the real world, rather than behind the closed doors of the sanctuary.

Grace to forgive and embrace in enormous measure, grace to hope in the goodness and greatness of God to make itself manifest amongst the mess of our communities. Truth about the real Jesus and not the Jesus of our own making. Truth about ourselves as individuals, truth about our communities, our nations, our race and our culture. Faith in God and His ability to redeem to the uttermost. Power to live, power to stand, power to testify, power to heal, power to deliver, power to provide, power to overcome and power to posses all that we are in Jesus Christ. That's the good stuff!

When the authentic church arises, I tell you that they shall dare to walk anywhere in the market place of religion, loaded with heavenly goods, stacked to the gunnels and wearing newly printed t-shirts that bear the simple message: "If we don't have it. You don't need it!" We've a ways to go that's for sure but this type of advertising needs to be seen and most importantly, needs to be backed by the reality of our possession of the same. "If we don't have it. You don't need it!" Imagine that.

Listen: *"Therefore we also pray always for you that our God would count you worthy of this calling, and fulfill all the good pleasure of His goodness and the work of faith with power, that the name of our Lord Jesus Christ may be glorified in you, and you in Him, according to the grace of our God and the Lord Jesus Christ." (2 Thessalonians 1:11,12 NKJV)*

Pray: Lord, I am not what I should be. Lord I fall far short of what I see in the Scriptures. Lord, forgive me, please heal me, deliver me and release me in such a way that Your grace, hope, truth, faith and power would be evidently manifest in my life. O Jesus, re-generate the regenerate today. Amen.

| Vol 02 | Q3 | NW00622 | September 12th |

Night-Whisper | **GIVE**

Saturn and the 7/11 store

I was investigating an area for a possible church plant. One of my tasks was to try and look at the community from every possible angle, see it in all its different shades as it were and so that particular night, I was out cruising with my video camera.

Matthew 26:11

For you have the poor with you always, but Me you do not have always. NKJV

The local 7/11 store was open, so out of the darkness I pulled into the parking lot in front of the store's bright and inviting lights and there was Fred. Off to the far right of my vision, the leather skinned full bearded and dirty castaway was skulking in the shadows. I stayed in the car and watched. As the late shoppers came and went, Fred would wait for a lull in the consumer traffic before walking out of the shadows, hunched and furtive like an old feral cat, moving towards the trash can. Here he would quickly claw and rummage through the surface layer of garbage, pick up some kind of maggoty messy morsel and then retreat into the shadows to examine it and eat it. He would do this silently, quietly and repeatedly until he was satisfied that the trashcan had been fully trawled. Thus expiated of investigation, he would move on to another store and another filth-ridden bin.

Now, I was out of the car and in the store when I saw Fred slip quietly off the scene and disappear into the shadows whilst I purchased a hot drink and some food for him. Coffee in hand, I came out and walked to the black back alley at the rear of the 7/11 and sure enough, there was Fred, now trawling the larger garbage bins.

After his initial surprise at someone following him around back with a hot drink, with thanks, blessing and prayer, the food and drink were very gratefully received. I remember that there wasn't much conversation. Fred "crossed" himself and looked up toward heaven, indicating to me that at least there was some former contact with an orthodox church, for Fred was a former Eastern block immigrant who didn't speak much

English and on top of that, it was evident that Fred was mentally ill. It was only a matter of time when someday soon, someone else would find Fred but this time he would be dead.

In lands of plenty, the poor are still with us, and the pain of it, the pitiful presence of it, still quietly lingers like the smell of sour meat around trash cans late at night.

In lands of plenty, the poor are still with us, and the pain of it, the pitiful presence of it, still quietly lingers like the smell of sour meat around trash cans late at night.

I thoroughly believe that how a nation treats its "down and outs" is indicative of its level of compassion. How we treat the one lost sheep is truly indicative of how we shall in the end treat the other 99. To me, there appears to be but four options for our rich nations regarding the pitifully poor. Eradicate them, ignore them, hide them or help them. The last of these four options, should be the only Christian option and make no mistake about it, the resources needed to do this will be enormous.

Maybe we should consider that the poor are God's outrageous gift to the rest of humanity? Maybe they are a sad and ever present picture of the true spiritual state of every fat cat and comfortable kitten curled up in front of a warm fire or a cold air conditioning unit? Maybe they are there, to always call forth selflessness from our utterly inbred selfishness? Maybe they are there, to embarrass our wallets and cause us to examine our spending programs, after all a few hundred billion dollars on a space program and a few thousand smart bombs, means we can know and see exactly where we choose to rain down vengeance upon our enemies and then watch the destruction via satellite in glorious Technicolor! Ooh and while I am talking of satellites and talking of glorious Technicolor, let's face it friends, most of us church goers know more of the conditions of Saturn's rings rather than the conditions behind the 7/11 on Johnson Street, on any street, on your street.

Maybe the real mentally ill aren't just trawling the trashcans of our major cities? Maybe many of them are in various positions of leadership? Now there's a thought! You will come across a needy person tomorrow, in some way, do try and reach out to them with the love of God.

Listen: *"He who gives to the poor will not lack, but he who hides his eyes will have many curses." (Proverbs 28:27 NKJV)*

Pray: Lord the needs of the poor are so great, that alone we cannot help to meet them. Nevertheless Lord, help us heap up blessings on ourselves, our communities and our nation by giving to the poor. In right ways, teach us how to do this O God, in Jesus name we pray, amen.

| Vol 02 | Q3 | NW00623 | September 13th |

Night-Whisper | **DESIRE**

Of chocolatiering shepherds

I have a confession to make today. I need to testify, I need to unburden myself, I need to make a declaration a shocking statement and maybe, I'm not sure but maybe, my journey to recovery shall begin. You see I am friends… a chocoholic.

Psalm 16:11

You will show me the path of life; in Your presence is fullness of joy; At Your right hand are pleasures forevermore. NKJV

Today in 1916, one of my favorite authors was born. A Welshman, Mr Roald Dahl. In WWII, Dahl was an RAF fighter pilot flying missions in Syria, Greece and Libya, being shot down and seriously wounded in the Libyan Desert. Indeed, he kept a piece of his femur, which had been removed in an operation, on his desk as a paperweight.

Though Dahl came from a tragic and abusive background he went on to write some of our most famous (even infamous) children's literature, writing world renowned books and screenplays as diverse as *The Twits, Chitty Chitty Bang Bang* and even a James Bond film, *Live and Let Die.* Yet I would still suggest, that his most well-known and best-loved work is *Charlie and the Chocolate Factory*, or the film of the book entitled *Willie Wonka and the Chocolate Factory,* where the main character, Charlie Bucket, a poor young boy living not far from and in sight of Wonka's Chocolate factory spends all his birthday money buying these delicious chocolate bars in the hope of finding one of five golden tickets which will "change the lives of those who find them." Imagine that! Living and being in sight of your desire and eagerly seeking a simple golden ticket which will give you access to life changing experiences, a golden ticket which will remove you from poverty and despair into, well into who knows what? Certainly everything that chocolate (rich, dark and plain, mmm…) gives you a taste of.

Now some of you will think I am being flippant today. Yet even John Bunyan that most famous of Puritan spiritual writers has his characters of Christian and Hopeful come to the Shepherds who are called Knowledge, Experience, Watchful, and Sincere for instruction. These shepherds, wonderfully, tend to their flocks in a place called the Delectable Mountains. Now this was obviously a place of chocolate! And while we are on the subject, yes indeed, I often wonder if the tree of knowledge of good and evil was in fact a cocoa tree?

Bunyan describes these delectable objects as mountains, which belong to the Lord of the hill and are full of "Gardens and orchards, vineyards and fountains of water; where also they drank, and washed themselves, and did freely eat." I would suggest Bunyan is trying to describe the gathering of the local church. No, it doesn't describe mine either. Yet imagine, dream if you will, what if it did describe our churches? Someone on a Sunday might just see that chocolate smile on our face and ask, "Where are you going this Sunday Morning?" "Oh, I'm off to the Delectable Mountains. Do you want to come?"

Here the shepherd's job is to feed men with the delights of God and not to be forgetful to entertain strangers. Though it is also their duty to teach and to caution those on the journey, after that, it is their very special delight to take pilgrims aside and through a telescope, make their distant destination fill their eyes and their hearts with gladness!

Delectable mountains. How wonderful. Here the shepherd's job is to feed men with the delights of God and not to be forgetful to entertain strangers. Though it is also their duty to teach and to caution those on the journey, after that, it is their very special delight to take pilgrims aside and through a telescope, make their distant destination fill their eyes and their hearts with gladness! Bunyan reports that with fear and trembling Christian and Hopeful would hold the shaking eyeglass and with the help of the shepherds to behold the welcoming and glorious gates of their only true home. The Golden Celestial city. (The streets no doubt actually paved with golden chocolate wrappers!)

I wonder if every lottery ticket, every shot of whiskey consumed by worn out men and every rolled dice of desperation is in fact the search for that seemingly elusive golden ticket? Every bet placed on a running horse, every popped pill, dark injection, forbidden but exciting sexual encounter, every gasp for satisfaction, every grasp for glory, is but a reaching for that golden ticket? Something that will, at last, deliver desperate men from darkness and make their lives changed for the good, changed for the better, changed forever and ever, amen! I wonder.

O Churches of God, O dear friends, O shepherds of the Lord of this celestial highway, please, please take us to the pastures of the Lord of this hill; deliver us to the delectable mountains and give us a glimpse of heaven, give us golden tickets. I speak to you shepherds today, give us golden tickets by walking us amongst the delectable mountains and giving us glimpses of the glory yet to be revealed! Experienced and experiencing, knowledgeable and sincere shepherds will always give their sheep rich, dark chocolate, all wrapped in golden entrance tickets. What kind of chocolatiering shepherd are you?

I speak to you shepherds today, give us golden tickets by walking us amongst the delectable mountains and giving us glimpses of the glory yet to be revealed!

Listen: *Then they came to Philip, who was from Bethsaida of Galilee, and asked him, saying, "Sir, we wish to see Jesus." (John 12:21 NKJV)*

Pray: Jesus, joy of man's desiring, Holy wisdom, love most bright; drawn by Thee, our souls aspiring, soar to uncreated light. Word of God, our flesh that fashioned, with the fire of life impassioned, striving still to truth unknown, soaring, and dying round Thy throne. Through the way where hope is guiding, hark, what peaceful music rings; where the flock, in Thee confiding, drink of joy from deathless springs. Theirs is beauty's fairest pleasure; theirs is wisdom's holiest treasure. Thou dost ever lead Thine own in the love of joys unknown.

| Vol 02 | Q3 | NW00624 | September 14th |

Night-Whisper | **COMFORT**

Of fathers, failings and formulas

"Every ant knows the formula of its ant-hill, every bee knows the formula of its beehive. They know it in their own being, not in our way. Only humankind does not know its formula."
Fydor Dostoyevsky

Isaiah 1:2,3

Hear, O heavens, and give ear, O earth! For the LORD has spoken:: "I have nourished and brought up children, And they have rebelled against Me; The ox knows its owner and the donkey its master's crib; but Israel does not know, My people do not consider." NKJV

Our verse for today brings God into a seemingly bad light. May I speak here as a mere mortal man and observe that it seems despite His hopes and His dreams, His attendant care and life-giving words, God still has rebellion on His hands. Let's face it friends, in our text for today God has seemingly failed as a Father! However, we understand this seeming failure for the tone and desperation of the latter half of today's verse is echoed in millions of Christian parents with wayward children. Yes, many of us recognize the despair in God's cry here.

Maybe some of you this morning, looking at the present chapters of the life story of your children, have taken the red inked stamp of "failed" and slammed it all over your children and especially over your parenthood. It would appear that in the rising generations especially, weeping is common amongst parents. I speak as a man, I speak as a mere mortal but this verse today, reveals to me that you are not alone. This verse shows the bewilderment and hurt, even in the broken fatherhood of God. Yes, it would appear that God has failed in His faithful and perfect parenthood. Or has He?

We view this verse from our own failings and so from a position of condemnation of both self and others. Of course, as sinners bringing sinners into the world and then trying to bring sinners up in a sinful world, we all fail at some point. We have to. There is no perfect parent. All of us need to repent of our many parental sins birthed in both the shades of zeal and in neglect. Well might we immediately pray, "Unfailing Father God, forgive us our many, many failings." However, God is perfect! He, unlike us, has no excuse for failing! Let me bring my criteria to You O great King and apply it! These verses talks of failed children and if that's the case O Lord. Then You, the Father of all perfection, failed at parenting O Father God, Yes if your children rebelled against you, then surely You failed as a father!

"I have nourished and brought up children, and they have rebelled against Me; The ox knows its owner and the donkey its master's crib; But Israel does not know, My people do not consider."

It's ridiculous of course to suggest God's failings here and so it should be for God does not fail as a Father! How could He? No, the despair of this verse is over the "forgotten formula" of His children. In this verse, all anthropomorphic in its communication, God wants us to know that He knows the despair of praying parents. He knows the bewilderment that rebellion brings. Friends, God the father knows your despair for your wayward children who in a multitude of bad and selfish choices, have forgotten the formula you laid up in them over the years!

Those of you whose loved ones have for today forgotten the father's formula need to take comfort from these verses. I counsel you to confess your failings, utterly reject condemnation of any kind, especially from the quiet looks of those seemingly successful parents around you and ask the Father to make His formula begin to bubble in the rebellious hearts of your wayward children. What I mean is, ask the Father to make the light to shine brighter in their darkness. Ask for His voice to echo deeper in their cavern. Ask for eternity to claim a larger expanse in a once open heart's now crowded house. Ask for conviction to cling and for conversation, consideration and conversion to come. Ask for the creators formula to fill the sinner with the forgotten knowledge of a Father's love. ***"I have nourished and brought up children, and they have rebelled against Me; The ox knows its owner and the donkey its master's crib; But Israel does not know, My people do not consider." Yes, God knows how you feel today.***

Listen: *"But when he came to himself, he said, 'How many of my father's hired servants have bread enough and to spare, and I perish with hunger!*

I will arise and go to my father, and will say to him, 'Father, I have sinned against heaven and before you, and I am no longer worthy to be called your son. Make me like one of your hired servants'." (Luke 15:17-19 NKJV)

Pray: Lord. We look at our own stories. How even now we are ignorant of things we should know. How even now, we are far short of the men and women we should be. From the acknowledgement of our owb personal failings then and into your abundant goodness, most merciful Father we gladly bring to You our own deaf donkeys and our own obstinate oxen. Have mercy on them Father. Have mercy on them we pray, in Jesus name, amen.

The God of guarantees

In this "thing" we call living, there are no guarantees of what we would deem to be success or happiness. The woman who has longed and prayed for a child, falls pregnant at last, only to give birth to a severely handicapped baby. The young man leaves Africa to study at seminary in America, works long nights at his job, holds his eyes open in the classroom, studies hard, studies late, studies years, only to be killed in a car accident the day before his graduation. The faithful couple who have been saving for years to retire to Florida and leave the rat race they have hated and arrive in the sun, only to find that too soon, far too soon, Alzheimer's robs one of them of the knowledge of the other and fills the void with daily fear. No sir, it is clear, that in this thing we call living, there are no guarantees of what we would deem to be success or happiness.

John 13:34

A new commandment I give to you, that you love one another; as I have loved you, that you also love one another. NKJV

The poet Tennyson writes about his sister's fiancé and his best friend Arthur Hallam, who died in Vienna today in 1833 of a brain hemorrhage just before the time fixed for the wedding. The final lines of the poem are known by just about everyone:

Tis better to have loved and lost
Than never to have loved at all.

Living takes much effort as we walk this sorry road of life. Loving however, well loving, takes enormous courage.

Loving calls for the greatest acts of selflessness, of forgiving, of chosen forgetting, of suffering, of redeeming, of weeping, of hoping, of dreaming better, dreaming bigger, dreaming beyond reason! Loving requires the greatest of courage, for it carries with it the greatest of costs and the greatest of rewards. Love may come with no guarantees, no certainties but what is life, what is living without loving friends? Even Tennyson confessed that these last lines carried more hope than he himself believed because you see, love demands the greatest of faith and courage! Real men love, and love no matter what. Maybe today some of you men need calling back to your vows, need to fit yourself like warriors and begin to be the courageous folk you are and love at last?

The world, sin and Satan, offer no guarantees of success and happiness. Oh, they might suggest they do but life proves that these offers are not worth the toilet paper they are written on.

The world, sin and Satan, offer no guarantees of success and happiness. Oh, they might suggest they do but life proves that these offers are not worth the toilet paper they are written on. Jesus is however, the God of guarantees. He has provided us with many promises that are yes and Amen, that are indeed both certain and true. The challenge we have is that the eternal God makes His promises not only last forever but come to realized fruition in the great forever. So, "Wait and see," He says, "Not one word shall fail." Those of us so bound by the finite have great difficulties apprehending by faith, the fruit of promises that are to be plucked from the infinite, plucked from the great eternal and eaten in our hearts in the here and now. "Wait and see," He says, "Not one word shall fail."

There is a promise however, that finds it fulfilment in the now as well as in the time to come. It is our rock to stand and fight upon; it is our banker that allows us to gamble on God; it is our light in the dark, dark night; it is our pleasant pill against depressions; it is the arms of love in all our loneliness, it is the promise of His "ever presence!"

Listen: *For He Himself has said, "I will never leave you nor forsake you." So we may boldly say: "The LORD is my helper; I will not fear. What can man do to me?" (Hebrews 13:5-6 NKJV)*

Pray: Loving Lord Jesus. You call us to the humanly impossible. You call us to selfless love. Once we see the demands of such love, the sacrifice, the pain as well as the pleasure, we draw back from that which requires such strength and such courage. Oh God, equip me like a strong warrior today that I might love and love again. Amen.

| Vol 02 | Q3 | NW00626 | September 16th |

Night-Whisper | **FAITH**

Bigmouth Bildad

Poet, philosopher, essayist and atheistic thinker, TE Hulme was born today in 1833. A pugnacious individual (it is rumored he was kicked out of one of his schools for using a knuckle-duster!) he roamed and wrote, until he was killed in action whilst serving as an artillery officer in WWI. One commentator writes of his poetry, saying that it had the ability to "bring the moon and stars back down to earth." I like that.

James 2:14-17

What does it profit, my brethren, if someone says he has faith but does not have works? Can faith save him? If a brother or sister is naked and destitute of daily food, and one of you says to them, "Depart in peace, be warmed and filled," but you do not give them the things which are needed for the body, what does it profit? Thus also faith by itself, if it does not have works, is dead. NKJV

You will have heard the saying that some Christians are "so heavenly minded that they are of no earthly use!" It isn't of course true but you get the drift don't you? I remember the time in fundamentalism when the term "social Gospel" was not only frowned upon but openly criticized. We Christians, after all, are charged with a message, which upon serious deliberation will set the eternal destiny of the individual. We are into the salvation of souls! No one would disagree with that and friends, as I write it, I tremble. What a commission! However, the seeming import and absolute conclusion of such a commission, some would say, is that we should not focus on the body, for the body is not eternal and therefore, any focus on this passing tent is an eternal waste, it is simply food for maggots. Mmmm.

It was Bildad, one of Job's friends, one of his comforters, who, when Job was in the deepest of distress, tried to turn Jobs eyes to heaven and open Jobs understanding to his own sinfulness. Bildad says: "How then can man be righteous before God? Or how can he be pure who is born of a woman? If even the moon does not shine, and the stars are not pure in

His sight, how much less man, who is a maggot, and a son of man, who is a worm?" Job 25:4-6

"Show me your stuff; show the world your stuff, because faith without works is dead!"

Yes Bildad, all this is true. However, let us now allow Job to respond in most majestic imagery. Job takes Bildad beyond the moon and stars and better than James T Kirk, with far reaching phrase goes where "no man has gone before". However, before that, he responds to Bildad with these down to earth questions "How have you helped him who is without power? How have you saved the arm that has no strength? How have you counselled one who has no wisdom?" Job 26:2-3. In Effect, Job says "Hey Bildad bigmouth, show me your faith by your works!"

Dear friends, in all our systematizing of theology, in all our imaginative unpacking of prophetic discourse, in all our irrelevant rules and regulations, in all our glorious gatherings, in all our heaven gazing and watchful waiting, let us be careful to always bring the moon and the stars back down to earth because God says "show me your stuff; show the world your stuff, because faith without works is dead!"

Listen: *Then the King will say to those on His right hand, "Come, you blessed of My Father, inherit the kingdom prepared for you from the foundation of the world: for I was hungry and you gave Me food; I was thirsty and you gave Me drink; I was a stranger and you took Me in; I was naked and you clothed Me; I was sick and you visited Me; I was in prison and you came to Me." (Matthew 25:34-36 NKJV)*

Pray: Lord, the need is so great. Yet you have called the crowds to follow You, hear Your words and caress the gates of Your kingdom and come in. Then You say to us "Give them something to eat!" Lord help us; give us fullness of faith and a dozen baskets to gather up the leftovers. Lord please help us to bring the moon and stars back down to earth. Amen.

| Vol 02 | Q3 | NW00627 | September 17th |

Night-Whisper | **BLOOD**

Of Chickens and contact lenses

Our world of high consumption leads to bizarre efforts in production. At the end of the twentieth century, the humble chicken outnumbered humans by 4:1. Mass production of these birds leads to natural pecking orders applied in the most unnatural of conditions. For example, put one hundred chickens in a pen and pretty soon you would see the number one hen become able to peck any of the other birds whilst they cannot peck back! The number two hen could then peck any bird except number one and so on, until those at the bottom of the pecking order, are in danger of being pecked to death! You see the problem with chickens is once they see blood, they become very aggressive. In such terrible factory production conditions, there is lot of blood, a lot of death and subsequent loss of profits and consequently, there is the need for a lot of chicken calming. Yes indeed, the last thing a producer needs is angry chickens!

Exodus 12:23, 24

For the LORD will pass through to strike the Egyptians; and when He sees the blood on the lintel and on the two doorposts, the LORD will pass over the door and not allow the destroyer to come into your houses to strike you. NKJV

The use of red light has a calming effect on the fowl. You see, in red light conditions, chickens cannot see the blood and so they are less aggressive. In addition to this, red light conditions also induce them to eat far less whilst producing the same quantity of eggs! Red light is good light if you are in chicken production, except of course for the additional electricity cost. Indeed, to save on electricity costs, one company actually makes red tinted contact lenses for chickens but that's another story, for another day!

It has been my observation that chickens of every kind, when seeing blood, move in for the kill. Fallen man especially has a very nasty way of pick, pick, picking on the weakest amongst us. Go into any school playground full of youngsters and see the terrible sight played out consistently day after day. Only the strong survive!

When it comes to "seeing red" there are two things of note for the Christian.

First, weakness in others should call forth mercy to our minds and love to our lips and limbs. Compassionate and selfless care should be the marks of the "Christ like" disciple. I wonder if compassion is caught rather than taught, seen rather than heard, modelled rather than made? Teachers, mentors and ministers, all please take note.

Our life is but a part, an important part for sure but nevertheless, a small, small part, of a big chapter, in a giant book, on the longest shelf, in the very largest of libraries.

Secondly though, when it comes to "seeing red," this is exactly what we want God to see! One of the things that struck me concerning Mel Gibson's movie, *The Passion of The Christ* was the predominance of the color red. Red, seemed to fill the screen. Red blood was everywhere, for friends, redemption is red! We need for God to see red. "Yes! Please great God, see the red of Your Son upon me today!"

Our life is but a part, an important part for sure but nevertheless, a small, small part, of a big chapter, in a giant book, on the longest shelf, in the very largest of libraries. So large, that space and time cannot accommodate it. This book is not our book and despite our egotistical fantasies, played out in every space movie ever made, man is not the center of this big, big book. We are in His story, and His storyboard, has placed into this cosmic epic, the absolute necessity of shed blood. Are you seeing the big picture? Are you seeing the rich red blood? Are you seeing His story, or are you looking at the world through colored lenses of someone else making? Get off the chicken farm friends!

A great man in another place wrote that in the stillness and the darkness before time dawned, the plot and the promise clearly stated that, "When a willing victim who had committed no treachery was killed in a traitor's stead, death itself would start working backward." God must see the blood. God must see red!

Let me ask you today, are you covered in His blood!

Listen: The next day John saw Jesus coming toward him, and said, "Behold! The Lamb of God who takes away the sin of the world!" (John 1:29 *NKJV)*

Then He took the cup, and gave thanks, and gave it to them, saying, "Drink from it, all of you. For this is My blood of the new covenant, which is shed for many for the remission of sins." (Matthew 26:27-29 *NKJV)*

Pray: Look Great God at the blood! Look at the rich red blood of Your Son and be satisfied. All I bring, all I bring, is the blood of my Saviors cross; a fountain filled blood to flood my sins away. Amen.

| Vol 02 | Q3 | NW00628 | September 18th |

Night-Whisper | **FAITH**

Making rain

Oliver Sacks in his book *The man who mistook his wife for a hat*, recounts the clinical tale of "Madeleine J" a congenitally blind woman with cerebral palsy, who had been looked after by her family at home throughout her life. Sacks recounts that, "Madeleine spoke freely and eloquently, revealing herself to be a high spirited woman of exceptional intelligence and literacy." He assumed this blind woman was widely read through her use of Braille. On enquiry though, her reply revealed that she did most of her reading through other people, that is, by listening to audio. Her hands could not hold a book or turn a page they were, as she put it, "useless Godforsaken lumps of dough that don't even feel part of me." Sacks, apparently was surprised to hear this, as cerebral palsy did not usually affect the hands and besides that, tests revealed that her sensory capacity was completely intact. Surprisingly though Madeleine J. could not recognize anything with her hands!

Matthew 12:13

Then He said to the man, "Stretch out your hand." And he stretched it out, and it was restored as whole as the other. NKJV

Sacks' theory for this gross incapacity was simple: she had been babied and protected all her life, so much so, that she had been prevented from developing a normal pair of hands! Madeleine J had perfect elementary sensations in her hands but was unable to integrate these sensations with perception. He wondered if now she was aged 60, that this normal development could still be encouraged.

His instruction to care assistants was, without being cruel of course, to make Madeleine J lay hold of her own food. Of course, she couldn't and so on many, many occasions, she went hungry! One day however, impatient and hungry, she finally reached out and grabbed a bagel and began eating. Within a year, I said within a year, her now alive and curious hands had turned her into the locally famous "blind sculptress of

St Benedict's". The late learning of this grossly handicapped woman had revealed an astonishingly artistic sensibility. The dormant and the blighted now fantastically flourished.

Now in our text for today, the man whose hand the Lord healed was, instantaneously and thoroughly fixed! In an instant, this one desperate man could now fully appreciate and totally utilize his restored appendage! Marvelous! Just Marvelous! In contrast, I want to suggest that millions of us gather on the Sabbath day with withered hands of worse condition than this man's ever were! As a Pastor, one of my chief observations is of our gross incapacity to reach out and lay hold of the goodness of God. This takes but elemental faith, yet the average Christian has such a massive disconnect between knowledge, perception and sensation that the inability to "rest and possess" in believing faith marks itself on us with withered hands and emptiness of every kind. Oh yes it does.

To our great consternation, God will not treat us like babies. He will have us whole and not handicapped and so in multitudes of difficult and embarrassing circumstances He comes and says to us, the withered and the wretched, saying "Stretch out your hands!"

To our great consternation, God will not treat us like babies. He will have us whole and not handicapped and so in multitudes of difficult and embarrassing circumstances He comes and says to us, the withered and the wretched, saying "Stretch out your hands!" As we do this, we feel great pain but if God is good to us, if God is good to us friends, He will consistently make things so difficult for us, that we have to keep on reaching out until a holy wholeness manifests itself in our hands.

Beloved of God, I am convinced that as we cripples connect perception with sensation then artists, writers, builders, fighters, carers, caresses, healers, helpers and a multitude of wonderfully whole and energetic Christians, shall be released into their destiny and out into the needy world. So, in the name of Jesus I say to many of you today, "Hey cripple! Stretch out your hand!"

Listen: *Then it came to pass the seventh time, that he said, "There is a cloud, as small as a man's hand, rising out of the sea!" (1 Kings 18:46a NKJV)*

Pray: Lord, when the effective fervent prayer, of righteous Elijah made headway in the skies, it was the seventh time. It was persistent reaching, strong and stretching prayer that formed the cloud the size of a man's hand that in turn, unlocked a 3 year drought and flooded the land. So with us O Lord, form our hands as we stretch our reaching hearts, come unload the wet heavens of Your blessing upon us, in Jesus mighty name. Amen!

People, pelicans and the ancient twitcher

I am in no doubt that there should be a law against greasy men wearing skimpy pink Speedos. Indeed, I have come to the conclusion that in our generation, when on the beach, there are only three safe places to look: out to sea, down at the sand, or up into the sky. It was the nauseating appearance of this bizarre Australian aberration (Speedos) spray painted on hairy old heavily greased former eastern-bloc men that caused me to lift my eyes once again to heaven and there they were, the pelicans!

Genesis 1:21

So God created every winged bird according to its kind. And God saw that it was good. NKJV

North American brown pelicans have fast become my favorite birds. Their strange pre-flood like bill give them a wonderful pre-historic quality and the largeness of the birds themselves, make them fascinating to watch in flight, as like old WWII bombers from 617 Squadron (the Dam Busters), they swoop down low over the water on calm and steady bombing runs, whilst the waves crash like furious flak bursting all around them. That day I looked up from the beach, there were two flocks of twelve, each flying in perfect "V" formation.

A team from the National Center of Scientific Research in Villiers en Bois, France, were able to measure the heart rates of eight pelicans as they flew in a V formation over Senegal. They reported that: "When flying alone, pelicans beat their wings more frequently than birds flying in formation. When in formation however, their heart rates dropped. Our results provide empirical evidence that compared with solo flight; formation flight allows birds to reduce their energy expenditure while flying at a similar speed." Their reason for this conclusion is that, "when birds fly in formation each wing moves in an up wash field that is generated by the wings of the other birds in the formation."

That's one theory for this way of flying and another theory for the existence of this fascinating form is that V formation geometry could simply be "Correlated with retinal features and the location of the eye on the head. In other words placement of the eyes restricts the field of vision and this motivates the use of a V formation in flight."

> *"Make sure to surround yourself with the right kind of strong good and company;"*

So in any event scientists at least conclude that the V formation of flight, saves energy, keeps the flock together, keeps them all going in the same direction and maybe teaches the younger birds, migratory paths. Pretty amazing eh!

It is not hard to discern the writings of God in all of this. Jeremiah (Jehovah will lift up) was a great twitcher, you know, a bird watcher, fully aware of various types and habits of birds in Israel. Under the guidance of the Holy Spirit he was moved to take examples of their habits and apply them both to the actions of God and the people of God. In the spirit of Jeremiah the ancient twitcher then, we might say that pelicans speak to us today and say, "Hey, don't forget the gathering of yourselves together;" they say, "Make sure to surround yourself with the right kind of strong good and company;" they say, "Two are better than one;" they say, "Follow me, even as I follow Christ."

I say to you today then folks, get to an assembly, find Godly friends and follow Christ in a V for victory formation. This is one of the ways that Jesus makes light, His most lovely yoke.

Listen: *Be ye followers of me, even as I also am of Christ. (1 Corinthians 11:1 NKJV)*

Pray: Lord, grow us up that we may with Holy confidence speak as our brother Paul did in inviting others to follow us, as we in turn follow You dear Master. Teach us Your way O God; teach us Your way, in Jesus name we pray, Amen.

| Vol 02 | Q3 | NW00630 | September 20th |

Night-Whisper | **FOCUS**

Magnetism, money and magnificent muscle

If you have ever been bullied as a young boy, then one thing you might eventually come to desire is muscle and fear. You will want to look like as much "bad news" as you can so you can instil fear in other people; fear that will keep them away and make them leave you alone. If you have experienced the debilitation that comes from physical weakness, then you may want to acquire this. Magnificent muscle after all, is might. Right?

> ***Psalm 73:7***
>
> *Their eyes bulge with abundance; they have more than heart could wish. NKJV*

If you have experienced the desperateness of poverty then you may also want to possess the power of money. It's true that Jacuzzis contain desperate and lonely people but my suspicion is, not many. Money of course does bring you happiness. Let's not lie about that one, friends. If you have experienced the closed doors, limitations and inabilities that financial frugalness finds you in, then maybe you will want to get money and lots of it!

Mighty money and magnificent muscle may be the standard tools for your average megalomaniac but they are also the chief sources of sought power and protection amongst us all! So, we find arms manufacturers always doing booming business, fitness centers packed to the gunnels with grunting sweaty men, supplement shops stacked with steroids and the property market will of course once again moving towards record highs as each day the power of possession tells it lies of "safety" and "security," forcing men and women to work every hour under the sun to gain more and more sterling, dollars, bucks, clams, money and muscle.

Channel surfing, I recently stopped upon a daytime chat show (Mogadon for the miserable!), showcasing two mothers who had been at one time, thieves. One had stolen $18k and served her time, the other, a diamond thief, had never been caught and boasted about spending over $40million. The first straight money she is earning is coming through her book and riding on the back of the rights of the film, which will be released soon having a famous Hollywood actress playing her as the thief. So get this, the women who steals $18k to pay her debts keep the roof over her head and feed her kids, gets caught and goes down, the other woman however, steals simply because she's an evil witch and then boasts about it freely because as she puts it, "she has been clever enough to make sure that there is no proof to indict her!" Both are thieves, one for the right reasons, if you know what I mean, the other for the wrong ones and she's the one that becomes a rich paid celebrity guest on a daytime chat show?

It's a strange world we live in but not a new one. David with consternation writes in ***Psalm 73:2-5 that his feet had almost stumbled and his steps had nearly slipped because he was envious of the boastful, having seen the prosperity of the wicked.*** As he puts it ***"For there are no pangs in their death, But their strength is firm. They are not in trouble as other men, nor are they plagued like other men."*** David says in effect, "What is happening here?! Where is God in all this injustice?!" You see friends, the deception of might and muscle is not a new one.

The magnetism of money and muscle amongst us must not be underestimated. Daily we are faced with their pull and daily, we must reset our thinking with the words of Jesus.

The magnetism of money and muscle amongst us must not be underestimated. Daily we are faced with their pull and daily, we must reset our thinking with the words of Jesus. Remember, in a moment a mere microbe can fell the tallest and toughest of individuals. In a moment, the desperate search to find a cure for a debilitating disease can rob you of all your money. In a moment, the stock exchange can crash and with it all your walls come falling down and all your streets be filled with mire. In a moment, both muscle and might can be seen for the dead and deceiving, dreadful idols they truly are.

Meditate upon the Word today and degauss your mind, for undoubtedly it has been warped with the magnetism of money and muscle. Let me ask you today, "Who's your daddy?"

Listen: *My flesh and my heart fail; But God is the strength of my heart and my portion forever. For indeed, those who are far from You shall perish; You have destroyed all those who desert You for harlotry. But it is* *good for me to draw near to God; I have put my trust in the Lord God, that I may declare all Your works. (Psalm 73:26-28 NKJV)*

Pray: Lord, be the strength of my heart and my portion forever. Take me to the sanctuary of Yourself and help me see correctly. O Lord, scour my eyes and scour my soul and help me tear down every false deceptive thought that has taken residence and my brain and root in my heart in Jesus name I ask it, amen!

| Vol 02 | Q3 | NW00631 | September 21st |

Night-Whisper | **BE!**

Seeking the sixth sense

"Proprioception" has been described as "the process by which the body can vary muscle contraction in immediate response to incoming information regarding external forces by utilizing stretch receptors in the muscles to keep track of the joint position in the body." In other words, proprioception is how we know where we fit in space; or better still, it's how we know exactly where our feet are, or our fingertips, or the position of our head. If we lose our sense of proprioception then we lose the sense of our bodily self. So much so that when it happens, as far our physical "being" is concerned; we are nowhere to be found! Oliver Sacks describes one of his patients having lost this sixth sense of "proprioception" as being akin to a disembodied lady.

Matthew 16:24, 25

Then Jesus said to His disciples, "If anyone desires to come after Me, let him deny himself, and take up his cross, and follow Me. For whoever desires to save his life will lose it, but whoever loses his life for My sake will find it. NKJV

Just about all of us are very well aware of where we are in space. However, "Who we are?" is a very different question. Now the sad fact, the very sad fact, is that many of us have not only lost our very own sense of self but have never ever discovered just who we are! And may I say that this is especially true of ministers, who for so long have in a very wrong, way become all things to all men that they may please but a few! Many Pastors have utterly lost themselves. So let this question burn into you today. "Who are you?"

Peer conformity is rife amongst Christians. I have seen whole sermon series constructed and preached, simply to massage "the agreed," the "set in stone" and "the popular view." Even if it's wrong! I have seen "protection of the pulpit" as a guilt edge law (no, I have spelt it correctly) in constitutions, simply to make sure no one rocks the boat. "If you want to be part of this club, you must believe our most intricate of parameters." People lose themselves in such cringing conformity and of those who have done so, are now sadly and simply, the sorry shell of who they should be and even of who they once were.

However in much more subtle ways, many of us have surrendered our distinctiveness to the imposed destinies of our parents or maybe, the deliberation of committees, or the desire of wives, the demands of our children and even to the social norms of a very sick church society. Many of us ceased to be a long, long time ago.

Before I continue friends, let me assure you that I am not speaking of disrespect to parents neither am I speaking of the desertion of our loving duty to children, nor bitterness against spouses, nor rebellion in the church. I am speaking of something far, far worse. The loss of ourselves, our true selves. So let me ask you again today; who are you?

Being a Christian should be an exciting journey into amazing discoveries about our true desires and our true destinies and not the shameful and shackled constrictions of slave ship conformity that so many of us experience.

In our text today Jesus is not saying that we should cease to be ourselves. He is saying that we should cease to be our selfish selves. There is a big difference. Consider this, for it has been my delighted observation to note that when we truly become more like Christ, we become more the person He created us to be. The more truly sanctified we become; the more we are released into our true selves. If this is true, then being a Christian should be an exciting journey into amazing discoveries about our true desires and our true destinies and not the shameful and shackled constrictions of slave ship conformity that so many of us experience. I tell you today, if you do not free yourself, you will kill yourself, so let me ask you again, who are you? Believe me, once you begin to know that, things will never be the same again!

Lest you are mistaken friend, I am indeed calling for "revolution!"

Listen: *And the evil spirit answered and said, "Jesus I know, and Paul I know; but who are you?" (Acts 19:15 NKJV)*

Pray: Lord, break the chains that hold Your creation. Lord let me seek only Your smiling face, Lord, above all thing let me be; that You would truly delight in me.

| Vol 02 | Q3 | NW00632 | September 22nd |

Night-Whisper | **FORGIVE**

The moorings of memory

Proprioception may give you awareness of your position and space but memories are the moorings of your place in time. Without your memory how on earth can you begin to fit and function in the now? Memory may not be a sense but we are senseless without it. The odd and Godless, shocking surrealist Luis Buñuel remarks, "You have to begin to lose your memory, if only in bits and pieces, to realize that memory is what makes our lives. Life without memory is no life at all, just as an intelligence without the possibility of expression is no life at all. Our memory is our coherence, our reason, our feeling, even our action. Without it, we are nothing."

Jeremiah 31:34

"No more shall every man teach his neighbour, and every man his brother, saying, 'Know the LORD,' for they all shall know Me, from the least of them to the greatest of them, says the LORD. For I will forgive their iniquity, and their sin I will remember no more." NKJV

Without dissecting the many propositions in this statement, let's just agree on the importance of memory. Not that it is of primary importance of course, for men are more than a collection of memories; yet memories do moor us in time and do define us to ourselves and to others. Memory can be such a blessing. Yet if our memories are ones of abuse, or ones of perpetrated or even perpetrating violence, or maybe hatred, then memory leads to regret, imprisonment and even torture. If memory then becomes the unrelenting torturer of the mind, then memory can also mean madness! So we can conclude than that our capacity to remember and our choice to forget are both paramount to our personal wholeness. You will notice I did not say *repress* memories but forget them, and *choosing to forget* them at that.

All of us in this sick world carry the scars of things we have done and had done to us. The memories of these things can be overwhelming and dreadfully debilitating. When we are brave enough, or desperate enough, or sick enough, I wonder if God would then have us face our knife edged problems, mourn them, grieve them, get angry over them, forgive them even and then choose to forget them; instead of using them like sharp pieces of broken vases to continually gouge the running poisoned puss out of the sores of our sorry souls? You see friends, I do believe there is a knowing forgetfulness that is rooted in forgiveness, that with it brings the healing and wholeness we so desperately crave. Most of us need to take an axe to the moorings that hold us in our unhappy harbors of hopelessness and start facing, forgiving and forgetting!

Most of us need to take an axe to the moorings that hold us in our unhappy harbors of hopelessness and start facing, forgiving and forgetting!

Don't think that this is without cost. Look at Calvary. Here God paves the way for us His children and shows us that His forgiveness is His ultimate goal. With payment made in full, the all-knowing God, chooses to forgive and to forget. This choosing of "forgetting" allows Him to enter into areas of the darkest destruction and then build a holy and an immovable city. Do you see that friends? Do you want that?

Listen: *"Behold, the days are coming, says the LORD, that the city shall be built for the LORD from the Tower of Hananel to the Corner Gate. The surveyor's line shall again extend straight forward over the hill Gareb; then it shall turn toward Goath. And the whole valley of the dead bodies and of the ashes, and all the fields as far as the Brook Kidron, to the corner of the Horse Gate toward the east, shall be holy to the LORD. It shall not be plucked up or thrown down anymore forever." (Jeremiah 31:38-40 NKJV)*

Pray: Lord, give me the courage, give me the package, give me the desire, give me the desperateness, give me the where with all; to face, forgive and choose to forget. Then O Lord, together, let us build upon this cleared devastation a most holy and immovable, eternal habitation for Your glory and my comfort, in Jesus name I ask it, Amen.

| Vol 02 | Q3 | NW00633 | September 23rd |

Night-Whisper | **SERVICE**

Doctorates for deacons

I used to visit regularly the local seminary for deacons. Jacks Diner is one of those "all American" places I love to go. It was late at night and this 24-hour gathering place was ticking over nicely. I sat on a blue vinyl stool at the white Formica bar and stared over into the cramped cooking area. Any second now Al Pacino, as the short order chef, would grab another slip of paper, furiously impaled on an old greasy aluminum prong beneath the brown fat matted heat lamps, where the neat cooked food waited to be whisked away by the wizened and over stressed, over busy, young- old waitress named Frankie.

***Acts 6:1-3a** Now in those days, when the number of the disciples was multiplying, there arose a complaint against the Hebrews by the Hellenists, because their widows were neglected in the daily distribution. Then the twelve summoned the multitude of the disciples and said, "It is not desirable that we should leave the Word of God and serve tables. therefore, brethren, seek out from among you seven men of good reputation, full of the Holy Spirit and wisdom, whom we may appoint over this business. NKJV*

As far as I know, the seminary is still decorated with shiny aluminum and magic mirrors that reflect flickering pink fluorescent lights and broken, not so new, neon signs. "Eat at Jack's!" The "J" almost certainly still flickering intermittently and drawing attention to itself.

The communion furniture at Jack's diner is common. Two miraculous royal blend never empty coffee pots eternally and slowly simmering on the side. Indeed, the brew is so powerful that even the decaf would keep a hardened platoon of tired soldiers awake for at least 3 days and nights leaving them fidgety for a fight. The coffee's aroma buzzes in unison with the neon lighting. Very soon Professor Frankie will swish into the classroom, pad in hand and begin the lesson.

It's a repetitive dance she has but over the years, it has served herself and others very well indeed. Listen and learn.

"Hey hun how you doin'? My name's Frankie and I'm your waitress for tonight. What's your name?"

Chewing gum and with hands on hips, the education continues.

"Do yoo need a few moor minutes hun? Let me get ya some caffee whilst yu decide what yer wantin."

The food order is given and then gently, openly and intricately examined.

"So, how do yer like yur eggs?" Hmhm.
"Fries or baked potadah?" Hmhm.
"Gravy? Saaad salad?" Hmhm.
"Sassage or baycun?" Hmhm.
"Canadian or American?" Hmhm.

The delivery will be hot and quick, arriving with affirmation from Professor Frankie,

"Man this sure smells guurd! Think I'll get me some O that thur myself!"

The consumption is never silent.

"More coffee hun?" or "Is everything OK hun? You like it?"

Searching eyes seem to be able to see through my off white and bourbon like stained plastic cup and somehow the coffee never gets below half empty and I mean, never! Whatever is left over (there are always left overs) are eventually removed and the final question is delicately broached,

"Dessert?"

The bill is written and out of respect, is placed face down on the table and with a smile, Frankie now flits away to serve another. She doesn't wait to count her money or inspect her tip. She expects you to be honest and if she has served you well, to be generous. Satisfied and well served I leave.

"Y'all come on back now."

Oh I will Frankie, I really will.

Kindness, fullness, warmth, consideration, attendant care and respect, will after years of selfless service earn any prospective deacon a doctorate in care. God's seminary at Jacks Diner together with Professor Frankie, are open and available 24 hours a day for your continuing instruction. "Y'all come on down now and learn a little."

Listen: *"You know that the rulers of the Gentiles Lord it over them, and those who are great exercise authority over them. Yet it shall not be so among you; but whoever desires to become great among you, let him be your servant. And whoever desires to be first among you, let him be your slave - just as the Son of Man did not come to be served, but to serve, and to give His life a ransom for many." (Matt 20:25-28 NKJV)*

Pray: Lord. Teach me to wash feet and wait on tables, to take care of the orphan and the widow. Lord teach me, pure and undefiled religion that is acceptable in Your sight, in Jesus name I pray, amen.

| Vol 02 | Q3 | NW00634 | September 24th |

Night-Whisper | **WITNESS**

Seeing songs

I seem to be one of those people who lately, cannot carry a tune in a bucket! Violence to vocal chords has limited my range of expression considerably. Nevertheless, the God of the Bible still encourages even me to sing!

Psalm 40:3

He has put a new song in my mouth - praise to our God; many will see it and fear, and will trust in the LORD. NKJV

I am reminded that the Scriptures speak not once of old songs but consistently of new ones. You see, there seems to be a freshness of expression that should be expected with each new generation, even with each new Christian. I wonder if every day, we should all be singing skillfully, new songs that contain shouts of joy?

Have you noticed that many songs have a "sell by" date? That's OK but the problem is when we insist on parceling the well overdue and well overdone up in books and laying them out before our congregations and insisting they then turn to page so and so and then drone on and on, whilst drowning in old froth, well, it is then that once new songs become simply old hat. It seems to me that worship should find a new voice, and yes indeed, a new expression in each new generation and in each new Christian.

Now let me really scare all our English readers of a certain age by saying that these new songs are animated. No, not the "Our God is so big, so strong and so mighty" or "If I were a Billy Goat" silly animations for the over 40s and early demented kind of songs, no, these are spirit animated songs. Let me explain.

The new songs, the living water springing up in our heart, welling up into praise, will both activate us and animate us. "Big Daddy Brubeck" got it right, for truly "There is rhythm in life!" Oh when we worship, we might raise our hands, we might even close our eyes and some of us might even get down and get with it but it's not that which the Scripture is talking about. Not really. It's about how the new song, like a great river is eroding all the old banks of long set feelings, habits and previous passions and replacing, changing and improving our inner landscape. So much so, that the outward cloth laid over us, is also fluctuating and morphing into new and winsome shapes, for you see friend, that cloth laid over our inner landscape is weaved into our countenance, our hands, our feet, our eyes, our actions, our relationships, our giving, our attitude, our fashion, our vision, our decision, our mission, and most especially, our mouth. Think about this though. All I have mentioned is in fact our mouth, for this new song is a song that is seen rather than heard! He has put a new song in my mouth - praise to our God; many will see it and fear, for sweet charity always brings the real rhythm of life.

There seems to be a freshness of expression that should be expected with each new generation!

Listen: *Then Moses and the children of Israel sang this song to the LORD, and spoke, saying: "I will sing to the LORD, for He has triumphed gloriously! The horse and its rider He has thrown into the sea! The LORD is my strength and song, and He has become my salvation; He is my God, and I will praise Him; My father's God, and I will exalt Him. The LORD is a man of war; the LORD is His name." (Exodus 15:1-3 NKJV)*

Pray: Lord as you re-lay in me, the foundations of your world, let me hear the singing sons of the morning raise such shout of praise, that they will shake the heavens once more. Amen and let it be so.

| Vol 02 | Q3 | NW00635 | September 25th |

Night-Whisper | **PRESENCE**

Robbing churches

Living in America exposes you to the largest of multi-media ministries, radio and television being the most expensive with respect to running costs. Though I am thankful to be able to see many Godly "word and spirit" related ministries on television, costly ministries do have the tendency to keep asking for your money and when you have to ask so consistently for the same thing, you tend to become innovative and in becoming innovative you become edgy and such edginess, has to be justified and such justification, leads to what so many have called, "The Gospel of Health and Wealth".

Philippians 4:19, 20

And my God shall supply all your need according to His riches in glory by Christ Jesus. Now to our God and Father be glory forever and ever. Amen. NKJV

Involved in church planting, I find that in the early stages you wear every hat imaginable. That of "fund raiser" is the one I hate the most. It takes me well outside of my comfort zone and into a high octane, dangerous and strange mixture of bombastic humility. How else can I describe the feelings and functions of a mystic missionary, a visionary but penniless entrepreneur, a righteous robber even? A robber indeed, for Paul in 2 Corinthians 11:7-9, hyperbolically adds this to his sins and vices, when in castigating the Corinthians he says, "Did I commit sin in humbling myself that you might be exalted, because I preached the Gospel of God to you free of charge? I robbed other churches, taking wages from them to minister to you."

It would appear from the Scriptures, that is not good to rob God but it is OK to rob churches! Am I being edgy? I see the red light of danger flashing in the corner of my eye.

Now, I may have related some of the following story previously but let me unpack it a little more. You see, there I was, returning from investigating an area for a possible church plant. A brother had placed $140 in my pocket before leaving home but I had been so well taken care of by the Pastor I was visiting, that I still had $100 left over. Arriving at the check in desk, tired and eager to get home, the lady looked at me quizzically and said, "I'm sorry sir, you are a week early for your flight." Sure enough, there was the date on my ticket. Either a human or technical error had placed me on a return flight, two weeks from my departure and not the one week I had intended. "Listen," she says, "I can transfer you to the flight today but there will be a cost of $100." I reached into my pocket took out the folded bills and laid them before her. "Let's do it!"

In times past, I have come home from wealthy churches and literally had to pick corn from the adjacent field to my house to feed my family that day.

In times past, I have come home from wealthy churches and literally had to pick corn from the adjacent field to my house to feed my family that day. I have gotten up in the morning and had apple sauce for breakfast with my children for it was all we had in the cupboard. That day though, I had $100 dollars. A prepared payment for a tired traveler. The spiritual journey of the Christian traveler is also a strange financial roller coaster as well. At times, it is unfathomable. For most of us, make peace with the fact that that this spiritual journey of ours will contain much abasing and little abounding! Now there's a sermon title for you today.

Listen: *"I know how to be abased, and I know how to abound. Everywhere and in all things I have learned both to be full and to be hungry, both to abound and to suffer need. I can do all things through Christ who strengthens me." (Philippians 4:12-13 NKJV)*

Pray: "Lord, neither fullness nor want is a sign of Your blessing O God. Yet I tell You dear Father, that if Your manifest presence is not with me, if I am not aware of Your "stickable" faithfulness, then truly, I am a pauper amongst the princes of this world. Lord, in all my gifts, in all my presents, let me know Your presence today. In Jesus name, amen and let it be so.

| Vol 02 | Q3 | NW00636 | September 26th |

Night-Whisper | **FEAR**

Inform NOK to flee the WTC

During our life, my wife and I have spent some time living in Florida - "the Sunshine State," and for the best part, dodged a number of nasty names. Thankfully, the "eye walls" of Frances, Ivan, Jeanne, Katrina and Rita all passed us by stealing only one side of the house in which we lived. Many in those times, had not been so fortunate.

Isaiah 13:6a

Wail, for the day of the LORD is at hand! It will come as destruction from the Almighty. NKJV

Before powerful hurricanes make landfall, the local authorities have the power to issue mandatory evacuation notices on areas close to the coast, where they fear the winds and associated tidal surge pose a serious threat to human life. Mandatory does not mean what you think though as people can in fact choose to stay! In cases like this it is reported that the local authorities, police, national-guard etc., simply visit the people staying behind, to get from them the names of their next of kin. Now imagine that conversation!

"So despite the warnings and impending disaster, you have decided to stay then?"
"Yup!"
"Well, we won't be here and we cannot provide you with any further help. You are on your own. Give us the name of your next of kin so we can inform them of your unnecessary demise!"

It's quite a sobering thing to have someone shake their head and ask you for the names of your nearest and dearest to so inform them of your impending death! It would certainly make me think about staying in the path of perilous and pernicious storms. Indeed, the safe and the sane would regard me as a fool hardy idiot to remain in such a condition but oh my friends, hasn't the blindness and deafness and all the other gross insensibilities of sin made fool hardy idiots of all of us, even of the whole wide world? For judgment is quickly coming upon us and yet, we choose to remain in its terrible path.

Our verse today proclaims to us on two levels.

First, Isaiah speaks to his contemporaries about the coming judgment from God's hand in that the rising world empire would like a flood overtake them and wash them away. If you read the whole passage you cannot escape the horror of what God Himself is about to do to His own people.

God is also so very, very scary, especially when He's on the rampage and I tell you, we had best be scared, we had best be frightened, we had best be fearful of Him in this cringing and trembling way.

As well as this, as in most prophetic discourse, there is also a secondary proclamation; in this case, it is an allusion to the final judgment: A coming day of unspeakable destruction and devastation. Jesus in anger, when He saw many of the Pharisees and Sadducees coming to his baptism, said to them, ***"Brood of vipers! Who warned you to flee from the wrath to come?" Matt 3:7-8*** Yes indeed, it's been a long time coming but coming it is!

Yes, God is Holy and needs to be respectfully "feared". However, God is also so very, very scary, especially when He's on the rampage and I tell you, we had best be scared, we had best be frightened, we had best be fearful of Him in this cringing and trembling way. Don't try to scale this horror down friends, don't try to dress God up in a white beard and a red suit, and don't create an idol of your own nice "enlightened" thinking about the Lord Most High! In the real sense of the phrase, God is awful! Did you hear that? God is awful and says and does awful things.

Like trembling Rahab of old, who knew of the coming destruction of her land and her people, we need to follow this wise prostitutes example and get our Next Of Kin into the redeemed house of shame, that now flies the crimson stained banner from the but one waiting window in the falling walls of this old and smelly Jericho. It is not a new message that should be on the lips of the church but it is a fearful and forgotten one that we should at the last, begin to proclaim again.

A day is coming when God shall judge the living and the dead. Inform your NOK to flee from the WTC.

Listen: *Your faith toward God has gone out, so that we do not need to say anything. For they themselves declare concerning us what manner of entry we had to you, and how you turned to God from idols to serve the living and true God, and to wait for His Son from heaven, whom He raised from the dead, even Jesus who delivers us from the wrath to come. (1 Thessalonians 1:8b-10 NKJV)*

Pray: Lord; no angry, self-righteous, mad, malicious and masochistic prophet is needed to spread this message of the fearful Wrath To Come. But rather, please send Your weeping Jeremiahs into the world once more, whilst there is still time O God. In Jesus name we ask it, amen.

| Vol 02 | Q3 | NW00637 | September 27th |

Night-Whisper | **REPENT**

Fat lips

The Scriptures do not appear to tell us what constitutes being overweight. Even the book of Leviticus has no measurement, no height to weight ratio for us to calculate this, or even and maybe especially, to repent of this sin. There I've done it. I've made the connection about being fat and sinning. Now you're really feeling awful, maybe even angry but please, allow me to continue for I wish to settle this silliness and then clarify correctness.

Matthew 11:19

The Son of Man came eating and drinking, and they say, "Look, a glutton and a winebibber, a friend of tax collectors and sinners!" NKJV

In the Old Testament, fat and fatness were used as signs of evident blessings. The people of God were to eat the fat of the land, delight themselves in fatness even! Indeed, listen to Isaac pronouncing the blessing, ***"Therefore may God give you of the dew of heaven, of the fatness of the earth." Genesis 27:28.*** So we shall agree that a little fat never hurt anyone and it tastes so good as well!

I eat well. I eat sugar, salt and fat, every single day. I enjoy food. I delight in eating food! In my opinion, life is more than food but it would be severely diminished without the enjoyment of it! I actually eat five or six times a day. No really, it forces my metabolism to work and burn up more calories. Yes, most of those meals are high protein but some of them are just jam packed with carbohydrates. I just couldn't function without them carbs. I just love 'em!

I am not overweight friends. Well not much anyway! Well just a little! The truth is that I have come, by observation and investigation, to know my body. I know how I react, in terms of energy and weight, to the food I am taking in and the task I am doing. It's a very simple routine. First, I weigh myself every morning and take (for me) some key measurements around my abdomen. Then I eat just about anything, making sure the combination of what I need and want are well matched. For me, if I put on weight and my waist size is not expanding too much, then I am putting on muscle mass. Eat on baby! If I put on weight and my waist size is also growing, then I need to alter the type of nutrition I am taking in. Eat less maybe but certainly eat different. Simple really don't you think? Try it and try getting to know yourself.

Truly fat people, have really fat mouths! Ooh and fat hearts! Now there is a sin to repent of.

Actually, it's not simple is it? You need to begin to love, respect and honor yourself before you will ever take time to truly get to know yourself. If you do not love and honor yourself, then maybe that is the sin. Like many of you, I have a terrible body image. However, I choose to honor myself. You must do so as well, beginning today. Repent of this sin of personal neglect and begin to love and respect yourself. How do you begin to do this with food? Well, in the United Kingdom, "king size chocolate bars are facing the axe" for the Food and Drink Federation want to give a sign to consumers to eat in moderation. There you have it. Why not begin in honoring yourself with some moderation! The opposite of moderation is of course, gluttony and gluttony is not just a sticky little word, it is a big fat sin. Indeed, gluttony in any thing is any action that is unrestrained or excessive. Excessive unrestrained anything, especially the excessive unrestrained consumption of food, is sin.

Now before you go hurtling off in the wrong direction, remember that Jesus was not an aesthetic. Indeed, because of His enjoyment of life and His association with those who lived in unrestrained excess, He Himself fell under the accusations of the self-righteous, the "at ease in Zion" if you will, the truly fat folk as it were, when they commented on His lifestyle saying, "The Son of Man came eating and drinking" and continued, "Look, a glutton and a winebibber, a friend of tax collectors and sinners!" Mmm? It seems that truly fat people, have really fat mouths!

Remember today, these three sins.

First: Whilst enjoying life to the full and delighting yourself in the gifts of God Most High, if you do not love and honor yourself, you are sinning.

Second: If you are unrestrained and excessive in anything then it is the sin of gluttony and it needs repenting of.

Thirdly, finally and most disturbingly, may I say that if you are sat at ease in selfish success of any kind, judging the little and the less, then I wonder if no matter how cut or thin you are, that you are the frightful fat folk of the Scriptures, the truly sinful, whose hard hearts are the malicious megaphones of fat and massive mouths.

Fat hearts! Now there is a sin to repent of.

Listen: *"They have closed up their fat hearts; With their mouths they speak proudly." (Psalm 17:10 NKJV)*

Pray: Lord, forgive me my fat mouth and my fat self-centered heart. Help me to bring love honor and health to this temple of Your Holy Spirit. In Jesus name, amen.

| Vol 02 | Q3 | NW00638 | September 28th |

Night-Whisper | **VICTORY**

Watchwords for warriors

It was Russell Crowe's General Maximus in Ridley Scott's film *Gladiator* that coined the phrase "strength and honor." Watchwords for warriors that's for sure, appealing to both men and women, summoning up senses and desires for both, no matter what the cost. "Strength and honor." I like that.

Joshua 1:18

"Whoever rebels against your command and does not heed your words, in all that you command him, shall be put to death. Only be strong and of good courage." NKJV

However, the victories and glory of Maximus, pail into insignificance when placed alongside those of General Joshua. In our verse today, from the lips of the leaders of the two and one half tribes settled already on the East side of Jordan towards the rising sun, we see reference to what I might suggest, are the watchwords of the warriors of God. "Strength and courage."

Paul as a prefix to dressing the Christian in the armor of heaven, begins with encouraging us to "be strong." Being a Christian is no easy thing. This side of heaven, it is not a call to "wimpage," it is not a call to ease, it's not a call to rest; it is a call to vicious and blood spilling battle. It is a call to the most violent of conflicts, it is a call to the clash of arms, it is a call to conquest. Such a call will not go without resistance but with the utmost ferocity, it will in turn be attacked. No wonder then that Paul prefixes his battle dressing with "be strong!" Resist, exert, endure, effect, energize yourself, be unmovable, "be strong!" Lean into the hurricane if you will, grit your teeth and snarl but whatever you do, don't turn, don't run, "be strong!" We must take heed of this exhortation, for I tell you friends, we are truly in a battle royal where the stakes are higher than we can ever conceive. To remain standing against such onslaughts you will need to be strong and you will also need great courage.

The English word "courage" has it's roots embedded in the old French word "cuer," that is "heart". Courage is a matter of the heart. If you are to stand and be strong in the face of such fierceness you must have courage, inner firmness, ingrained fortitude, desperate determination, terrible tenacity, a screaming resistance that roars back at the enemy and dares to bear its own teeth in terrible display.

Courage is a matter of the heart. If you are to stand and be strong in the face of such fierceness you must have courage, inner firmness, ingrained fortitude, desperate determination, terrible tenacity, a screaming resistance that roars back at the enemy and dares to bear its own teeth in terrible display.

I do think that there will come a day when we shall roll up our sleeves and show our scars and say, "I got this when..." or "this happened as... " or maybe "this is to remind me of... " For I wonder, if those who aspire to be God's true generals, like His own supreme commander, the Blessed Savior Jesus Christ the Lord, King of Kings, Prince of Peace and God over all, shall along with Him, also walk the streets of heaven bearing red badges of courage, even all the marks of their own involvement in conquests, battles and victories?

O Christian, is the Holy Spirit saying to you today, "Prepare yourself! For in three days you shall go over this Jordan. Only be thou strong and very courageous."

Listen: *"You therefore, my son, be strong in the grace that is in Christ Jesus. You therefore must endure hardship as a good soldier of Jesus Christ. No one engaged in warfare entangles himself with the affairs of this life, that he may please him who enlisted him as a soldier. Therefore I endure all things for the sake of the elect, that they also may obtain the salvation which is in Christ Jesus with eternal glory. This is a faithful saying: for if we died with Him, We shall also live with Him. If we endure, We shall also reign with Him." (2 Timothy 2:1-12 NKJV)*

Pray: Lord I pray for the fixed heart of Queen Ester, to be kept from for the lacking determination of King Joash, to be given the swinging arm of Elijah, the blind strength of Samson, the wiliness of Jael, the wisdom of Joshua, the eyesight of Moses, the mouth of Peter, the loving and embracing arms of

John, the courage of the thirty and the dedication of the three. O God I pray that I would at last, be true, be true, be true, be true to Thee. Amen.

| Vol 02 | Q3 | NW00639 | September 29th |

Night-Whisper | **FEAR**

Of worms and watchwords

Isaiah 41:14

"Fear not, you worm Jacob, You men of Israel! I will help you," says the LORD and your Redeemer, the Holy One of Israel. NKJV

Yesterday we looked at the watchwords of the warriors of God; them being, "strength and courage." Large shields are these magnificent words, sharp swords even strong steeds, iron gates, fearsome friends that are always marching onwards together, the valiant vanguard of any advance. Yet just as the largest and strongest of athletes can be felled by a mere microbe and left sweating and moaning in a gibbering heap, so these two great words, strength and courage, can in a New York minute, have their foundations eaten away by a small and little, wriggly worm. Such eating away, will double us up with unexpected pain and like the burst and dissipated waters from premature twins, our now cringing cowardice will first give birth to weakness and then to death. The worm I speak of is fear. Once fear takes root friends: kingdoms fall! Selah.

In my experience and observation, the introduction of this worm of fear is one of the chief weapons in the armory of the enemy. Like most vile and viral agents it needs to have a good breeding ground, it needs to have the right climate to multiply its madness. That climate is doubt. Doubting the faithfulness of God; doubting the good intentions of God; doubting the capacities of God, doubting especially the goodness of God. "He's deserted me. Did I really hear Him? Maybe He won't help me. Maybe He can't help me? Maybe He's against me? I wonder if He wants to harm me really?"

Doubt is always the precursor to fear. So may I suggest that to remove and kill the worms of fear, we need first to remove the climate of doubt. How then does the damp despair of doubt begin to clothe the mountain tops of strong courageous hearts and envelope them like cold thick fog? May I suggest that three things give rise to this deadly climate.

The first is, discouragement. Fighting of any kind has its setbacks. A "right hook" from the enemy may violently turn your head and for a moment, rock your world. When this happens, suck it up, cover up, get your breath back, bob, weave, stick your left out, then get back in there, this time watching out for that which hurt you so much the last time. So first of all, do not let hard blows discourage you.

Keep looking in the right place. Only one corner out of four holds the eyes of encouragement and the instruction for victory that you require.

Secondly, lack of listening. God always gives instructions before the battle. Always! Listen to this and follow closely. Note as well that in conflict, God will always provide times of rest, so when you get back to your corner, listen. Receive the refreshing water, the cool wind of the flapping towel, the grease and the fixings, but whatever you do, listen and listen hard. If we think we are not hearing from our master, our trainer, our coach, then we are in deep distress. The feeling of seeming desertion and being totally alone will shrink and shrivel our hearts to the size of old walnuts. Secondly then, be sure to listen to God.

Lastly, keep looking in the right place. Only one corner out of four holds the eyes of encouragement and the instruction for victory that you require. Look to that corner, again and again and again. Don't get disorientated, don't get misled, and above all, when in need of encouragement, direction and help, keep looking to God's corner.

Discouragement, lack of listening and misdirected gazing, will all cloud your sky, will set your sun and will bring down the cold fog of doubt in double quick time. Such cold isolation will breed the worms of fear and those eaten by them will wriggle like them, convulsing on the devil's dire and dirty hook, their strength and courage, stripped and strained away, their face now all yellow with cowardice. Today then oh maggoty eaten friend, get off the hook, get up, get on, listen intently and this time, look in the right direction.

Listen: *"O man greatly beloved, fear not! Peace be to you; be strong, yes, be strong!" (Daniel 10:18-19 NKJV)*

Pray: Lord. Revive me. Shine bright in my sky, burn away the fog of doubt, set me on my feet, strengthen me and help me today O my God, my strength and my redeemer. Teach me to be more than a conqueror through Him who loved me and gave Himself for me. Amen.

| Vol 02 | Q3 | NW00640 | September 30th |

Night-Whisper | **HONOR**

The sound of the chamber pot

The Great War (1914-1918) devastated Britain and France. The loss of life in unceremonial and industrial slaughter was overwhelming and later marked in every city, town and village by memorials marked with multitudes of the inscribed names of the dead. These two countries never again wanted another European War.

1 Chronicles 16:25-27

For the LORD is great and greatly to be praised; He is also to be feared above all Gods. For all the Gods of the peoples are idols, but the LORD made the heavens. Honor and majesty are before Him; strength and gladness are in His place. NKJV

Signed today in 1938 the Munich Pact seemed to ensure that Anglo-German relations would never again break down and disturb the peace of Europe. Sure, Czechoslovakia was to be carved up piecemeal and Hitler given his piece of silver but nevertheless, peace was ensured, and no more would tens of thousands die unnecessarily. Chamberlain, the then British Prime Minister, returned to England from Munich, rested, relieved and triumphantly waving the signed paper pact, declaring both, "Peace with honor" and "Peace in our time." Later at 10 Downing Street, he is reported to have added, "My good friends, for the second time in our history, a British Prime Minister has returned from Germany bringing peace with honor. I believe it is peace for our time. Go home and get a nice quiet sleep." In less than a year, Hitler's invasion of Poland would plunge Europe and the whole world, into years of total war.

There are two hard lessons for us to learn here. These lessons not only apply nationally but individually; not only apply materially but spiritually as well. Remember then first that those intent on bloody conquest can never be appeased. Never! Secondly, that there is no peace without righteousness.

Fatigued and recovering warriors need to take note of this. Knowing our desire for peace and our need for recovery and space, the Devil will come and speak an alluring peace to us even attempting to make pacts of peace with us. I am personally familiar with the "draw back and I'll leave you alone" offers of the enemy. Be it ever so subtle, be the offer of withdrawal ever so tempting, let us remember the lessons of history and pursue righteousness, giving no place to the Devil. I wonder sometimes, if the peace of the whole world depends upon the righteous stand of often tired and weary warriors? Friends, never be deceived by the Devil's offers, nor think that on accepting them, that a nice quiet sleep will ever follow. When the Devil speaks peace, do not rest but keep on resisting! For all you are really hearing is the sound of his urine whizzing down the sides of a chamber pot and quite frankly, that's as much as his words are ever worth. A pot of pee. Never forget that.

When the Devil speaks peace, do not rest but keep on resisting! For all you are really hearing is the sound of his urine whizzing down the sides of a chamber pot and quite frankly, that's as much as his words are ever worth. A pot of pee. Never forget that.

Listen: *"Be sober, be vigilant; because your adversary the devil walks about like a roaring lion, seeking whom he may devour. Resist him, steadfast in the faith, knowing that the same sufferings are experienced by your brotherhood in the world. But may the God of all grace, who called us to His eternal glory by Christ Jesus, after you have suffered a while, perfect, establish, strengthen, and settle you. To Him be the glory and the dominion forever and ever. Amen." 1 Peter 5:8-11*

Pray: Lord. Give us Your peace. Help us to settle and even sleep well upon the roaring seas, because we are cradled in the hammock of Your great righteousness and might. Oh let righteousness and peace always be the bed fellows of all my weariness. Amen.

DID YOU REMEMBER?

DON'T FORGET TO ORDER YOUR NEXT QUARTER OF NIGHT WHISPERS.

Check us out more at WWW.NightWhispers.com

Buy at WWW.WhisperingWord.com

THE MISSION STATEMENT OF THE 66 BOOKS MINISTRY

WWW.66Books.tv | Our Mission is:

1. "To proclaim Jesus, the Savior of the whole world, from the whole Bible, because He is wonderful!"

2. Indeed, we are constrained by the love of God, to communicate the rawness of the Bible to real people, in real ways, and our driving and major project of '66Cities' shall take us to the 66 most influential cities of the 250 nations of the world in the next 25 years. That's 16,500 cities!

3. We are aiming to build relationships with grass roots, real people, that is, ordinary people, who, in their own countries and cities, want to do extraordinary things for Jesus and the Kingdom of God, to bring a Biblical Gospel message that is relevant to now, in a world that has come to believe that Jesus is irrelevant to their lives.

THE 66 Books MINISTRY

If you would like to partner with us in this great task. Then we want to hear from you! Contact me today on vr@66books.tv

MORE ABOUT 'THE 66 BOOKS MINISTRY'

WWW.66Cities.com | By the year 2047, by the grace of God and according to His will and favor, The 66 Books Ministry shall be preaching consecutively from each of the 66 Books of the Holy Bible, the Gospel of the Lord Jesus Christ in 16,500 of the most influential cities of the world on an annual and ongoing basis!

We do not underestimate the quality teams of trained people that this will take, together with the need for vast amount of materials and finances which will also have to be raised. However, as most futurists indicate that the growing global population will be gathered mostly in major world cities in the coming years, there is a necessity laid upon the church to present and proclaim the God of the whole Bible, through the primacy of preaching in these cities. We are convinced that this is a paramount and pressing concern.

"For since, in the wisdom of God, the world through wisdom did not know God, it pleased God through the foolishness of the message preached to save those who believe" 1 Corinthians 1:21NKJV

"Preach the Word! Be ready in season and out of season. Convince, rebuke, exhort, with all longsuffering and teaching." 2 Timothy 4:2NKJV

The church is looking for a revival. The 66 Books Ministry, however, is trying to start a revolution of a return to the preached Word, from the whole of the Bible as a precursor to any and all coming revival.

For "whoever calls on the name of the Lord shall be saved." How then shall they call on Him in whom they have not believed? And how shall they believe in Him of whom they have not heard? And how shall they hear without a preacher? And how shall they preach unless they are sent? As it is written: "How beautiful are the feet of those who preach the gospel of peace, Who bring glad tidings of good things!" Romans 10:13-15 NKJV

We are unashamedly looking for and seeking to foster a massive, huge, releasing, transformative, and exceptionally disruptive reversal and revolutionary change, both within the church and then in the world. We are not just another mission trying to do the same as every other mission. We are intent on revolution!

To this revolutionary end, we have no fear of seeming failure and will cultivate that audacious atmosphere within our ministry. We want to attract grass roots people who are people of faith risk takers, for we believe it is people of such life hazarding attitudes that are used by God to make breakthroughs in the world for the Kingdom of God. Hanging back for fear of seeming failure, hanging back and waiting for the trained professionals, both wastes the time of the church time and kills the spirit of victory.

In that spirit then, we therefore are believing that this task can be accomplished by such people within the time frame we have given ourselves.

Fully assured then, that we are in full obedience with the great commission of our great God and Savior Jesus Christ, we do, with great confidence in Him, turn ourselves happily to this so great a task in the hope that, like a happy hound straining at the leash to be let loose, we believe that many other people will smile along with us and be part of this brand new grass roots 21st Century Global City Mission.

If you want to know more and want to be part of what we are doing then go to www.The66BooksMinistry.com or call us in the USA on **855 662 6657**, or email V.R. directly on vr@66Books.TV

AUTHOR BIO | PURPLE ROBERT

It won't take too much investigation for you to find out that Purple Robert is in fact, Victor Robert Farrell (Born 1960 and alive until now and still kicking) was born in Chesterfield England to Scottish parents with Irish grandparents, which is an obvious recipe both for writing and emotional disaster if ever there was one!

He grew up a culturally excluded Roman Catholic (his parents were divorced,) which is one of the reasons why he hates religion with a passion, and that's an interesting enough fact by itself, because he is also an ordained protestant minister to boot.

Purple Robert. became a Christian whilst serving on board a Polaris Submarine at the end of the cold war. He has gone on to do many things, including being a broadcaster, App developer, performance poet, and the long-time author of 'Night Whispers,' which is read in over 100 counties and is also translated into Spanish (see www.Night Whispers.com)

Currently, Purple Robert is also President of The 66 Books Ministry: a grass roots global city mission endeavor. I suppose it is this concoction of background and experience which means Purple Robert's communication is always raw and emotive. After all, and as he says, *"If Christianity can be relevant on a Monday morning, several hundred feet underneath an unknown ocean, in a pornographic sewer pipe carrying enough nuclear weapons to destroy a continent whilst hiding from the Russians, then it can be relevant anywhere and everywhere!"*

Purple Robert sees himself as a servant of the 'Word of the Lord' to tasked communicate the God of the whole Bible. His proclamation of the same is done in very raw terms to very real people, is both his burden and his passion.

May 26th | Reading 147 of 366

MORNING → HISTORICAL BOOKS

BOOK 11 of 66 → 1 KINGS 16,17

Signpost Words → **'AN ANSWER'**

Highlight Verses → **1 Kings 16:31-34**

And it came to pass, as though it had been a trivial thing for him to walk in the sins of Jeroboam the son of Nebat, that he took as wife Jezebel the daughter of Ethbaal, king of the Sidonians; and he went and served Baal and worshiped him. Then he set up an altar for Baal in the temple of Baal, which he had built in Samaria. And Ahab made a wooden image. Ahab did more to provoke the Lord God of Israel to anger than all the kings of Israel who were before him. In his days Hiel of Bethel built Jericho. He laid its foundation with Abiram his firstborn, and with his youngest son Segub he set up its gates, according to the word of the Lord, which He had spoken through Joshua the son of Nun. NKJV

Some Observations →

This is nothing but an extended killing time, and it is God who is slaughtering His wayward nation. Decade after decade the decadent mobster kings steer the people more and more out of the way of the Lord. Dogs lick up the blood from slaughtered corpses, birds peck the watery eyeballs out of the maggot eaten heads. Death and destruction stalk the land, yet still the people rise up to pray to an idle and engage in sexual sin. The mercy of God is seen on two legs and heard from one mouth, even the prophets of the Lord. Now, dropped from heaven, out of nowhere, in answer to the madness of Ahab the loon, a prophet like no other arrives on the scene. Elijah the Tishbite

A Call To Action →

Fine pulpits and finer churches, are rarely the abode of the prophet.

EVENING → PAULINE EPISTLES

BOOK 46 of 66 → 1 CORINTHIANS 15

Signpost Words → **'ASSURANCE OF SALVATION'**

Highlight Verses → **1 Corinthians 15:1-11**

Moreover, brethren, I declare to you the gospel which I preached to you, which also you received and in which you stand, by which also you are saved, if you hold fast that word which I preached to you — unless you believed in vain. For I delivered to you first of all that which I also received: that Christ died for our sins according to the Scriptures, and that He was buried, and that He rose again the third day according to the Scriptures, and that He was seen by Cephas, then by the twelve. After that He was seen by over five hundred brethren at once, of whom the greater part remain to the present, but some have fallen asleep. After that He was seen by James, then by all the apostles. Then last of all He was seen by me also, as by one born out of due time. For I am the least of the apostles, who am not worthy to be called an apostle, because I persecuted the church of God. But by the grace of God I am what I am, and His grace toward me was not in vain; but I labored more abundantly than they all, yet not I, but the grace of God which was with me.... NKJV

Some Observations →

The two 'wee' words we Evangelicals dislike to discourse upon are 'if' and 'unless.' I believe that once we are saved we are always saved, 'IF' we continue on receiving, believing and standing. I believe that once we are saved we are always saved, 'UNLESS' we prove ourselves to be unfaithful and reprobate in forsaking the Christ of the Scriptures. Paul did not believe he was saved by our works, yet by grace he worked his little heine off!

A Call To Action →

Continuance in the work of grace is the key to your own assurance.

JOIN THE FELLOWSHIP OF THE BOOK

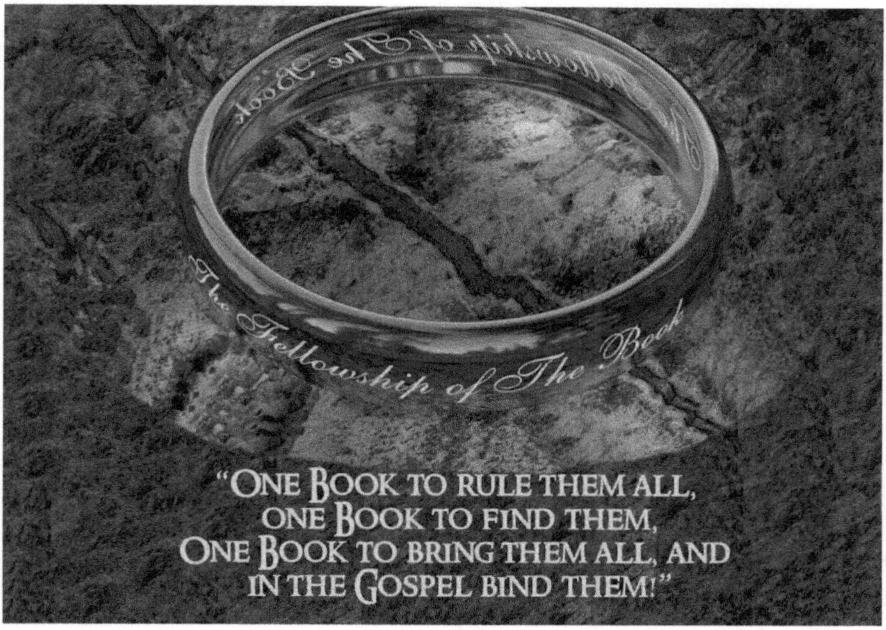

The Fellowship of The Book
"ONE BOOK TO RULE THEM ALL,
ONE BOOK TO FIND THEM,
ONE BOOK TO BRING THEM ALL, AND
IN THE GOSPEL BIND THEM!"

WWW.TheFellowShipofTheBook.com

The Fellowship of The Book is a Daily Bible Reading Fellowship. It is a morning and evening devotional of four books available each quarter of the year. It includes

Signpost Words
Highlight Verses
Some Observations
Call To Action

Consecutively, Chronologically and in many other ways, Read The Bible Thru in 1 just one year, with both Morning and Evening reading to keep your mind focused on the Lord of the Word and the Word of The Lord. Buy this and several other ways to 'Read the Bible Thru in a Year Books' at www.whisperingword.com

ANOTHER BOOK BY THE AUTHOR, VR

Habakkuk A Prophecy For Our Time

As the Church in the West is found to be mostly dead and covered with Laodicean lukewarm vomit, as The Lord, slips the dead things silently over the side of the storm tossed ship into the dark oblivion of the waves of secular humanism and rising Islam, what remains will need to be fortified with steel to live in a quickly changing anti-Christian world of persecution. There is no better prophecy more equipped to speak to such a remnant who shall be so very besieged. Welcome to Habakkuk, 35 of 66, a prophecy for our time.

Buy at www.whisperingword.com

ANOTHER BOOK BY THE AUTHOR, VR

The 66-Minute Bible

I am told that there are 788,258 words in the King James Bible and of these 14,565 are unique. That's a lot of words! I have been reading the Bible for nearly forty years on an almost daily basis. It still remains to me the most exciting book on the planet, however, it never gets any easier. Bible reading is a spiritual discipline and for me the emphasis is on discipline. I created this resource to aid you in your Bible reading, it gives your brain a sixty second overview of the Bible, a loose enclosure to herd the narrative of the book into something that can be seen as a whole. It was never created to be a substitute, but an aid. Just saying…… Friends, welcome to the most exciting book on the planet! V.R.

AN INTRODUCTION TO 'PURPLE ROBERT'

Some Dangerously Different Devotionals!

Now, before I go any further, this guy comes with warning shots! The opening parts of his currently seven volumes pf poetic works says quite clearly, *"If you are easily offended by low level expletives...* ***Go no further. Do not read this book!*** *If you are prudish in any way ...* ***Go no further. Do not read this book!*** *If you do not want to be challenged...* ***Go no further. Do not read this book!*** *If you want to be stroked into unchanging sleep and into the stupor of remaining as you are...* ***Go no further. Do not read this book!*** *If you hide under the respectable covers of a comfortable religion...* ***Go no further. Do not read this book!*** *If you are frail in faith and dishonest about life under this sun...* ***Go no further.*** *If you have no real integrity regarding the state of your own heart,* ***then do not read this book!*** *If however, you are grown up, honest and have a basic human integrity, ENJOY!"* So, there you go, you have been warned!

Purple Robert is a Performance Poet and a Metaphysical Biblical Realist. If you want to hear some of his work and get hold of the 66 Poems each of the Seven volumes contain, then go to www.PurpleRobert.com and purchase them today.

Also Buy at Buy at www.WhisperingWord.com

www.ingramcontent.com/pod-product-compliance
Lightning Source LLC
Chambersburg PA
CBHW022115080426
42734CB00006B/143
* 9 7 8 1 9 1 0 6 8 6 1 2 6 *